American Business:
A Two-Minute Warning

Ten Changes Managers
Must Make to Survive
into the 21st Century

C. Jackson Grayson, Jr.
Carla O'Dell

THE FREE PRESS
A Division of Macmillan, Inc.
NEW YORK

Collier Macmillan Publishers
LONDON

The Free Press
A Division of Macmillan, Inc.
866 Third Avenue, New York, NY 10022

Collier Macmillan Canada, Inc.

Printed in the United States of America

printing number
2 3 4 5 6 7 8 9 10

Library of Congress Cataloging-in-Publication Data

Grayson, C. Jackson (Charles Jackson)
    American business, a two-minute warning: ten changes managers must make to survive
into the 21st century / C. Jackson Grayson, Jr., and Carla O'Dell.
        p.   cm.
    Bibliography: p.
    Includes index.
    ISBN 0-02-912680-0
    1. Industrial management—United States. 2. Industrial management—Japan. 3. Industrial
productivity—United States. 4. Industrial productivity—Japan. 5. Economic forecasting—
United States. 6. United States—Economic conditions—1981-   I. O'Dell, Carla S.
II. Title.
HD70.U5G69 1988   87-19391
658'.00973—dc19   CIP

We dedicate this book to the past—to the late Mr. and Mrs. C. J. Grayson, Sr., who passed away during the planning and writing of this book. Their lives provided a rich legacy for us.

We also dedicate this book to the present—to our families, who sacrificed more than we did in order that we might write it: to Chris, Michael, Randy, and Daniel Grayson and to Olive, Patrick, and Harry O'Dell.

Finally, we dedicate our thoughts and hopes to the future—to the men and women working across America whose actions will ultimately determine the outcome of the last two minutes of the game.

Contents

Preface and Acknowledgments

In 1972, *Newsweek* asked in a cover story, "Can the U.S. Compete?"

In 1987, fifteen years later, *Business Week* asked in its cover story, "Can America Compete?"

Can America compete?

Of course it *can*. The real question is *"Will* America compete?" Will American firms sufficiently sense the competitive danger and act, will American firms adjust their operations to be competitive, do American firms still have the drive, the "eye of the tiger" necessary to make difficult adjustments?

Not yet.

In 1982, Tom Peters and Bob Waterman described in their pathbreaking book *In Search of Excellence* the characteristics of firms judged to be excellent, and the need for American firms to restructure in order to remain competitive. Five years later, in a 1987 *Fortune* article, Tom

Peters sadly concluded that the efforts to date added up to a ''failure to come to grips with the magnitude of the problems we face. There are no excellent companies in the U.S.''

Despite fifteen years of warnings and at least five years of supposedly active restructuring to create excellence, the United States is, as yet, not adjusting adequately to the challenge. Meanwhile, the United states has steadily lost ground.

Now the question has an added dimension: Will America adjust-in-time?

This book is about adjustment: the need for adjustment, the resistance to adjustment, the needed speed for adjustment, the fate of nations that did not adjust, examples of successful (and unsuccessful) adjustment of American firms, and what we recommend as the critical ''Agenda for Adjustment'' for business and government.

Why are we so concerned?

America now stands, at the end of the twentieth century, where England stood at the end of the nineteenth—the strongest economic power on the face of the earth, yet facing strong challengers from abroad. Britain did not respond to warnings, and it began its descent into the ranks of also-ran economies in the last decade of the nineteenth century.

If America does not adjust, then a cover story written at the beginning of the twenty-first century might read: ''America: A Second Britain.'' *U.S. News and World Report* already asked in a February 1987 feature story, ''Will the U.S. Stay Number One?''

This book is our ''two-minute warning.''

It is written in the hope of awakening Americans to action before the end of the century. By then it will be too late.

One of us, Grayson, came away from his post as Chairman of the U.S. Price Commission (1971–73 price controls) firmly convinced of three things:

- U.S. productivity growth was then on a declining trend, but most Americans were not aware of it.
- Foreign competitors were outperforming the United States in productivity and quality. Most Americans were unaware or unconcerned.
- Government controls, subsidies, and protection were not the answer. Officials were not convinced.

In 1977, Grayson formed the American Productivity Center, a non-profit education, research, and consulting center in Houston, Texas, to focus attention on the problem. O'Dell joined the Center in 1978, convinced that the piecemeal efforts managers, employees, and unions were making would not be adequate to the challenge.

That was a decade ago. Today, we are both convinced of three things:

- Though far more Americans are aware of the problem and some firms are responding, U.S. productivity growth is still largely stagnant.
- Foreign competitors have almost caught up to the United States in productivity, and if trends continue, the United States will not be the world productivity leader in the twenty-first century.
- Government controls, subsidies, and protection are not the answer. The danger is increasing that many will, in desperation, seek those government solutions.

We shall let the chapters speak for themselves, but there are five points we want to make up front.

First, this is primarily a book for managers and union leaders. It is not a technical book on productivity or why U.S. productivity is in trouble, nor a book on economic policy, though we certainly discuss all three in Parts I, II, and V. The primary focus is on what the private sector can and must do to renew America's competitiveness—and the consequences if we do not.

Neither is this a history book, though we refer often to history to obtain examples and useful "lessons" in Part III. The historical parallels are both fascinating and alarming. We think thoughtful readers are concerned, as are we: "Can what happened to Britain happen to us?"

In Part IV, we talk about what managers, unions, and employees are doing to address ten "tough issues," the issues that stand in the way of competitiveness and renewed growth. And we recommend what we think they must do. Those issues are our private sector "Agenda for Adjustment."

In Part V, we cover the role we see—and do not see—government playing to restore American competitiveness.

Finally, in Part VI we give our assessment of our most formidable competitors. Though the United States still has some strong European competitors, we concentrate on Asia, for that is where we think our greatest challengers are. Of those nations, we focus most on Japan: its strengths, weaknesses, and the dangerous myths that could keep Americans from making the right responses.

Second, this book is not an ideological defense of the American market system. We believe that, for the United States, relying almost entirely on the private sector is the best way to achieve high productivity, competitiveness, and a rising standard of living. Government does have a role, esepcially in education, but its role is limited.

This is a pragmatic view, not derived from blind ideology. We even point out in the next-to-last chapter that the Asian nations have achieved a mix of government and business that, for them, is highly effective in achieving economic growth.

Third, we are "critical U.S. lovers."

John Gardner described two kinds of lovers that do their fellow citizens and institutions no good. The first are "unloving critics" who criticize without concern, who browbeat and denigrate the very object of their supposed affection.

The second are "uncritical lovers," who overlook faults, cover up, deny all shortcomings, and refuse to hear or admit any negative information. They block change, thereby hurting the one they profess to love.

Our role is of a third kind, as "critical lovers." We point out faults, mistakes, and flaws in the American management, union, and governmental systems—problems we had a hand in shaping. And yet we love this nation. We criticize in the hope of awakening people and institutions to the need for change. A British author, Fred McKenzie, wrote a book in 1901 warning the British of their danger of decline, and he faced the same problem:

> I have not hesitated to state unpleasant truths, and to state them plainly, though well aware that in doing so I lay myself open to a charge of lack of patriotism and lack of confidence in my own people.

We are critical lovers of America.

Fourth, we are not blind Japanophiles. We think the Japanese are good. Very good. They will not be defeated by a higher-valued yen or economic sanctions. They will not stop competing. But we also point out many of their weaknesses and problems, as well as myths about the Japanese, the most dangerous of which is that the Japanese, as well as other nations, have "converged" and cannot possibly overtake the United States because they are "copiers" and can't create. The British can testify to the falsity of that thesis.

We also stress that competitiveness is not a contest of "us" versus "them," winner take all, the good guys and the bad guys. Nations that compete economically are not enemies. They are customers, suppliers, military allies, and co-developers of technology. Economic growth is a win-win game, and the poor people of the earth need all the help we can give them.

The danger is that Americans will fear strong competitors and let changes due to shifts in comparative advantage degenerate into mindless bashing, a world trade war, or even worse.

It is in the hope of helping to avert that disaster that this book is written.

Fifth, we are optimists.

Though we join others in warning the United States about its eroding competitiveness, this is not a fatalistic or pessimistic book.

We see much reason for optimism. For every example of industrial decline we can offer counter-examples of renewal. Stories of trouble in Big Steel run beside the accomplishments of agile steelmakers like Nucor, Chaparral, and Worthington. Americans are the beneficiaries of electronic highways carrying new world-class operating system knowhow and employee commitment strategies from one time zone to another instantaneously. All over the country, in industry after industry, firms are scrambling to adjust to competition. "Restructure or die" is the battle cry. As we shall show, our approach to restructuring is more difficult than the financial maneuvers that pass for restructuring in the business press.

This book is the product of two people who have worked closely together for years on the productivity and competitiveness issue with managers, union leaders, academics, and government leaders. What you will find in these pages is both concern and hope.

We owe an enormous debt of gratitude to a great number of people, not all of whom can be acknowledged in this brief space. But we must single out a few.

The first is the staff of the American Productivity Center. Their work over the past ten years has contributed heavily to our understanding and knowledge. They supplied data and case studies, and they stand ready to assist all who wish to know more and explore changes.

A few members of the APC staff in particular stand out: David Jones, who assumed leadership as President of APC while Grayson was writing; Bonnie Donovan, whose editing and advice saved us space and avoided many errors; Vivian Howser, whose assistance was invaluable at the computer and in the files; Brian Parker for managing, tracking, and caretaking the competitiveness data; and Anne Ogden for keeping the world at bay as we wrote. Our deep appreciation to the APC staff members who read and offered many thoughtful and useful comments on drafts: Don McAdams, Blair McDonald, Diane Riggan, Marty Russell, and Carl Thor.

At the risk of omitting some outside of APC, we also want to acknowledge all those who helped us with perspective, ideas, and judicious
comments: Robert Cole, John Dailey, Elliott Danzig, Frank Gibney,
Charles Hatfield, Tom Melohn, Olive O'Dell, George Sadler, Ralph
Saul, Ed Utz, Ezra Vogel, John Wolf, and our editor, Robert Wallace.

We have also benefited greatly from authors listed in the references
and reading list, all of whom we can recommend most highly.

Our debt of gratitude to our family and friends is high: Their tolerance
and understanding go far beyond the call of duty. Only family would
put up with this.

And finally, to the business people, union leaders, and government
officials with whom we have worked and talked over the years, we can
only broadcast a general and heartfelt thank you.

We'd better get moving. The referee has just blown the whistle
signaling the two-minute warning.

C. J. G. and C. O.
Houston, Texas

Prologue

And then they tried wordmagic.
"Conditions are fundamentally sound,"
they said—by which they meant to
reassure themselves that nothing was
really changed, that things were as they
always would be, forever and ever. Amen.

But they were wrong. They did not know
that you can't go home again. America
had come to the end of something, and to
the beginning of something else.

You Can't Go Home Again
—Thomas Wolfe

—*Part I*—
Time Is Running Out

—1—
The Two-Minute Warning

In 1896, a book was published in England entitled *Made in Germany*. Its author, E. E. Williams, a journalist, delivered a strong warning to English citizens:

> The industrial glory of England is departing, and England does not know it. There are spasmodic outcries against foreign competition, but the impression they leave is fleeting and vague . . . the nation at large is yet as little alive to the impending danger as to the evil already wrought.

Williams gave example after example of increasing foreign competition, especially from Germany. He urged British managers and union leaders to wake up, be more competitive, and "lock their stables while there is still something inside them."

England did not respond.

In 1901—six years later—another alarm was sounded by the British author F. A. McKenzie in his book *The American Invaders*. McKenzie warned Britons of the strong competitive thrust coming from America, the erosion of British competitiveness, and the need for British managers to take action before it was too late:

> The future still lies before England if England will but have it. And it is in the hope of arousing her to a slight sense of the real need of immediate action that this is written.

England still did not respond.

From its nineteenth-century position as number 1, the world's economic leader by far, Britain fell to where it is today: number 11 in GDP/capita, at the bottom of the league of developed nations with a standard of living about equal to that of East Germany.

A WARNING

It is now 1988, almost a century later. Paraphrasing Williams and McKenzie, we are delivering a similar warning to American citizens:

The industrial glory of America is departing, and it is in the hope of arousing her to a sense of the real need for immediate action that this is written.

Ours is certainly not the first warning.

There have been newspaper and magazine articles on America's eroding competitiveness, speeches, reports, surveys, even a Presidential Commission on Competitiveness. Yet, the response to date is inadequate. "Americans are awake," said one Japanese, "but they are not yet out of bed."

We will show that (1) U.S. competitiveness has seriously eroded, (2) the international competitive challenges are far stronger than most people yet realize, (3) the U.S. response to date is inadequate to meet the challenges, and (4) not only *can* the United States lose its world economic leadership, but *at the moment it is losing.*

Note carefully that this is not an obituary or a prediction. We do not say that the United States *has lost,* nor do we say that the United States *will lose.* But we do say most strongly that whether we like it or not, the United States *is losing.* If trends of the last twenty years continue, the U.S. standard of living will shrink relative to other nations, and eventually it will lose its world economic leadership.

The single, most fundamental determinant of the U.S. economic future will be productivity. Productivity, more than any other factor, determines a nation's standard of living and is the best single indicator of its economic performance over the long run. In the end, it determines the rank of nations. History shows that the nation that is the productivity leader eventually becomes the dominant world leader—economically, militarily, and politically.

The United States has been the world productivity leader for almost a hundred years. But in recent years U.S. productivity growth has been dismal, both relative to its earlier years, and even worse relative to international competitors.

Other nations are catching up. For the past thirteen years, 1973–86, Japan grew almost six times faster, France and Germany over four times faster, and even England three times faster than the United States. If those trends continue, five nations—Canada, Germany, France, Norway, and Belgium—will pass the United States in productivity level by the turn of the century, and Japan will pass the United States level in the year 2003—fifteen years from now.*

Of these competitors, Japan is the most formidable. Japan is now the second largest economy in the Free World and is the world's largest creditor nation. It has seven of the ten largest banks in the world and manufactures half of the world's ships, two-fifths of its TVs, and over one-third of its semiconductors. For many nations, Japanese, not American, management has now become the model for the world. Japanese workers are well educated, technologically sophisticated, and very determined. Japan is building a formidable high-technology infrastructure, the quality of its products is world-renowned, and Japan's productivity gains in the postwar period have outstripped the rest of the world.

Some mistakenly assume that Japan's productivity growth is "finished" because of the higher-valued yen, increasing world protectionism, and rising competitiveness of the Asian NICs (newly industrializing countries). Japan does face those and other problems, which we discuss in Part VI, but it also has some fundamental strengths to draw on and historically has shown remarkable ability to adjust to adverse circumstances. The United States underestimated the Japanese in the past. It would be unwise to do so again.

If present trends continue, Japan will emerge in the first decade of the twenty-first century as the productivity leader of the world, and the

---

* There are many ways to measure productivity, and international comparisons of productivity are especially difficult because of data comparability and exchange rate fluctuations. The various measures and their limitations are discussed in Chapter 3.

United States will drop to a number 2, number 3, or a lower position in productivity rank.

For a long time, however, U.S. total GNP will still be larger than that of other nations, for the United States still has great wealth and a large population. It will also continue to exert world influence for many decades because of its size, military power, and past history. But in productivity level, GNP/capita, financial power, and overall dynamism, a continued lack of productivity growth will eventually take its toll, as it did in England. U.S. economic leadership and world influence will slowly weaken, and Japan will assume its place as the economic leader of the twenty-first century.

The twenty-first century begins in thirteen years.

CONSEQUENCES

Some of the consequences of the U.S. productivity slowdown are already being felt by Americans.

Real compensation per hour at the end of 1986 was no higher than it had been in 1969. Median household incomes in real terms were 8 percent less at the end of 1986 than they were in 1973. Families that used to double their incomes in their lifetime now have no hope of that. A young man leaving home in the 1950s and 1960s could expect by age thirty to be making 33 percent more than his father did when he left home. No longer.

The prospect of a steady job, promotion, pay increases—a rising standard of living—is the heart of the American Dream. That prospect is fading, forcing Americans to confront dramatic changes in standard of living, expectations, values, and the future of their children.

To try to sustain their standard of living, American families are sending more people to work, and they are also going deeper and deeper into debt. As a result, the United States has moved in just four years from being the world's largest creditor nation to being the world's largest debtor nation, the largest ever recorded in the history of mankind. Americans are borrowing, not earning, their standard of living. They are living beyond their means, and they can't keep it up forever. To put it plainly, the jig is up. The nation must grow faster or live on less.

All this happened not because of foreign competition or supposedly "unfair" foreign trade barriers, but because of the U.S. productivity slowdown.

At the same time, however, strong international competitors are adding to the economic pressures: tough, determined global competitors the likes of which the United States has seldom, if ever, faced. It is not just "more" competition; it is different competition.

Those competitors are technologically sophisticated, well educated, and willing to work hard and put in long hours with lower pay. They have absorbed much of American scientific knowledge and equaled, even bettered, some of U.S. technological capability. They work with their governments on a cooperative basis and share a national consensus around the importance of productivity and growth. *Those competitors cannot be stopped by protectionist barriers or currency devaluations at the national level, or by business as usual at the firm level.*

WARNING SIGNALS

All this has not happened overnight. Contrary to popular belief, U.S. productivity growth and competitiveness did not drop suddenly in the late 1970s or early 1980s. The decline has been under way for almost twenty years.

Look at Exhibit A.

U.S. productivity growth is dead last. The U.S. standard of living growth has all but halted. The U.S. share of world exports has declined in industry after industry. Imports of manufactured goods, often of higher quality, have invaded most U.S. markets. Debt has climbed steadily upward to unprecedented and alarming proportions. Personal savings rates have hit all-time lows. The vaunted lead in high technology is diminishing. The U.S. educational system has deteriorated.

These warning signals are not all symptoms of declining U.S. competitiveness. Some occurred because of the U.S. productivity slowdown and would have occurred whether the United States traded internationally or not. Some reflect predictable comebacks by other nations from war-torn conditions.

But collectively, they portray a growth slowdown in a nation that has become addicted to growth, has an expectation of rising standards of living, and is accustomed to being number 1 in the world. Being "number 1" is not important because of any American ego trip. It is important because of what happens when a leader slips to number 2 or number 3 or lower: degenerative impacts on social goals, national security, and education and rising inflation, protectionism, and divisiveness.

In that sense, these data *are* a warning. The implications for Americans will be staggering. Only war could have a comparable impact on the

Exhibit A: WARNING SIGNALS

PRODUCTIVITY

- U.S. productivity growth has slowed to a crawl. In 1973–86, it was only 0.4% in GDP/employee, and 0.8% in GDP/hour.
- Productivity in the U.S. services sector (now about 68% of GDP) has been almost zero since the start of this decade.
- U.S. productivity growth for the past thirteen years has ranked *dead last* among the advanced nations. Japan grew in that period about six times faster; even England grew almost three times faster.
- The U.S.A. will rank sixth in productivity level among developed nations at the beginning of the next century, and Japan will overtake the U.S.A. in the year 2003, *if* the most recent thirteen-year trends continue.

COMPENSATION/STANDARD OF LIVING

- Families that used to double their incomes in their lifetime now have no hope of it. Median household incomes in 1986 in real terms were 8% less than they were in 1973.
- Hourly earnings at the end of 1986 were no higher than in 1969. Real gross weekly earnings were lower than in 1962.
- A thirty-year-old American male in 1973 earned in 1986 dollars an average of $25,545. Today, a similar thirty-year-old earned only $18,236–one-fourth less.
- Americans are spending more than they are earning to the tune of about $10,000 per family per year.
- The per capita income of Japanese citizens, at current exchange rates, is now larger than that of American citizens. In the third quarter of 1986, annualized Japanese GNP/capita was $18,000, the U.S. $17,700.

DEBT

- The U.S.A. is the world's largest debtor nation. From a net creditor position of $141 at the beginning of 1982, the U.S.A.

Exhibit A (continued)

shifted to a net debtor position of $264 billion at the end of 1986, a swing of $405 billion in just five years.
- The total debt of American citizens—government, business, and personal—is now over $7 trillion, about $35,000 for each man, woman, and child in the U.S.A.
- Foreign debt is estimated to reach $700–$900 billion by 1995. Americans will have to spend about 1% of their GNP just to service the foreign debt.

SAVINGS, INVESTMENT, PROFITS

- The U.S. personal savings rate is the lowest of all industrialized countries—3.9% of GNP in 1986. The Japanese rate was about 17% and the West German 12%.
- Of the advanced nations, Japan leads the world in capital formation. In 1985, the Japanese gross fixed capital investment as a share of GNP was 28%; the U.S. 17%.
- Twenty years ago, the average real pretax return on manufacturing assets was almost 12%. Today, it is about 7%.
- The world's seven biggest banks (in assets) are all Japanese. Citicorp is number 9 and Bank of America is number 25.

R&D/HIGH TECHNOLOGY

- The U.S.A. spends more on total R&D than any other nation. However, it spends less on civilian R&D as a percentage of GNP (1.9%), than Germany (2.6%) and Japan (2.8%).
- Since 1965, seven out of ten U.S. high-technology industries have lost world market share. In 1985, the U.S.A. had a larger trade deficit with Japan in electronics than in passenger cars.
- Japan graduates almost as many engineers per year as the U.S.A.: In 1985, Japan graduated 71,000; the U.S. 78,000. On a per capita basis, that's about twice the U.S. rate.
- In 1960, about 20% of U.S. patents were granted to foreign inventors. In 1986, they accounted for almost 50% of all

Exhibit A (continued)

U.S. patents. Hitachi in 1986 received more U.S. patents than any other company, including GE and IBM.

FOREIGN TRADE

- The 1986 U.S. merchandise trade deficit was an all-time high of $156.2 billion—the largest trade deficit ever recorded by any nation in history.
- The U.S. now imports 66% of its TVs and radios, 63% of shoes, 47% of machine tools, 28% of passenger cars, and 25% of computers. The U.S. Commerce Department predicts foreign cars will take 37% of domestic sales by 1990.
- High-technology electronics has had a negative trade balance since 1984. In 1986, there was a $13.1 billion deficit, almost 50% larger than 1985.
- Protectionist barriers created by the American government cost American consumers an estimated $66 billion annually.

EDUCATION

- The average achievement level of high school students on SATs is lower than it was twenty-six years ago, when Sputnik shocked America.
- In international tests of mathematics and science, Japanese students consistently come in first, Americans consistently near the bottom.
- Of the 24,000 U.S. high schools, 7,000 offer no physics, and 4,000 no chemistry, 2,000 no biology. Only one-third of U.S. high school students take a science course in any given year.
- Almost two-thirds of seventeen-year-old U.S. students in one study could not put the Civil War between 1850 and 1900; half could not identify Winston Churchill or Joseph Stalin.
- The U.S. national high school dropout rate is about 25%; Japan's, 10%.
- The Bureau of the Census estimates that 13% of U.S. adults are illiterate in English. Other studies show that one-fourth to one-third of American adults are *functionally* illiterate.

lives of present Americans and their children. To use Thomas Wolfe's words at the front of the book, "America has come to the end of something, and to the beginning of something else." The components of American world economic dominance and the American Dream are disappearing, one by one, like the fading grin of the Cheshire Cat.

The United States must act or decline.

INCONCEIVABLE?

America lose the leadership? The initial reaction of many today is the same as it was in England in the latter part of the nineteenth century when, after almost a century of unprecedented economic power, the British were warned by people like Williams and McKenzie that England could lose the leadership. Williams wrote:

> Now to tell a strong man, conscious of his strength to an over-weening degree, that he is in danger from a half grown youngster, is to invite his derision. He goes on vocalizing *Rule Britannia* in his best commercial prose.

The United States has known almost total economic, military, and political world domination since the end of World War II. It has been a model to the world of dynamism, management, and economic strength. Most Americans alive today have never lived in a world in which they were not number 1.

Because the decline has been so gradual, and the problems not yet a full-blown crisis, Americans find it difficult to come to grips with the thought there really is a serious challenge. While some can intellectually accept the possibility, they have a hard time imagining what it would be like to be a second- or third-rate power. But we point out (only half facetiously) that, like the test-tube baby, the possibility may be incredible, but it is not inconceivable. Throughout history, other nations as powerful in their day as the United States have lost.

The question is *not* whether the United States can restore the unquestioned, unchallenged economic dominance it had in the 1950s and 1960s. It cannot. That era is over. Finished. It is unlikely to return, at least not in our lifetimes.

The *real* question is whether the United States can revive its stagnant domestic productivity growth, restore a rising standard of living, respond to the rising global competition, and keep world economic leadership.

It can. But will it—like England in the late 1800s—fail to respond, in which case "the industrial glory of America will depart."

CHALLENGE AND RESPONSE

This is not the first time in history that a leading nation has been challenged by pursuers. Arnold Toynbee, the historian, characterized the struggle as a series of "challenges and responses."

A young nation grows and prospers when it successfully finds responses to the challenges that face it, as did the United States when it was challenging England and the rest of the world for economic leadership.

As time passes, the challenges change. But the leader doesn't. The leader sticks to the old responses and suffers decline and eventual failure.

Why did declining nations in the past not adjust? Did they know at the time of the danger? Did they try to prevent their fall? And, most important, is it America's turn now to decline?

To gain some insight into these questions, we turned to history to see if there might not be some "lessons" that might be helpful in looking at the U.S. competitive position today and how American business and government are responding. We found ten such lessons, which we share in Part III. We are well aware that the world has changed drastically and that history does not have to repeat itself, but we believe there are enough similarities to make these lessons worth heeding even today in the global economy.

One overarching message throughout the history of the rise and fall of nations is that the downfall of leaders is due mostly to *internal,* not external, causes. The leader, however, tends to look outside itself to find the reasons for its problems and avoids internal adjustment.

Blaming others is much easier than adjusting one's habits, institutions, attitudes, or traditions. Looking inside often means admitting errors and faults, and acknowledging that others might be as good as yourself, that they may have come up with better ideas, and that you can learn from them.

For those reasons, down through history nations have postponed or avoided adjusting internally and have declined. England was no exception: "There was," as Williams said, "a tendency to look for external causes of difficulties rather than to their own possible inadequacies."

We see some of those symptoms in the United States, both in the private sector and in government.

Konosuke Matsushita, executive adviser at Matsushita Electric, said in 1979:

> We are going to win and the industrial West is going to lose out; there's not much you can do about it, because the reasons for failure are within yourselves.

Is he right? Can the United States adjust?

FIRM-LEVEL RESPONSES

Some American firms *are* responding vigorously to the new competitive challenges, as we shall show in our "Agenda for Adjustment" in Part IV. These firms are developing a continuous improvement mind-set, automating, simplifying their structures, increasing employee involvement in real business issues, tying pay to performance, and improving quality. Some have always operated that way; others are rapidly adjusting to the new world of competition.

That's the good news.

The bad news is that as yet only a relatively small number of firms are making the kinds of changes required. The majority of American firms are not responding at all, doing very little, or engaging in a flurry of activity, much of it short-term cost-reduction, layoffs, slam-bang automation, and closings of inefficient operations. They will secure some short-term improvement but little lasting productivity growth. Such efforts give the appearance of adjustment but have not changed the core way firms do business.

American quality in products and services still suffers by comparison with leading competitors. A comprehensive study of "flexible manufacturing systems" in both the United States and Japan described the U.S. efforts as a "desert of mediocrity." Many management layers have been peeled away, but many of the surviving layers still do not function as a team. Human resources get a little more notice from senior management now, but compared to attention given to financial, legal, and marketing strategies, people strategies—involvement, man–machine operating systems, rewards—are still hind dog.

While some union leaders are working hard to find ways to work with managers and still be reelected, too many are trying to go back to the days of the power struggles, adversarial tactics, and confrontations that they know so well.

In short, not enough managers or union leaders have fully realized what they are up against, nor are they yet making the fundamental adjustments inside their organizations. We see neither in the data nor in the actions of most firms or unions across the nation *sufficient* change to alter the basic trend toward economic decline.

That is why this book's "Agenda for Adjustment" for firms and unions, Part IV, is principally about internal adjustment issues—not strategic planning, market segmentation, investment criteria, asset management, automation techniques, or bargaining strategies. Those are all important. But none of them will work well if managers, employees, and union leaders do not face the really "tough" issues of internal adjustment inside their organizations.

These internal adjustments are where the battle will be won or lost. As *Business Week* said in its April 1987 Special Report "Can America Compete?," the "gods of growth dwell in the details."

Government Responses

At the governmental level, the problem is not a lack of response, but too much response and response of the wrong kind.

Politicians have suddenly discovered "competitiveness."

They now feel they must "do something" about it, and in line with historical precedent, they focus mostly on external factors and avoid tough internal adjustments. That means calling foreign competition "unfair," drafting protectionist legislation labeled as trade policy, and blaming others "for the mess we're in." They are turning competitiveness into a buzzword and using it as a flag in which to wrap everything they've always wanted to do, and more. At the same time, they are avoiding other actions, like reducing the federal budget deficit, and neglecting some badly needed changes, like altering the educational system.

Of course, unfair trading practices and overvalued currencies need attention. We agree. But those are not the main reasons the nation faces a standard of living decline and eroding competitiveness. Most of the actions to date—protectionism, bashing, retaliatory bilateral actions—do not work on fundamental causes. They build walls, delay adjustments, protect inefficiency, and alienate trading partners. Devaluation of the dollar as a competitiveness strategy only makes the United States progressively poorer; it also does not work on the fundamental matter of productivity improvement. Exchange rates in the end only ratify underlying economic conditions.

Unfortunately, all of this activity is reported daily in the press, feeding an exaggerated belief that the causes are external and that government can enhance economic welfare and competitiveness.

It isn't that we believe the government has no role. It has a role, but it is a limited one, as we spell out in Part V.

OUR RECOMMENDATIONS

Our recommendations throughout the book are based on (1) ten years of work with firms, unions, and government in the American Productivity Center; (2) analysis of productivity data and trends; (3) our combined personal experience in consulting, academia, business, and government; (4) our personal visits to Japan and Europe; and (5) the lessons we have learned from our reading of history.

They center on productivity. The United States must revive its productivity growth so that it reaches a rate equal to or better than other nations'. Our view also is that the bulk of the change—with the exception of education—must come from the private sector, not from the government. There is no other lasting way.

Americans should not let the stockmarket, currency values, or recent manufacturing productivity gains delude them into thinking the battle is over. Far from it. It's just beginning.

DOOMSDAY?

This is no Doomsday book.

The United States is still the world's largest economy. It is a huge nation full of natural resources and possessing tremendous wealth, military power, entrepreneurship, innovation, and world influence. In consumption per capita, the U.S. standard is the highest in the industrial world. It has low inflation, a low degree of public ownership of industry, and a tax burden—federal, state, and local—lower than that of other advanced nations, with the exception of Japan.

The United States is still the largest homogeneous market in the world, and the nation is politically stable. Mergers and acquisitions help keep the U.S. economy more dynamic than many other nations. It is a nation with heart and spirit, with a reservoir of free and imaginative people who are energetic, creative, and resourceful, especially when they are aroused.

Although we project trends that show a diminishing leadership for the United States, we are well aware of the folly of mechanically extrapolating trends. *Trends do not have to continue.* They can change.

That is why we are writing this book, to change the direction in which the United States is headed before it is too late to do anything about it, and to make the point forcefully to Americans: *Grow or decline.*

THE TWO-MINUTE WARNING

In football, when the end of the game is two minutes away, the referee signals the "two-minute warning," a time-out to give each team a chance to assess its own and its competitor's strengths and weaknesses, review its game plan, adjust its offense or defense, and renew its spirit of teamwork, drive, and will to win.

This book is written as a two-minute warning to the United States. Americans have less than two decades to turn around the direction of the current game. Every day Americans postpone action is a day lost.

Competitors are not going away, and the competition is going to get tougher. H. Ross Perot, founder of EDS, warned, "We've got some first class teams on the field, and they're tearing our heads off." A semiconductor equipment executive, D. Paul Petach, Velco Instruments, expressed it even more dramatically, "Grab your socks, your pants are lost!" And George Butts, vice president of Chrysler, has said, "I'm convinced what we've seen up to now wasn't really a battle at all. It was just a skirmish: The real battle is still to come. Scary? You bet!"

Almost exactly a century ago, when E. E. Williams issued his warning, England was still the wealthiest and strongest nation in the world in almost any way you wanted to measure it—militarily, scientifically, economically, culturally—with the possible exception of educationally. England did not pay much attention at first to the challenges from the United States and Germany. And when it finally did, it was too late to respond.

We don't want that to happen to the United States.

Our book, like Williams's, is written as a warning, in the belief that, as Williams put it, "a warning is better than an obituary notice."

Can the United States adjust and respond? We think so.

We think things *can* change. But we had better hurry.

When we used the analogy of the two-minute warning in one meeting with some business executives, one excited CEO jumped to his feet and shouted, "And there are no time outs left!"

—2—
Consequences

"I'm scared," he said. "We lost our steel industry, our shipbuilding industry, our TV industry—almost every major industry—to the Japanese. Now we may be losing our semiconductor industry.

"If I lost my job, how will I be able to raise my family and send my kids to college? What will they do when they grow up if we keep losing our industries? How can we sustain our competitiveness? How can we keep our heads up?"

There are many people in the United States who could have spoken these words. They were spoken by a fifty-three-year-old engineer in Silicon Valley to Sheridan Tatsuno, author of *The Technopolis Strategy*, voicing what is, or should be, on the minds of all Americans—the consequences should U.S. productivity continue to stagnate and competitiveness continue to decline.

The speed and breadth of the repercussions to date have surprised many Americans. But they are only beginning to perceive the full implications.

The political, social, geopolitical, and economic consequences will be far-reaching. We point out seven that will dramatically affect the nation and its citizens.

1. STANDARD OF LIVING

The most tangible and personal impact will be in the pocketbook. Americans have already been hit there. Look at the incredible drop in growth of real hourly compensation (business sector):

Decade	Compensation Growth
1950s	3.7%
1960s	2.9
1970s	1.1
1980s	0.1

Back in the 1950s, earnings grew at a fast clip of 3.7 percent. At that rate, people's incomes doubled in nineteen years. The 1960s were not bad either, with growth at 2.9 percent—slightly slower, but hardly noticeable: Incomes doubled in twenty-four years, still within a working career. A wage earner could look forward to one or two cars, a single-family home, a dishwasher, a color TV, and possibly a vacation home, a boat, and sending the children to college. It became the American Dream.

Then, in the 1970s, things began to change.

The rate of increase dropped to 1.1 percent. At first, inflation masked the decline, but pretty soon people began to notice they didn't have as much left over at the end of each month. It would now take sixty-three years for incomes to double—two generations.

And things got worse. In the 1980s, income growth all but halted—a rise of only 0.1 percent—one-tenth of 1 percent. The American Dream of always being better off than one's parents now was ended. At that rate of increase, it would take 720 years to double incomes! In fact, from 1973 through 1986, real average hourly wages in all nonagricultural sectors in the United States *fell* by about 6 percent.

If, instead of the drastic slowdown, productivity had continued the trend of the earlier postwar decades, the American people would right now have a level of real income 42 percent higher than they have, almost $10,000 per person per year.

Clearly, it's not just the present generation that is affected. *American children cannot look forward to the rising standard of living their parents had.*

The impact can be dramatically illustrated by taking the case of a thirty-year-old male who started out earning $11,924 (in 1984 dollars) in 1949.

As shown in the following table, prepared by Professor Frank Levy and Richard Michel, by the time a thirty-year-old had reached forty, his real earnings had *risen by 63 percent*—a nice rapid gain in ten years. Another thirty-year-old starting in 1959 also had a nice rise in income. His earnings increased by 49 percent in ten years.

But now take a thirty-year-old male starting in 1973. He started higher at $23,580, but by the time he hit forty, his real average earnings *declined by 1 percent*. Finally, by 1983, a thirty-year-old starting out was making the same as his counterpart in 1959!

Year	Avg. Earnings (1984 Dollars) Achieved by Age 30	Avg. Earnings (1984 Dollars) Achieved by Age 40	Change
1949	$11,924	$19,475	+63%
1959	17,188	25,627	49
1973	23,580	23,395	−1
1983	17,520	??????	?

Prior to 1973, each generation of U.S. citizens could expect to be about twice as well off as their parents. That was because productivity was growing fast. Such is no longer the case. When productivity slowed to a crawl, so did real wages. The two are tied together: There is no way growth in living standards can be revived without a revival in productivity growth. Among the advanced nations of the world, the United

States and Britain are battling it out for last place in growth of standard of living.

This stagnation hasn't really surfaced yet as a public issue, because Americans are trying to cope in several ways.

First, they are "downsizing" the American Dream. Single persons are delaying marriage. Families are postponing children and buying smaller houses. Prospects of a vacation home, saving for retirement, and college for the children are fading.

Also *Americans are working more hours*. In the 1950s and early 1960s, most of the income growth came from productivity, not from working more hours. From 1948 to 1965, almost 90 percent of real growth in the business sector came from productivity improvement, only 10 percent from an increase in hours worked.

But that changed when productivity growth slowed down. Between 1973 and 1986, only 36 percent of real growth came from productivity growth, so 64 percent of it had to come from an increase in hours worked. More members of families went to work to try to sustain total income. The proportion of the total population at work increased from about 40 percent in 1970 to almost 50 percent today. Women, in particular have entered the workforce in dramatic numbers. Levy and Michel estimate that among married couples 25–34 years old, 47 percent of the wives worked in 1973. Today, two-thirds of all young wives are working. But even with more wives working, the average income of two-parent families actually declined by about 3 percent from 1973 to 1984. Thus Americans are working *more,* but not more productively.

The third way they are coping is by *going into debt.*

2. DEBT

Americans are getting "another day older and deeper in debt"—consumer debt, business debt, foreign debt, and government debt.

All of these are, in one way or another, an attempt by Americans to live beyond their means—trying to forestall a sagging standard of living.

A debtor's game plan can work in the short run. It sustains living standards at least on the surface. But as a long-run strategy for an individual or a nation, it's an illusion and a disaster.

It is one thing to pile up national debt that Americans owe to themselves. They can tax themselves and pay it off. And if consumers and businesses go broke from too much debt, at least it's "all in the family."

Foreign debt is another thing.

Foreign capital is now flowing into the United States in record proportions. Americans are, in effect, using foreign savings to support their standard of living.

Like a dissolute heir in just three years Americans ran through $141 billion 1982 inheritance in net foreign assets that had accumulated over two-thirds of a century.

Then, as the United States needed more money to sustain its standard of living and to make up for a lack of savings and stagnant productivity, Americans borrowed from abroad. At the end of 1986, the United States owed $264 billion to foreigners—a shift of $405 billion dollars from assets to liabilities in just five years!

The rapid shift from being the *world's largest creditor* to the *world's largest debtor* in the short space of five years is staggering and unprecedented in history.

Foreign debt could easily reach $700–$900 billion in the early 1990s; some estimate as high as $1 to $2 trillion. The interest on the rapidly growing debt and eventual amortization has to be paid outside the United States, and the amounts could reach huge proportions. To pay off the debt itself, the United States will have to run trade surpluses, mostly in merchandise trade. If productivity does not increase, then such a surplus can be achieved only by more currency devaluation, thereby further lowering living standards.

Also interest on the debt will cause Americans to pay tens of billions to foreigners and could consume 1 percent of American GNP. Americans are passing the buck to their children and grandchildren. They are using borrowed savings and growth to live well today at the expense of tomorrow. Americans are literally mortgaging their children's living standards in order to live better today.

This scheme of massive foreign debt accumulation can't go on forever. At some point, foreigners will cry, "Uncle!" They will call some part of the debt, thus forcing Americans to lower their standard of living to pay off. Otherwise, interest rates will have to rise in order to compensate foreigners for the added risk.

Americans cannot, for much longer, hide declining productivity gains under an increasing wall of debt.

3. INFLATION

As debt rises, the temptation will grow to create inflation, so that the debt can be repaid with cheaper dollars.

Also, inflation may get restarted simply because people refuse to accept the fact that their standard of living is falling, and try to preserve it with wage increases. However, if productivity is not growing, such wage increases are inflationary. Each American thinks that she or he can raise his or her wages faster than the inflation rate and be the exception. As Lester Thurow, Professor of Economics at MIT, puts it:

> Everyone can blame inflation on someone else, usually the government, and not have to confront the fact that his wages are stagnant because his productivity is stagnant.

4. DIVISIVENESS

As the American pie stops growing, or actually shrinks, people start struggling over shares of the diminishing pie. Income inequality usually increases in slow growth.

Envy begins. Since no one likes a smaller income, especially if the neighbors are doing better (next door or in Tokyo), the feeling grows that "they" must be doing it at my expense. Internationally, people seek foreign devils on which to blame their misfortunes. Foreign "bashing" increases, and economic nationalism replaces international cooperation.

Domestically, people turn to government to allocate the income "fairly." The mood grows ugly and divisive. The sense of community diminishes. Groups accuse one another—"fat-cat unions, greedy managers, wealthy corporations." Intergenerational conflict increases as younger people with stagnant incomes resent the debt they're saddled with. As Joseph Bower says, "Thus doth slow growth make competitors of us all."

5. DEFENSE

When the economy declines, eventually military power erodes. No nation can maintain a military force of any size without resources to equip and maintain it.

Also, as economic strength wanes, it becomes harder and harder in a democratic society to fund defense when social programs suffer from a shortage of resources.

Conversely, a prolonged high emphasis on defense can weaken an economy. It has happened repeatedly in history that older powers have bled themselves economically to maintain political and military empires. It could be happening again today.

Russia and the United States are preoccupied in a huge struggle over territory, space, and military power, spending huge sums on defense and relatively neglecting productivity and competitiveness. Meanwhile, other nations are building up economic strength and competitiveness. Over a long period of time, as Richard Rosecrance has pointed out, the winner could well be the economically strong nations. Military might and global influence always rest, over the long haul, on a strong economy.

6. FOREIGN INVESTMENT IN THE UNITED STATES

In 1968, J. J. Servan-Schreiber published a book called *The American Challenge*. He documented the mammoth investments Americans were making in Europe and warned Europeans of the "economic invasion" by Americans:

- "American industry has gauged the terrain and is now rolling from Naples to Amsterdam with the ease and speed of Israeli tanks in the Sinai desert."
- "American firms continue to carve up Europe at their pleasure."

The "modern equivalent of Ceaser's legions," another author called American companies, "arrogant and irresistible as they continue to plant their standards in the very citadel of their foes." Americans couldn't understand then why Europeans didn't appreciate what was being done for them. After all, wasn't America providing them with capital, know-how, and good management?

Twenty years later, foreign capital, especially Japanese capital, know-how, and management are beginning to flood the United States. It will be interesting to see how Americans like the consequences of "The Japanese Challenge."

7. NUMBER 2

The last major consequence of continued stagnant productivity will be that the United States will no longer be number 1. It will slip to number 2. Or 3. Or . . .

No big announcement will be made as that occurs. It will happen gradually over time. In fact, if you could ask people who were living at the time when the United States passed England in the 1890s, they would probably say, "I didn't know it was happening."

The United States will simply become slowly "relatively poorer," as its competitors grow faster. England, for example, continued as a world power for more than twenty years after it lost the lead. But it was steadily weakening, militarily and economically. It did not "crash" until the period between the two great wars.

Even today Britain, though "fallen" as a world power, still enjoys freedom through democracy, wins more Nobel Prizes per capita than any other nation in the world, and is a very pleasant place in which to live and visit. Although its income per person is still growing, relatively it is at the bottom of the league, with a GDP/capita in purchasing power terms that is less than in the United States, Canada, Norway, Sweden, Denmark, Belgium, Netherlands, France, Germany, and Japan. Even Italy, once far behind, has drawn even with Britain in GDP/capita.

The lower-productivity nation will always have some niche assigned to it—the production crumbs not valued by more efficient nations. It can remain competitive only by lowering its real wages and its standard of living.

The low-productivity nation thus pays for its relative inefficiency by getting less and less for its exports, by dropping its standard of living lower and lower, and by being assigned a lower rank in the world economy—one commensurate with its mediocre performance.

Some of these international effects of relative U.S. economic decline are already being felt.

America is no longer as universally wooed, feared, loved, or respected. No longer can Washington make its economic policy decisions with disregard for what other nations will do. The United States is less able to dictate the pace and direction of world economic policies without the concurrence of other nations. As C. Fred Bergsten of the Institute of International Economics points out, "The United States is the world's largest debtor but it continues to think like a creditor—dispensing advice to the rest of the world . . . while its own budget remains in huge deficit." *Pax Americana* is weakening, and the United States is no longer seen as a paragon, model, or invulnerable leader.

And if America falls still further economically, prestige and influence will diminish even more.

Americans will not like, as one diplomat put it, to be assigned to a new seat "below the salt" at the table of nations.

URGENCY

"Why are you sitting there so calmly in your seats," Henry Kissinger once said to an audience after he had briefed them on a particularly unsettling world situation. "Why aren't you out running the streets, spreading the alarm!"

We feel the same way.

Given the consequences that have already occurred, and ones that may occur, we also wonder why people aren't more up in arms, doing something to revive American productivity and competitiveness.

Americans have postponed the effects of low productivity and declining competitiveness for more than fifteen years, and the string is running out.

The United States is like a football team that has led for three quarters of the game. It suddenly finds that the opposition has scored several quick touchdowns, and the lead has shrunk to one point. The ball is on our own 20-yard line, and they have possession.

Two-minute warning.

Our economy is changing structurally. Growing debt will not be easy to reduce. Foreign investments in U.S. real estate, factories, and distribution channels will not be easily dislodged. Attitudes about foreign quality are becoming fixed.

Twenty years of relative decline is going to make it hard to restart our engines. It would be bad enough to discover one day that you were behind, but it is even worse to find out that you are unable to catch up.

GLACIAL CHANGE

It's not that Americans don't know that changes are occurring in world competitiveness. They read the headlines, watch the evening news, and if an individual is in a competitively impacted industry, he is made painfully aware by loss of job or cuts in pay.

But most people are *not yet* directly affected by rising international competitiveness. In fact, they have benefited from lower prices and improved quality for some foreign goods. They may see a few domestic problems, but nothing big. They have a job. Inflation is down. Things don't seem so bad.

The national statistics reporting declining competitiveness—"warning signals"—may be disturbing for the moment, but they are soon forgotten. They're like hurricane warnings from the Weather Bureau, hard to get very excited about when the sun is shining and the air is calm.

Because the U.S. decline is not arriving with a big bang, like a Sputnik, most Americans aren't yet fully awake to the danger. A big bang would at least arouse a strong response that might jar loose a more rapid and deeper level of adjustment; break up vested interests; sweep aside complacency, defensiveness, and old, inadequate responses; and end the search for external devils to blame.

Absent such a crisis, America could suffer the fate of the boiled frog.

THE UNITED STATES—A "BOILED FROG?"

There is a well-known lab exercise in which biologists drop a live frog in boiling water. Predictably, he jumps out immediately.

Then the frog is put in cool water, and the temperature is very slowly brought to a boil. The frog will stay there until he is boiled to death.

For almost twenty years now, the United States has been sitting in slowly heating water, complaining some about the rising economic discomfort, waving fans, and wishing someone or something would turn down the heat. But the heat is still rising, and the United States is still sitting there.

The United States is in danger of becoming a "boiled frog" by the end of this century.

Humans and nations are not frogs.

They can be warned. They can take readings on the water temperature to determine the degree of danger. They can review the past and look into the future. That's what we hope to do with the warning in this book.

The slowly warming water the country has been sitting in is the new, global economy that has been heating up around the United States. The best way to gauge the temperature is to look at the most fundamental indicator: *productivity*.

—Part II—
The Productivity Challenge

—3—
Productivity

What went wrong?

The root cause of America's economic stagnation and eroding competitiveness can be summed up in two words: *productivity stagnation.*

The solution for maintaining a rising standard of living and continuing economic leadership of the world can also be summed up in two words: *productivity growth.*

Unfortunately, U.S. productivity growth over the past few decades has been terrible. In this chapter, we discuss:

- The link between productivity and competitiveness
- Definitions and measures
- U.S. productivity scoreboard
- International productivity scoreboard
- Productivity goals

PRODUCTIVITY AND COMPETITIVENESS

"Competitiveness" is now on the national agenda.

In a way, that's good. More people are paying attention to the issue. It's also not so good, for some people are confusing symptoms with causes, misinterpreting measures, and inappropriately selecting measures to fit their particular purpose.

Let's try to sort out some of the confusion.

Two frequently cited measures of competitiveness are *trade balances* and *exchange rates*. Both are related to competitiveness, but *neither* is a true measure of competitiveness.

Trade balances are affected by a number of factors other than productivity: exchange rates, national budgets, differences in international growth rates, and others. The large U.S. trade deficit is often cited as a sign of poor competitiveness, but trade deficits are neither good nor bad by themselves.

Poor nations, like Afghanistan and Nigeria, can have trade surpluses. Rich and competitive nations often have trade deficits. The United States, for example, ran a trade deficit when it was growing rapidly in the nineteenth century, and trade was mostly in balance during the 1970s, when U.S. productivity was declining.

Exchange rates are also related to competitiveness but likewise are influenced by a host of other factors. First, the United States ran a trade deficit when the dollar was *low* several years ago. Second, roughly half of the U.S. current trade deficit is with nations whose currencies did not strengthen against the dollar. Third, not all competitiveness is determined by price; much is determined by design, quality, delivery, and service.

We argue that the best measure of competitiveness is productivity, and the best way to restore American competitiveness is productivity growth.

Economists argue that a nation can be competitive *regardless* of its productivity level. That is, if productivity drops, all the nation has to do to remain competitive is reduce wages and depreciate its currency until the nation is once more competitive. If that doesn't make it competitive, then do it again. And again.

Think of it as holding an international "markdown sale" until products and services move. Any nation, even Chad and Ethiopia, can become "competitive" (using the economists' definition) at some standard of living, however abysmal.

We don't buy that definition of competitiveness, nor do we recommend it to Americans. Manipulating the exchange rate to lower the dollar is a poor competitiveness strategy. As we shall point out repeatedly, fighting America's competitive problems with a lower dollar means *competing with lower wages and a lower standard of living,* not with higher productivity.

We define competitiveness as having two components:

- Maintaining a rising standard of living
- Keeping the economic leadership of the world

That being so, our definition of competitiveness is similar to that used by the President's Commission on Industrial Competitiveness:

> The ability of the U.S. to produce goods and services that sell in international markets while also maintaining or improving a standard of living equal to or better than competitors'.

The only way to satisfy those conditions for competitiveness is through *productivity—productivity growth that equals or surpasses that of competitors.*

John Young, chairman of Hewlett-Packard, who chaired the Presidential Commission, said in private correspondence to Grayson, "We have discovered over the course of the last eighteen months that the basis of American competitiveness is the relative growth of productivity compared to our major trading partners."

Any competitiveness measure not tied to productivity is deficient.

DEFINITIONS AND MEASURES

First, what is productivity?

It is what you get out for what you put in: *output/input.*

It's a ratio. If it increases, you are growing. If it decreases, you are declining. It's as simple as that.

It is the optimal use of *all* resources—labor, capital, material, energy, and technology. It includes both "physical capital" and "human capital." It is universal. It is not unique to capitalistic societies or to profit-making organizations. It is as applicable to universities and hospitals as it is to Xerox, Russia, or Bangladesh.

Productivity is not the same as production. Productivity can result in either more production or less. Productivity includes both "efficiency" *and* "effectiveness."

It is a common error to equate productivity with firing workers, reducing costs, or just doing the same things only faster: "speed up." For years, productivity has been saddled with an image of Charlie Chaplin in *Modern Times,* strapped to an eating machine, flailing away at an ear of corn on the cob like a typewriter gone berserk. Productivity improvement can also include adding workers, increasing costs, improving quality, and *doing things differently or doing different things.*

The firm or nation that provides the output (product or service) at the lowest cost and highest quality is the most productive—the most efficient *and* effective. And over time the most productive nation—war aside—will lead the world economically.

How is productivity measured?

Measures

Bear with us for a few pages, while we give a brief explanation of the key productivity measures. It gets a bit technical, but don't skip it, for when you read in the newspapers that "Productivity Rose This Quarter," you need to know what measure is being reported.

The three most commonly quoted statistics are:

- *GDP/capita.* GDP (gross domestic product) divided by the entire population; a measure of national wealth, but not a good productivity measure, as GDP is divided by every man, woman, and child whether he or she works or not
- *GDP/employee.* GDP divided by the employed labor force; a better productivity measure, but does not account for the differences among nations in hours worked
- *GDP/hour.* GDP divided by hours worked or paid; the best productivity measure, but generally not available internationally for comparisons.

Note that we use "GDP" (gross domestic product), not "GNP" (gross national product). GDP is very similar to GNP, but excludes overseas earnings of a nation's citizens. GDP is used most often when comparing economies of nations.

There are several other things you need to know about productivity figures in order to understand and use them:

1. Levels and growth rates
2. Trends
3. Sectors and industries
4. Exchange rates
5. Quality

Productivity *levels* and productivity *growth rates* are both useful. A "level" refers to a particular point in time—a snapshot—of where a nation is. A nation can compare its level to itself in another time period or to the levels of other nations. For example, the Netherlands had about 86 percent of the U.S. productivity level in 1986,* as measured by GDP/employee. Canada had 95 percent.

Growth rates measure the "change" in productivity levels between specified time periods. For example, Germany grew at an average rate of 2.2 percent (GDP/employee) in 1973–86. The United States grew at a rate of 0.5 percent.

Trends are rates of change over a multiyear period, such as ten to fifteen years or longer. Trends are best for making comparisons of basic strengths, since they are persistent and don't change rapidly with fluctuating events. Frequent revisions often bounce short-term numbers drastically.

Sectors and industries are divisions of an economy. The two broadest sectors are "goods" and "services."

"Goods" includes manufacturing (the largest part), farming, construction, and mining—altogether about 30 percent of the economy. "Services" includes everything else—business services, wholesale and retail trade, public utilities, communications, transportation, finance, insurance, and real estate.

Other breakdowns used in the book refer to "business sector" (all businesses in the private sector), "nonfarm business sector" (farms excluded), or "nonfarm, nonmanufacturing," 90 percent of which is services.

Finally, sectors can be broken down further into specific *industries,* such as petroleum refining, railroads, airlines, hotels, banks, and the like. All these breakdowns are intended to provide more information for analysis of what is happening inside an economy.

Exchange rates are the medium by which currencies are converted to some common denominator to be compared.

---

* The year 1986 was the latest year for which many of the international comparisons used in this book were available. While more current U.S. figures are available, data from international competitors often lag as much as two or three years.

Two kinds of exchange rates are used:

- *Market.* Exchange rates prevailing at a selected point in time. Market rates sometimes fluctuate for many reasons unrelated to productivity.
- *Purchasing power parity.* An adjustment to the market rate to reflect differences in inflation rates between nations. This comes closer to productivity comparability among nations by comparing baskets of goods and services.

Note that a *quality* measure was not mentioned. Despite its importance for competitiveness, no national or international quality measures exist because of measurement difficulties.

Now that you know how score is kept, what's the score?

U.S. PRODUCTIVITY SCOREBOARD

Let's take U.S. productivity first.

Productivity growth, whether measured in the "business economy" or "nonfarm business economy," has steadily declined since the high growth years of the 1950s and 1960s (GDP/hour):

Period	Business Sector	Nonfarm Business Sector
1948–68	3.2%	2.6%
1968–73	1.8	1.5
1973–86	0.9	0.7

The average annual growth rate in both sectors was less than 1 percent for the thirteen-year period 1973–86—approximately one-fourth the rate of the 1948–68 period.

Recovery?

Hasn't the United States improved its productivity growth record in recent years?

Somewhat. Productivity in the nonfarm business sector (the most commonly reported sector) rose at an average rate of 1.6 percent the years 1982–86. The better growth was partly due to business cycle growth and perhaps also due to steps taken by firms to improve efficiency by closing inefficient plants and offices, cutting costs, reducing inventories, automating, and other measures. That's the good news.

The bad news is that, first, even this growth rate is insufficient to remain competitive with other nations growing at a faster rate. Second, the U.S. growth rate should have been much higher, for these were supposedly economic "recovery" years, and the pace of increase has been disappointing. *Productivity gains in this business cycle recovery have been lower than in any similar recovery in the entire postwar era.* And, if we average the recession of the early 1980s with the recovery years to get a full cycle, productivity grew at only 1.2 percent, about half the rate of the postwar period prior to the 1980s.

And, alarmingly, the growth rate is tapering off. The year 1985 showed negligible growth of 0.5 percent, and for 1986 it was only slightly better at 0.7 percent in the nonfarm business sector. Nonfinancial corporate productivity growth was zero. For the moment at least, the United States seems to have lost the rhythm of growth.

Those figures are for the total economy. Let's look inside the economy. An APC estimated breakdown shows that manufacturing has clearly done better than nonfarm, nonmanufacturing.

	Output per Hour			
	Nonfarm	=	*Mfg.* ($^{1}/_{3}$)	*Nonfarm, Nonmfg.* ($^{2}/_{3}$)
1959–69	2.4%		2.7%	2.2%
1969–79	1.1		2.3	0.5
1979–86	0.9		3.1	(0.2)
1986	0.7		3.5	(0.7)

Note that U.S. manufacturing productivity growth picked up in the 1980s, and was better than in the 1960s and 1970s. Also, for the first time in thirty-seven years, U.S. manufacturing productivity in 1986 rose more than in nine other industrial nations. This is encouraging.

However, if the gains came mainly from one-time cost reduction and cleaning out of inefficiencies, then even the better manufacturing statistics are not indicative of a fundamental turn for the better in productivity performance, but are only temporary and transitory gains.

Also, on a longer trend basis, U.S. manufacturing productivity growth trails major competitors. For 1979–86, U.S. manufacturing productivity growth was only 55 percent of the rate achieved by Japan. And over an even longer term, 1960–86, U.S. manufacturing productivity growth was 35 percent of Japan's and 61 percent of Germany's. Against eleven foreign countries, the productivity trend in manufacturing has consistently been below average performance for a *quarter of a century*.

The biggest productivity problem, however, is not in manufacturing productivity but in the "nonfarm, nonmanufacturing" part of the economy. Since 90 percent of this sector is "services," we shall refer to it hereafter as "services."

Services Productivity

Services productivity has shown no growth since the start of the decade. Because it is roughly twice as large as the manufacturing sector, its low productivity growth pulls down the national average. And the services sector continues to grow.

Services are now about 68 percent of GNP, employ 74 percent of the workforce, and are about 25 percent of exports. The most dramatic shift has been in the composition of employment. Figure 3–1 shows the large decline in agricultural employment, the small decline in the goods sector, and the explosive growth in services sector employment. Furthermore, almost nine out of every ten new jobs from now until the mid-1990s will be in the services sector.

Much information about the services sector is distorted. The cry that the services sector is growing at the expense of manufacturing and that the United States is "deindustrializing" is not true. Not true as yet, at least. What is true is that while *employment* as a percent of GNP has declined in manufacturing, the share of GNP originating in manufacturing has remained almost a constant 21 percent of GNP: In 1950, manufacturing was 21.4 percent of GNP; in 1986, it was 21.7 percent.

Another distortion is the image that some have of the services sector as providing only dead-end, low-paying jobs in barber shops, launderies, and fast food outlets—the "Taco Bell economy." The truth is that the lower-paying, consumer-service jobs are only about 10 percent of services employment.

Services also provide jobs for academics, U.S. Senators and Congressmen, journalists, 85 percent of U.S. high-paying professions such as law and medicine, and nearly three-fourths of well-paid managers. Services industries purchase as much as 80 percent of the nation's high-tech computing and communications equipment, and many are very capi-

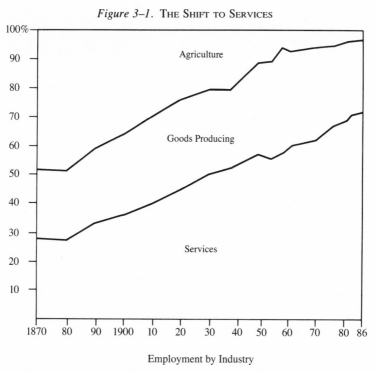

Figure 3–1. THE SHIFT TO SERVICES

Employment by Industry

SOURCE: U.S. Bureau of the Census, 1987.

tal-intensive, like communications, transportation, and public utilities.

It is also inaccurate to say that *all* services industries have low productivity levels or growth rates. American Productivity Center (APC) figures show that some do better than manufacturing:

	GDP/Hour	
	1985 Level	*1979–85 Growth*
Manufacturing	$18.73	3.1%
Services		
Real estate	$58.86	(1.4)
Public utilities	52.65	1.8
Communications	33.50	3.9
Trade	14.18	1.3
Finance, insurance	13.98	(1.3)

Note that real estate and public utilities have higher productivity levels than manufacturing, and communications even has a higher productivity growth rate than manufacturing. Even so, total services productivity growth is very poor. When it is added in with manufacturing, overall U.S. productivity growth is stagnant—less than 1 percent.

U.S. productivity growth is in trouble.

Some dismiss the productivity slowdown as just a "measurement problem." Not likely. All economic parameters—GNP, profits, costs—have measurement problems. All have arbitrary and often distorting conventions, inaccuracies in capturing information, and imprecision in valuing intangibles. Productivity measures are not better or worse. They need improvement, as we discuss in Part V, but the deficiencies are not serious enough to give large distortions, especially over time, and errors are as likely to be above as below reported figures. In other words, the slowdown is real, not just a measurement problem.

No matter whether you peg comparisons to GDP/capita, GDP/employee, or GDP/hour; whether you use market or purchasing power parity exchange rates; whether you use "labor" (hours paid) or "total factor" (labor and capital) productivity measures—the results are the same: *The United States has steadily lost ground in productivity growth relative to its own past and relative to competitors.*

International Productivity Scoreboard

The U.S. productivity lead is evaporating.

Satchel Paige gave Americans some well-intentioned, but bad, advice when he said, "Don't look back. Somebody might be gaining on you."

Not "somebody"—a whole bunch is gaining! And Americans had better look back to see who they are, why they are running faster, and what Americans can do to keep world leadership.

Two of the commonly cited measures of international competitiveness are real *GDP/capita* and *GDP/employee*. We said earlier that GDP/capita is a good measure of standard of living but not a good productivity measure. But given that one part of our definition of competitiveness also includes a rising standard of living, then GDP/capita becomes relevant.

The United States ranks at the top in level of current income per person (GDP/capita), but note that other nations are growing faster:

| | Real GDP/Capita | | |
	1986 U.S. Dollars *(Pur. Power)*	*Relative Level U.S. = 100*	*Growth Rates 1973–86*
U.S.	$17,395	100.0	1.4%
Canada	16,270	93.5	2.2
Norway	14,967	86.0	3.8
Germany	12,813	73.7	2.0
Japan	12,357	71.0	2.8
France	12,260	70.5	1.8
Netherlands	11,775	67.7	1.1
U.K.	11,443	65.8	1.3

Purchasing power exchange rates were used for GDP/capita exchange rate conversions. If current "market exchange" rates, which reflect major currency shifts were used, in 1987 *the average Japanese citizen was the richest in the industrialized world.*

Now, look at the relative rankings of nations as to productivity, as measured by GDP/employee: (See Figures 3–2 for a graph of productivity levels and 3–3 for growth rates).

| | Real GDP/Employee | | |
	1986 U.S. Dollars *(Pur. Power)*	*Relative Level U.S. = 100*	*Growth Rates 1973–86*
U.S.	$37,565	100.0	0.5%
Canada	35,670	95.0	1.2
Netherlands	32,415	86.3	0.7
France	31,667	84.3	2.2
Belgium	30,543	81.3	2.0
Germany	30,390	80.9	2.2
Norway	30,114	80.2	2.4
U.K.	26,448	70.4	1.5
Japan	25,882	68.9	2.8

Figure 3–2. GDP PER EMPLOYEE
U.S. = 100

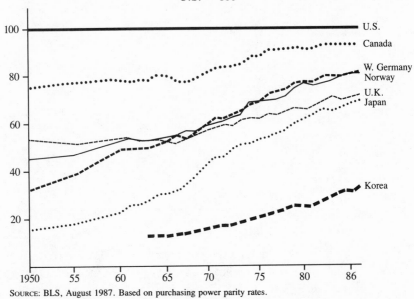

SOURCE: BLS, August 1987. Based on purchasing power parity rates.

The United States is still number 1 in productivity *level* by this measure. The nation still has time to take action and keep the lead.

However, other nations are growing much faster and rapidly catching up. Look at the right-hand column. Japan grew almost six times faster than the United States, Germany and France over four times faster, and even England three times faster. The United States ranks *dead last* in growth rates of all industrialized nations over the past thirteen years.

If this keeps up over a period of years, it is inevitable that other nations will overtake the United States in productivity level and pass it by, regardless of how far it is ahead right now. (That's what happened to England in the nineteenth century, as we shall show in the next chapter.)

Let's illustrate.

Germany is now at 81 percent of the U.S. level in GDP/employee. Germany has grown at 2.2 percent from 1973 to 1986, and the United States has grown at 0.5 percent.

If we project those growth rates into the future, at what point will Germany overtake the United States? About eleven years from now, in the year 1999.

Using the same method for other nations, the following are the

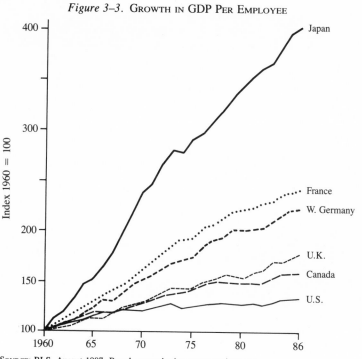

Figure 3–3. GROWTH IN GDP PER EMPLOYEE

SOURCE: BLS, August 1987. Based on purchasing power parity rates

years these nations will equal or pass the United States in GDP/employee level, assuming continuation of 1973–86 trend growth rates:

Canada	1994
France	1996
Norway	1998
Germany	1999
Belgium	2000
Japan	2003

By the year 2003—*if these trends do not change*—the U.S. will rank seventh in this group of nations.

It may surprise some to see Japan as the last in this group to pass the United States. As you can see from the table, Japan's GDP/employee in 1986 was only about 69 percent of the U.S. level. The reason is that while Japan's performance in manufacturing, is equal to or better than the U.S. level (some private estimates put Japan at 100 to 110 percent of the U.S. manufacturing productivity level) its agriculture, distribution, and transportation sectors pull down the overall national score.

One objection to this extrapolation might be that only one interval (1973–86) is used. What if others were selected? The following table shows approximate years in which various nations would overtake the United States if growth rates in different time intervals were used for the projection.

Year of Overtake of United States
Projecting Various Trend Intervals

	1950–86	1973–86	1979–86	1982–86
Belgium	1990	2000	2007	Never
Germany	1994	1999	2013	2035
France	1994	1996	2002	Never
Japan	1995	2003	2005	2025
Canada	1995	1994	2012	2025
Norway	1999	1998	2004	2000
U.K.	2030	2022	2026	2074

Which is the "correct" trend interval to use? There is no "correct" one. The future is unknown to all of us.

Using the first column—going back to 1950—does not seem reasonable, for the interval contains many years of extremely rapid "catch-up" growth by other nations that have since slowed. The last column, 1982–86, uses more recent numbers and provides a more optimistic result. However, this interval must be viewed with caution since it spans only economic recovery years and not a whole business cycle. The middle columns seem to offer the best periods to use to look ahead.

The second column, the 1973–86 interval, covers a full business cycle and still gives weight to recent numbers.

That projection shows that five nations will equal or overtake the United States by the year 2000.

The third column, using a 1979–86 projection, shows that six nations will equal or pass the United States by the year 2013.

Extrapolation

We emphasize that these are trend projections and trends can change. Also, we are well aware of the fallacies in any mechanical, uninterrupted extrapolation over a long period:

- If a fourteen-year-old boy continued his growth rate for decades, he would be a monster by age twenty-five.
- A bacterium unimpeded in its division would produce a mass a million times larger than the sun in thirty days.
- If the population of the earth continued to expand at the present rate, Isaac Asimov calculates that by A.D. 6826 the total mass of human flesh and blood would equal the mass of the known universe.

Clearly, judgment—and guessing—is called for in making any extrapolation. The examples are not a prediction but an illustration of what will occur *if* trends do *not* change: Other nations will pass the United States.

Aren't other nations inevitably going to slow down now that they have almost caught up to the United States? Not necessarily. Nothing in history says they have to slow down so far that they have to stay behind the leader. Other nations converged on England late in the nineteenth century, and today England ranks number 9 in GDP/employee level. (See p. 86.)

Sector and Industry Productivity

The national numbers we have been using are very broad measures, comparing performance of whole economies with one another. In the real world, the United States does not compete with Japan. U.S. car makers compete with Japanese car makers, U.S. chemical producers with their Japanese counterparts, and so on. But comparative international statistics at the "sector" and "industry" levels are not published by the U.S. Bureau of Labor Statistics, with one exception: manufacturing. Even here the data include *only growth rates,* and not levels.

However, special studies have been made by some economists and by the American Productivity Center to make international comparisons of productivity at the sector and industry levels.

One such study was that done at APC by George Sadler and Eliot Grossman in cooperation with the Japan Productivity Center. The study, using GDP/hour, calculated productivity levels and growth rates by industries in the United States and in Japan:

Industries	Levels (1983)		Growth Rates (1980–83)	
	U.S.	Japan	U.S.	Japan
Food and tobacco	$13.72	$ 7.23	1.6%	0.1%
Finance, insurance	8.29	14.72	−0.2	7.1
Pulp and paper	13.26	10.79	5.8	6.4
Chemicals	16.41	22.50	3.5	13.5
Elec. machinery	11.78	20.42	3.0	15.2
Transp. equip.	11.57	12.17	3.8	3.6
Wholesale and retail trade	8.77	4.81	2.8	0.5

Note that in this sample the Japanese do better in chemicals, electrical machinery, and transportation equipment, and surprisingly well in finance and insurance. The United States does better in food and tobacco, trade, and pulp and paper.

A clear message to those industries with comparatively lower productivity levels and growth rates is that they had better improve. To those still ahead, keep running. Today's lead can evaporate quickly.

Soviet Union

Notice that we've not included the Soviet Union in the international comparisons of productivity. That does not mean there is a lack of interest in productivity on the part of the socialist system. All of the Soviet Union's leaders have acknowledged the importance of productivity, and so did Karl Marx.

The Soviet Union is usually left out of such comparisons because the data are so poor. Reliable productivity figures are hard to come by because of data secrecy and the difficulties of making comparisons with artificial exchange rates and state-determined prices.

Best estimates by informed observers are that Soviet productivity is about 50 percent of the U.S. level, and the Soviet growth rate has been steadily declining.

Soviet growth in the 1960s wasn't too bad—on the order of 5 percent for GNP growth and 3 percent for productivity. But in the 1970s and into the 1980s, the Soviet economy slowed.

	Real GNP Growth	*Productivity*
1965–70	5.3%	2.9%
1970–75	3.7	1.3
1975–80	2.2	1.1
1980–85	2.1	1.3

The Russian economy has about ground to a halt, and Russian living standards have almost stopped rising. Their level is estimated to be somewhere near where Italy was in 1947 or 1948.

Mikhail Gorbachev's ambitious five-year economic plan calls for a national income growth rate of 4.1 percent and labor productivity growth at 4.6 percent. Without a dramatic step up in productivity, there is no way to achieve his stated five-year objectives.

In urging higher productivity, Gorbachev has used words like "reform," "radical restructuring," and "increased management autonomy." He urged the creation of worker teams, called "brigades." Tass, in September 1986, called for pay to be linked to performance and quality:

> The main aim is to enhance the entire pay system, to create a direct dependence between the amount and quality of work and pay, and to make the growth of pay dependent on the increase of labor productivity.

Gorbachev complained to the Soviet Communist Party's Central Committee that management was "unwieldy" and "inefficient" and had a "fossilized mentality." Sound familiar? If change is difficult in Western societies, it is compounded tenfold in the Soviet bureaucracy, as Mr. Gorbachev is learning.

However, we hope that Mr. Gorbachev attains some measure of success, for, as Will Durant pointed out, when nations have contested for power in history, "the nation that has lost in the economic competition, if it is stronger in resources and armament, has made war upon its enemy." A Malaysian proverb puts it more graphically: "When the trough is empty, the horses will bite."

America faces twin dangers from a Japan that wins too well and a Russia that loses too badly.

PRODUCTIVITY GOALS

What should America's productivity goal be?

We suggest a goal of 2.5 percent annual growth (GDP/hour, nonfarm business) from now to the year 2000.

Clearly, a 2.5 percent average growth would be quite a reach, considering the growth trends in different intervals of recent years:

1973–86	0.7%
1978–86	0.6
1982–86	1.6

The last time the United States achieved a 2.5 percent productivity growth rate on a sustained trend basis was 1961–69. The world has changed much since then, so it will not be easy to revive growth at that rate. Why not set a lower goal of, say, 1 or 1.5 percent? That would seem more reasonable.

The first problem with settling for a lower rate is that U.S. incomes would continue to move upward very slowly, at a far slower rate than what Americans want or have come to expect. To make it worse, for many years to come, more than 1 percent of U.S. GNP growth is going to be siphoned off to pay interest on foreign debt, leaving zero or only a very small increment to American incomes from 1 to 1.5 percent growth. Even the Reagan Administration's goal of 1.9 percent growth from 1987 to 1992 is too low.

An expected average increase of 1 percent in hours worked, and a 2.5 percent increase in productivity would generate an average annual increase in real GNP of 3.5 percent, a rate that would generate rising incomes and probably retain U.S. economic leadership.

A second reason for not aiming for a lower goal is that some competitors are growing faster, at productivity growth rates of 2 to 3 percent. A U.S. trend rate lower than theirs would mean a continued gradual and steady erosion of its lead.

Those differences of 0.5 percent or 1 percent may sound ridiculously small to be discussing in such detail, but the difference between a 1

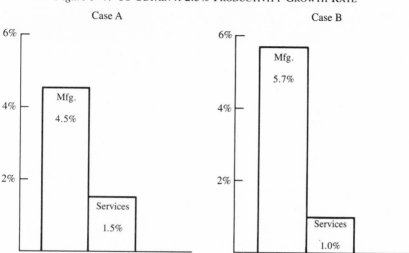

Figure 3–4. To Obtain a 2.5% Productivity Growth Rate

percent and 2 percent growth rate over a long period of time is like the difference between night and day. A small difference of 0.8 percent spelled the downfall of England in world productivity leadership.

For all these reasons, we think the United States should aim for no less than a 2.5 percent annual growth rate trend.

To achieve that goal, many industries and firms will have to do much better than 2.5 percent growth, for some will have small or negative gains. Improvements need to come from both the manufacturing and services sector. There are many combinations of growth rates in the two sectors that will achieve a 2.5 percent growth; two are illustrated in Figure 3–4.

In Case A, manufacturing productivity grows at 4.5 percent, and services at 1.5 percent. When each is weighted by its share of private economy GNP, the combined total is 2.5 percent for the overall economy. In Case B, manufacturing would have to grow at 5.7 percent, and services at 1.0 percent to reach 2.5 percent.

Many other combinations are possible, but no matter what combination is chosen, long-term improvements have to come in *both* manufacturing and services, but especially in services.

Services Productivity

Improving services sector productivity is not impossible. The services sector has both the necessity and the opportunity to become an overall highly productive sector. Highly intelligent and creative people work in this sector, and nearly 80 percent of the high-tech investments in recent years in computers and communications are in services industries.

Services are not immune, however, to increased foreign competition. As Quinn and Gagnon pointed out in a 1986 *Harvard Business Review* article, services must not make the same mistake as manufacturing; they must not wait to be overrun by more competitive nations and "follow manufacturing into decline."

Japan's services sector is still inefficient compared to the United States, but as they have done in manufacturing, the Japanese are beginning to move in services. Signs are already around in banking, insurance, hotels, brokerage, and more to come as Japan is chased out of some of its manufacturing sector by low-wage Asian nations. In fact, data from Angus Maddison going back to 1950 show that in services sector productivity *growth,* Japan has led all nations.

Ironically, the Japanese might help the United States achieve the 2.5 percent goal. The GDP of the United States reflects a production within the U.S. domestic borders, regardless of who owns the plants. So, if the Japanese own and operate U.S. plants with high productivity, they will not only provide jobs for Americans, but their figures will boost American productivity growth. Unfortunately, the profits and/or interest will flow back to Japan. Productivity counts in the GDP of the United States; cash flow counts in Japan's GNP and adds to its wealth.

Can the 2.5 percent be achieved?

Not the way we are running our businesses now. There has to be a major restructuring of firms, new ways of managing, different attitudes, better education, a new long-term orientation, and more attention to quality.

The old game plan simply won't do it.

Before we give our "game plan"—our "Agenda for Adjustment"—for reaching the goal, we shall spend a few chapters putting this goal into perspective. *We want to show why the United States has to move its productivity growth to a higher rate or suffer the fate of other nations in history that failed to do so.*

And now, as F. Scott Fitzgerald said in the introduction to one of his stories, "Pull your chairs up close to the precipice, and let me tell you a story." A story in this case of "The Decline and Fall of Practically Everybody."

—4—

The Decline and Fall of
Practically Everybody

We are often asked, "Is the United States in the early stages of a decline similar to that of England?"

Maybe. The parallels are eerie.

Must the U.S. follow in their path? No. There is still time to adjust, provided the U.S. "adjusts-in-time."

Before we present our agenda for adjustment, we believe it valuable to go back in history to see what happened to other productivity leaders and to look at the challengers who overtook them. This is not a history book. The intent is to see if the past can be helpful in shaping U.S. responses today. From our reading of history, it can.

In this chapter, we present (1) a short history of productivity in the world, with special emphasis on (2) the rise of England to world power through productivity, (3) the competitive challenge to England from Germany and the United States in the late nineteenth century.

In Chapter 5, we look at the rise of the United States to world economic power, the decline of England, the fabulous American "growth machine" of the 1950s and 1960s, and the subsequent U.S. economic stall. In Chapter 6, we ask what happened: "Was it the butler?"

And then, in Chapters 7 through 9, we present ten "lessons from history" that should be heeded lest the United States suffer the same fate as others before it who failed to respond to challenges.

But first, in our reading of the history of productivity, we found some surprises.

THE HISTORY OF PRODUCTIVITY

We presumed, as do most people, that "growth" by productivity started fairly rapidly after man stopped his nomadic wanderings, around 8000 B.C., and settled down to agriculture, or that it accelerated around 4500 B.C., when the first "civilizations" and tools were formed.

That's not quite right.

Look at Figure 4–1.

It's a plot of estimated growth in per capita income from 8000 B.C. until today. The graph dramatizes that there almost no growth in income per person from 8000 B.C. until the eighteenth century—almost a 10,000-year period.

It wasn't until the eighteenth century that any acceleration in growth appeared. Then it shot up in that towering growth "spike."

This surprises people. Weren't there some wealthy civilizations? Didn't the Romans have a high standard of living for their day?

Yes, so did Athens, Babylon, Egypt, Persia—all accumulated fabulous wealth.

But their wealth didn't come from growth as we know it today. It came primarily from taking it away from one another: bashing each other with thighbones, plunder, expropriation, and "beggar-thy-neighbor" trading.

The lack of growth from productivity wasn't from a lack of technology. Ancient China, Greece, Rome, and India all had technology of a relatively high order. China, for example, was once the technologically dominant civilization of the world, leading the way in papermaking, the development of the magnetic compass, movable type, and gunpowder. China was far ahead of Europe.

"Their failure to attain sustained growth," Herman Kahn argues,

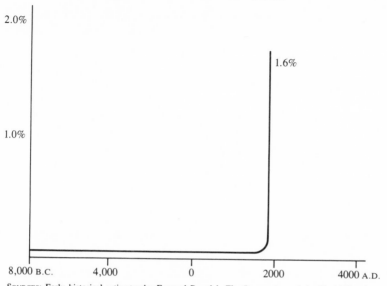

Figure 4–1. GROWTH IN GDP/CAPITA

SOURCES: Early historical estimates by Fernand Braudel, *The Perspectives of the World* (London: Fontana Press, 1985); and Angus Maddison, *Phases of Capitalist Development* (Oxford: Oxford University Press, 1982). Modern day figures by the Bureau of Labor Statistics, U.S. Department of Labor. The idea was stimulated from a graph of growth in world population by Herman Kahn, *The Coming Boom* (New York: Simon & Schuster, 1982), p. 30.

''stemmed from societal and cultural attitudes which constituted social limits to economic growth.'' Rapid growth meant upsetting ruling ideologies, vested interests, and the balance of power. They suppressed growth, as did other ancient societies.

Also, while gross world product did grow slowly, population grew just as fast, so income per person stayed almost stable. The only time the standard of living rose rapidly in preindustrial societies was when the Black Death and other epidemic diseases struck Europe in the Dark Ages. Population fell, more land was available, and incomes rose slightly. (Not exactly a recommended growth policy, however.)

In all, in the preindustrial world, growth was so slow as to be scarcely noticeable from one generation to another. For example, annual income rose, over the two-hundred-year period from 1500 to 1700, from an estimated $215 per capita to $265 per capita (in today's dollars), an average annual growth rate of 0.1%.

Fortunes and empires were built mostly on trade wars, armies, and cannon power (a technological advance over thighbones). It was mostly a ''win–lose'' world.

Growth Through Productivity

Growth through productivity—"win–win"—is really an invention of Western civilization, and it is only about 200–250 years old. Growth began to accelerate slowly in the early eighteenth century, and since then, only three nations have led the world in productivity growth.*

Who are those three leader nations?

Before answering, let's define "leader."

We use leader to mean the nation that leads in the *level* of productivity. Other nations growing faster might be called "growth leaders" (e.g., Japan today), but they are not yet the leader in the level of productivity.

First Leader?

Now, who was the world's first productivity leader?

The Netherlands.

Most people immediately assume England, as the home of the Industrial Revolution, was the first leader. However, Angus Maddison, former chief economist of the OECD, names the Dutch as the world's first real productivity leader, pacing the world for most of the eighteenth century—from about 1700 to 1785.

In 1700, Dutch GDP/capita, about $440 per person, was a little over 50 percent greater than England's $288. The Dutch weren't industrialized as we use the word today, but they still had a great deal of industry: sophisticated processing of woolens and linens, brewing, ceramics, soap making, shipbuilding. The Netherlands had a bigger fleet than England, and its activity in international banking, insurance, and shipping was on a much larger scale per capita than England's.

The Dutch were described by Norman Gall as the "Japanese of the

---

*The historical productivity data cited in this chapter and elsewhere in the book come largely from the seminal work of Angus Maddison. Along with everyone else interested in historical productivity, we owe him a great debt for his painstaking research and writing during his years as Chief Economist for OECD and during his retirement. *Phases of Capitalist Development,* the work used most often here, is listed in the References.

seventeenth century," for they, like the Japanese three centuries later, built a trading network that spanned the world. "Cheap" Dutch textiles invaded the home markets of Genoa, Venice, and Milan, wiping out many of their industries.

The Italian historian Carlo Cipolla has said, "The Dutch had a genius, if not an obsession, for reducing costs."

> The Dutch succeeded in selling anything to anybody because they sold at very low prices, and their prices were competitively low because their costs of production were more compressed than elsewhere . . . they endeavored to maximize their profit by maximizing the volume of sales.

The Dutch led the world for about eighty-five years, grew rich and powerful, and felt very secure.

But the British were coming.

For most of the eighteenth century, the English were behind the Dutch in productivity level. But Dutch average productivity growth slowed, even turning slightly negative (−0.1 percent during the latter part of the century, whereas the British began to accelerate to about 0.4 percent.

The British gained on the Dutch in both agriculture and trade. By 1760, England had pushed the Dutch aside to become the world's biggest trading nation.

It was in the last quarter of the eighteenth century that England began really to move ahead, as the first effects of the Industrial Revolution were felt. Hargreave's Spinning Jenny (1764) permitted a sixteenfold productivity increase in spinning soft welt. Arkwright's spinning frame (1768), Watt's steam engine (1776), and other technological developments began to increase the rate of England's productivity growth. The word "productivity" first appeared in print in 1766 (not in England, interestingly, but in France), and Adam Smith's *Wealth of Nations* was published in 1776. The stage was set.

The Industrial Revolution got off to a slow start, however. England's average rate of growth moved up to only about 0.5 percent a year for the last few decades of the eighteenth century. But that rate of growth—plus Dutch stagnation—was sufficient for the British to make steady gains on the Dutch.

It is estimated that England passed the Dutch in productivity level around 1785.

England became number 1.

Second Leader: England

Most of the nineteenth century belonged to Britain. It was the technological wonder and workshop of the world; its power, its wealth, and its lead over other nations was immense. Its per capita income was one-third greater than that of France and twice that of Germany.

England turned out two-thirds of the world's coal, and more than half of its iron and cotton cloth. London was the center of the world's financial markets. England's merchandise dominated in all markets of the world, its manufacturers feared no competition, it had free and open trade. England was, as David Landes, Professor of History, Harvard University, wrote, "the very model of industrial excellence and achievement."

By the middle of the nineteenth century, Britain was at the peak of its power. The famous "Crystal Palace Exposition" in 1851 in London was a worldwide exhibition of all the marvelous machines of the Industrial Age.*

It tripled its earlier rate of productivity growth to 1.5 percent between 1820 and 1870, the most rapid period of economic development in the whole of British history—its "go-go" years. By 1870, England's trade was greater than that of France, Germany, and Italy combined, and three times that of the United States.

The sun never set on its empire, and it commanded economic, military, and political power far beyond its share of world population. They became complacent, idealized themselves and their own past, and didn't look back to see if anybody was gaining.

They should have. Two major competitors were coming up fast behind them: Germany and the United States.

English Warnings

No one can date the exact time when England began to recognize the growing economic strength of other nations, but sometime in the 1880s the rising competition—particularly from Germany—began to be discussed more and more often in the British press, Parliament, and business circles. You could roughly equate that period with the early 1980s—

---

* The original Crystal Palace in London burned in 1936. Its concept and architecture were faithfully re-created in Dallas, Texas, in 1985. The building, known as "Infomart," was created by Trammell S. Crow to bring together the products not of the Industrial Revolution but of the "Information Revolution"—an imaginative concept and a striking building.

almost exactly a hundred years later—as concern started rising in the United States about international competition.

One of the first public documents was the finding of a Royal Commission in 1885 that in the actual production of commodities, the British had few if any advantages over the Germans and that the Germans "appeared to be gaining in ground on British business."

A London *Times* editorial in 1886 declared:

> The Germans are beginning to beat us in many of the qualities which are the factors of commercial success. They are content with smaller profits; their clerks work for lower salaries, they speak all languages; they are bound by no hard and fast traditions. . . . If we are to hold our own against them we must be content to adopt once more the methods which we used to practice when our trade was in its infancy, but which we seem to have largely forgotten.

A British worker wrote to the *Times* in October 1887 that one could hardly pick up a newspaper without seeing something about "this German craze" and that "we are constantly being told that they are supplanting us in everything."

The Colonial Office, in 1896, after an elaborate survey of trade competition in the Empire, found that the accusations against German "unfairness" in trade were false:

> It is the bitter truth that our commercial defeat is the result of commercial inferiority, and that we shall never manage to hold our own against our continental cousins unless we humbly confess that fact and seriously seek to remedy it. The sooner we go to school to Germany, instead of preaching morality to her, the better for ourselves.

The London Board of Trade issued a Blue Book in October 1898, containing 171 reports from consuls all over the world, which "lamented and condemned the shortcomings and supineness of the British trader."

The *Times* editorialized on November 14, 1898, that "Barbarossa (Germany) is not only awake, but wide awake, while the British merchant tosses uneasily and only half awake on his monopolist pillow—with the stuffing out."

E. E. Williams, the British author of *Made In Germany*, whom we quoted at the opening of this book, not only gave a strong general warning to the nation in 1896 but also specified how British managers were not responding to German competitiveness:

- "They rely to much upon the superiority of England already acquired, and take too little trouble to perpetuate that superiority."

- "[T]heir methods of conducting business in many English houses is as rigid as their own cast iron."
- "[I]t is mainly in the training of the employees and in the possession of scientific skills that Germany excels."
- "[T]hey do not know as many languages . . . and they do not take the trouble to study the needs of their foreign customers."
- "[The Germans] have come to England to learn our methods on the spot."

Williams even scripted a "day in the life" of a typical Englishman using German goods (see Figure 4–2).

Williams warned English manufacturers against using the excuse that Germans were doing better because of "cheap labor" and hoped that what had already happened would be an "object-lesson" to other industries "who may perchance take heed in time."

However, Germany was not the only country competing with England in foreign and domestic markets.

The Americans were also coming.

Figure 4–2. FROM *Made in Germany*

You will find that the material of some of your own clothes was probably woven in Germany. Still more probable is it that some of your wife's garments are German importations; while it is practically beyond a doubt that the magnificent mantles and jackets wherein her maids array themselves on their Sundays out are German-made and German-sold, for only so could they be done at the figure. Your governess's fiancé is a clerk in the city: but he was also made in Germany. The toys, and the dolls, and the fairy books which your children maltreat in the nursery are made in Germany: nay the material of your favourite (patriotic) newspaper had the same birthplace as like as not. Roam the house over, and the fateful mark will greet you at every turn, from the piano in the drawing-room to the mug on your kitchen dresser, blazoned though it be with the legend, A present from Margate. Descend to your domestic depths and you shall find your very drain-pipes German made. You pick out of the grate the paper wrappings from a book consignment, and they are also "Made in Germany." You stuff them into the fire, and reflect that the poker in your hand was forged in Germany. As you rise from your Hearthrug you knock over an ornament on your mantelpiece; picking up the pieces you read, on the bit that formed the base, "Manufactured in Germany." And you jot your dismal reflections down with a pencil that was made in Germany. At midnight your wife comes home from an opera which was made in Germany, has been hero enacted by singers and conductor and players made in Germany, with the aid of instruments and sheets of music made in Germany. You go to bed, and glare wrathfully at a text on the wall; it is illuminated with an English village church, and it was "Printed in Germany." If you are imaginative and dyspeptic, you drop off to sleep only to dream that St. Peter (with a duly stamped halo around his head and a bunch of keys from the Rhineland) had refused you admission into Paradise, because you bear not the Mark of the Beast upon your forehead, and are not of German make. But you can console yourself with the thought that it was only a Bierhaus Paradise any way; and you are awakened in the morning by the sonorous brass of a German band.

SOURCE: E. E. Williams, *Made in Germany* (London: William Heinemann, 1896), pp. 10–11.

—5—
The Rise and Stall
of the United States

Few Americans alive today remember a time in their lives when the United States was not number 1.

A whole generation of Americans have grown up, as Steven Schlossstein put it in *Trade War,* when the U.S. was the biggest kid on the block, "the largest GNP in the world, the highest per-capita consumption, the strongest currency, the best technology, the richest in natural resources, the most food, the most churches, the most countryclubs, the most everything."

But it wasn't always that way.

Not back in 1776.

When England was only a few years from overtaking the Netherlands, the United States was an underdeveloped nation.

1776

The year 1776 contained some interesting writing. On July 4, 1776, George III of England supposedly wrote in his diary, "Nothing of importance happened today." He had no way of knowing that on that day across the ocean a nation was born that would overtake England.

Several important documents appeared in 1776. Two were:

- The Declaration of Independence, which charted America's course to political strength
- *The Wealth of Nations,* by Adam Smith, which charted American's course to economic strength and freedom

Not as well known is that in the *same* year—1776—another document was published:

- *The Decline and Fall of the Roman Empire,* by Edward Gibbon, which we can only hope was not an ironic joke of history charting the decline and fall of America

Adam Smith ranked the nations at that time in the order of their level of economic performance (excluding, as he said, nations with "naked savages"). The Netherlands was number 1, England number 2, and the North American colonies (the thirteen colonies and Canada) were fourth:

1. Netherlands
2. England
3. France
4. North American colonies
5. Scotland
6. China

As we related in the previous chapter, about 1785 the Dutch fell back, and England forged ahead to world leadership.

The United States was no economic challenge to England at that time. GNP/capita in the advanced nations was estimated to range from $180 to $440, expressed in today's dollars, and the United States was near the bottom. Still struggling to create a new nation, it was heavily engaged in agriculture, estimated at 90 percent of employment, as contrasted with 40–50 percent in England and the Netherlands.

The American shift into heavy industry did not begin until almost forty years after Britain's. Even when the early Americans began to industrialize, only a few were inventors. They drew heavily on the British for ideas for improving productivity. The French observer of America, Alexis de Tocqueville, described America as a "land of copiers," but copiers who quickly made products better than the original ideas. New England textile mills hired craftsmen who had worked in, or toured, British textile mills so they could copy British ideas and techniques. (American history schoolbooks see this as "Yankee ingenuity," Lester Thurow points out, while British schoolbooks see it as American theft of British technology.)

U.S. employment began to shift away from agriculture into industry and services, so that by 1870, 50 percent of the work force was in agriculture, 24 percent in industry, and 26 percent in services. As American manufacturing grew stronger, American goods began to invade British markets overseas and at home. The U.S. share of world trade in manufactures grew from 3.4 percent in 1883 to 9.8 percent in 1899.

During most of its growth, the United States had high tariffs to protect its fledgling industries, but England was a wide open market. A British author wrote of the "invasion" by the Americans:

> American brains, enterprise, and ingenuity are to-day ousting British traders in the battle for commerce in many lands. . . . America has already far outstripped us in iron and steel making . . . is seriously competing with us in cotton, and is planning to take from us our export coal trade.
>
> The real invasion goes on unceasingly and without noise or show in five hundred industries at once. . . . Americans are selling their cottons in Manchester, pig iron in Lancashire, and steel in Sheffield. They send oatmeal to Scotland, potatoes to Ireland, and our national beef to England. It only remains for them to take coals to Newcastle.

There was both admiration and bitterness in this book by F. A. McKenzie, entitled *The American Invaders*. As Williams earlier described the daily life of a Britisher using *German* goods (Figure 4–2), McKenzie also dramatized how *American* goods had invaded every aspect of British life. The average Britisher, he said, "rises in the morning from his New England sheets, he shaves with a Yankee safety razor, pulls on his Boston boots over his socks from North Carolina," and at the end of the day,

> . . . when evening comes, he seeks relaxation at the latest American musical comedy, drinks a cocktail or some Californian wine, and finishes up with a couple of "Little Liver Pills" "Made in America."

THE PASSING LANE

By 1870, Maddison estimates that the productivity growth sweepstakes (GDP/hr.) looked something like this:

	1870 Productivity Levels (England = 100)
England	100
Netherlands	93
Belgium	93
U.S.	88
Germany (7th)	54

Note that the Netherlands, though it had lost the lead, had not dropped too far back. It was tied with Belgium for second place at 93 percent of England's level. Germany, though growing at a faster rate than England, was still very far back as a result of Germany's late start and the Franco-Prussian War of 1870.

The United States was in fourth position but growing at 2.1 percent, faster than everybody else. The United States overtook the Netherlands in the 1870s, Belgium in the 1880s, and moved over in the passing lane to overtake England.

Meanwhile, England's growth rate fell to 1.2 percent. "In a sense," Landes said, "the Empire began to die in January 1860." After that, "the British lines bend over like wilting flowers." Though the difference between the U.S. growth rate and England's was only 0.8 percent, it was enough for the United States to pass Britain in the 1890s.

Third Leader: The United States

The United States became the world productivity leader–number 1—a position it holds today, ninety-seven years later.

Though the United States passed Britain in productivity level, Britain continued to grow, even after the spirit of leadership and productivity growth had slowed. But the United States continued to grow faster. On the eve of World War I, the U.S. productivity level was 25 percent greater than England's, and on the eve of World War II, 42 percent greater.

Britain really didn't visibly crash until the period between the two great wars, and then "The sun, which as every schoolboy knows never set on British territory and British trade, went down below the horizon."

England dropped back in the pack.

The "Go-Go Years"

When World War II ended, the U.S. productivity lead was enormous.

Under wartime production, U.S. productivity soared, benefiting from new technology, flexibility in the labor force, and labor–management–goverment cooperation. The United States showed, as Frank Gibney, vice chairman of Encyclopaedia Brittanica and author of two excellent books on Japan, said, that "no other nation could land so many Coca Cola machines so quickly on a beachhead."

American economic power was truly overwhelming. Most other nations had their productive capacities blown up, their operations in chaos, and manpower decimated. European productivity levels were only 30–40 percent of the U.S. level. Japan was only at 14 percent of the U.S. level. The American production machine was intact, new technologies had been learned during the war, and consumer demand was set to burst forth.

The economy grew at the high average annual rate of 3.2 percent. The number of businesses grew. Population grew, government grew. TV sets, automobiles, washing machines, houses, boats and electrical appliances spewed from the factories. America produced 80 percent of the world's cars and 52 percent of the world's steel.

Growth seemed easy. Almost a right.

Americans wanted it all, and they had it all. Daniel Bell called it the "ampersand" society: Guns & butter & equity & compassion & foreign aid & tail fins & rock and roll.

Almost anything business tried was successful. Managers looked like geniuses. As one writer put it, "Being in the right place at the right time wasn't hard. There were so many right places."

U.S. management techniques were carried across the world by U.S.

managers and by American management professors teaching computers, decision trees, DCF, MBO, strategic planning. W. Edwards Deming was invited over to Japan to teach the Japanese something about quality, and they listened. U.S. academics became gurus: Maslow, Herzberg, Drucker, Likert, Feigenbaum.

"American" and "management" became one word.

Competition

Competition? What competition?

As Schlossstein put it, "Their players were mostly dead, their playing fields destroyed, their coaches old and tired. It was a perfect setup." Tom Peters, co-author of *In Search of Excellence*, likened the postwar period to "a 16–0 season and we won 16 games by forfeit. There were no competitors. . . . It was like we were living on an island and had no international competition."

Americans didn't pay too much attention to the teams of Japanese who swarmed across the United States to learn American managerial and production techniques. It was amusing and, well, sort of flattering. They asked good questions and took pictures and lots and lots of notes. Managers and academics briefed the Japanese with all the patience of parents teaching children, unaware of the Japanese saying that the greatest compliment you can pay your teacher is to surpass him.

It was estimated over a ten-year period that more than 10,000 Japanese visited the United States and went home to implement (and improve on) what we preached. They expressed genuine appreciation for what they had learned.

Americans also failed to notice that productivity was growing in Germany and France at 5–6 percent a year, and in Japan at 8–10 percent.

Diamonds in the Sky

The good times continued to roll.

At 3.2 percent productivity growth, incomes doubled in a little over twenty years. Every generation was twice as well off as its parents. Americans came to regard 3.2 percent growth almost as fixed as π. It was assumed the good times were in sustained orbit and would go on forever.

High outputs concealed waste and poor quality, but that didn't matter.

The United States was a rich nation in a poor world. The United States didn't have any competition, and people could buy anything and discard it. The Kleenex society.

Americans accumulated so much wealth the problems were not how to improve manufacturing processes or product quality (''give 'em leather, they can smell it''), but how to fill time and opt out of the rat race. Life was almost the way Woody Allen described it later: ''In order to be successful, all you've got to do is show up 80 percent of the time.''

Americans worked at play (''Pop counterculture'') and played at work (''Don't buy a car built on Monday or Friday''). These were the years of small-is-beautiful, the Whole Earth, encounter groups, the ''Scarsdale Hell,'' psychedelic drugs, Synanon games, the ''Politics of Joy,'' drop out/tune in/turn on, and the inner life of whales.

No hard choices about government programs. The pie got bigger and bigger, so there was something for everyone: farm programs, social programs, the environment, investment, defense. It was America's Golden Age. The American Century. The Go-Go Years.

After the longest period of sustained growth ever, the Nobel economist George Stigler was quoted in *Time* as saying, ''Economics is finally at the threshold of its Golden Age—nay, we already have one foot through the door.''

Goethe's warning that ''nations can endure anything but a succession of prosperous days'' was a bit of delicious irony. The United States was the exception that proved the rule.

Or so Americans thought.

Then, the most incredible thing happened.

As the Midnight Cowboy said of something else, ''The dern thing quit.''

Growth Interruptus

After almost twenty years of high growth and happy-days-are-here-forever, growth started to slow.

It didn't happen overnight.

In fact, there was little awareness in the land that anything was different.

But something was. It most definitely was. The slowdown wasn't visible at first, for it didn't affect things right away, and the seeds had been germinating for years. The signs were around, but people didn't see them or mistook them for cyclical ''hiccoughs.''

But the decay had already set in.

The old reliable—productivity growth—began to falter. The first phase of the slowdown, around 1968, went relatively unnoticed. Things had gone too well to quit now. Productivity growth, after an annual average of 3.2 percent from 1948 to 1965 (GNP/hour, business sector), declined to a rate of 2.1 percent from 1965 to 1973—a 35 percent drop.

Then came OPEC, and to everyone's surprise and disbelief, there was actually *negative* growth of −2.1 percent in 1974, the first one in American history since productivity figures were officially recorded.

That was followed by a series of slumps, a second round of oil price hikes, and escalating inflation. Productivity growth, except for cyclical upticks, continued to slow.

From 1973 to 1977, productivity growth (business sector) dropped to 1.1 percent, almost a 50 percent drop. Then from 1977 to 1986, it declined even further to an 0.8 percent rate, a further 27 percent decline. All in all, from a 3.2 percent growth rate in the first two decades of the postwar period, productivity growth declined by 75 percent.

It was like a 78 rpm record being played first at 45 rpm, then at 33⅓. The sound was terrible.

WHAT HAPPENED?

The United States has moved through three major postwar phases from (1) unbounded optimism to (2) affluence and redistribution to (3) sobering up and realism.

A "downsizing" of the American Dream is what some call it, "an end to dreaming in color."

The children of the "me generation" hung up their street clothes, graduated from college, cut their hair, read "Dress for Success," put on ties and jackets, and struggled to mold their ideals into realistic goals. Many college graduates, with the exception of those still panning gold in investment houses on Wall Street, began to start at the bottom to learn the business, or to go into business for themselves.

America is sobering up after a growth binge.

Note that this chapter is entitled "Rise and Stall of the United States," not "Decline and Fall." What happens now is up to Americans.

Why did we take the time to recount this? Don't most Americans know all this?

Yes, many do. But many do not. Those in the management ranks then, say aged 35–50, are now 65–80. A whole new generation of managers have now come up beneath them who did not experience that heady period as managers.

Even those who lived through that fabulous era as managers are only now realizing what an incredible period those go-go years were, how high the United States flew, how little competition there was, and how far the United States has fallen.

Many have also forgotten how hard the United States struggled to get to the leadership position in the nineteenth century and how it resorted to some of the same tactics and practices used by its challengers today: copying, invasion of markets, protection, international investment, and paying attention to customers and improvements.

We want to remind Americans that though they generally know about the decline of Britain from greatness, they never *really* think it could happen to the United States. It seems that neither nations nor animals, seeing another die, can imagine it happening to them. But it can.

To recap the longevity record of the three productivity leaders:

	Leader	*Years as No. 1*
1700–1785	Netherlands	85
1785–1890	England	105
1890–????	United States	98

Is there to be a fourth number 1? Who? When?

Now, in the late hours of the twentieth century, our country is somewhat like a salmon lying in a pool of historical exhaustion, and people are asking, "What happened to America?"

"Where did we go wrong?" "Who did it?"

"Was it the butler?"

—6—
Was It the Butler?

Near the end of the movie *Casablanca,* Capitaine Renault, the police chief, sees Humphrey Bogart shoot the German officer, sighs, turns to his subordinates and says, "Round up the usual suspects."

In a way that's what economists have done in searching for an explanation for the productivity slowdown. They've rounded up the traditional macroeconomic productivity suspects.

- *Capital investment.* Insufficient levels of capital investment have reduced gains from productivity-improving technologies and capital–labor substitutions.
- *R&D.* Insufficient investment in R&D has decreased innovation and technological improvements.
- *Age/sex labor force composition.* A heavy influx of women and youth into the work force has added too many inexperienced workers.

- *Energy.* Sharply increased energy prices have made much equipment obsolete and caused labor–capital substitution.
- *Inflation.* Rising prices and shrinking real profits have reduced capital for investment and increased uncertainty.
- *Others.* Excessive government regulation, tax disincentives, heavy environmental expenditures, and more.

To the traditional economists' lists, we've added other suspects named by businessmen, other academic disciplines, and consultants and compiled them in the fifty-nine-item matrix shown in Figure 6–1.

There is wide disagreement on the degree of influence that each suspect has contributed to the slowdown. Some feel, for example, that reduced capital investment caused only 10 percent of the slowdown. Others think it caused 50 percent. Some think high energy prices have had a large impact. Some say management.

Nearly every researcher, even after exhaustive econometric calculations, has been left with as much as 40 to 50 percent of the slowdown simply "unexplainable." No wonder the slowdown has been called by many a "mystery."

If we believed the typical economists' suspects to be the main causes, our recommendations in this book would be different.* We would be advocating public policies around fiscal and monetary policies; policies that encourage capital investment, savings, and R&D; increases in government training programs; and subsidies for some sectors. We do not, because:

- Even after a turnaround in the last few years of some of the supposedly negative influences, productivity has not yet returned to its earlier growth rates.
- Almost all of the "noneconomic" factors that influence productivity are left out of the economic models because they are not quantifiable.
- We question the direction of causality of some of the explanations. For example, an arithmetical correlation between productivity improvement and capital investment does not prove that investment causes productivity. It is just as likely to be the other way around: Capital flows to opportunity; productivity causes investment.
- The slowdown began as far back as 1968, before some of those

---

* Despite indications to the contrary here and there in this book, we have nothing against economists. We agree with a friend who has said, "Up to 25 percent of the guests at a university dinner party can come from the economics department without spoiling the conversation."

Figure 6–1. SLOWDOWN SUSPECTS

	MACRO	MICRO
H A R D W A R E	• High tax rates • Insufficient R&D • Low savings and investment • Excesssive regulation • Inflation • Restrictive antitrust • Fluctuating economy • Bureaucratic delays • Government paperwork • Government waste • Low government productivity • Excessive defense spending • Energy prices • Materials shortages • Protection, quotas, OMAs • Subsidies to inefficiency • Too high government as a percent of GNP	• Obsolete plants • Obsolete machines • Insufficient plants/machines • Inadequate R&D

S O F T W A R E	• Low education standards
	• Illiteracy
	• Adversarial relations with private sector
	• Changing work ethic
	• Shifts to service sector
	• High crime rates
	• Shifts in values, attitudes
	• Focus on self
	• Psychology of entitlement
	• Litigious society
	• Special interest lobbying
		A. *Management*
		  • Short-term focus
		  • Inattention to operations
		  • Inattention to quality
		  • Overstaffing
		  • Excessive analytic management
		  • Inattention to human factors
		  • Excessive attention to legal affairs
		  • Excessive attention to mergers
		  • Insufficient training
		  • Excessive executive pay
		  • Resistance to change
		  • Decline in risk-taking
		  • Adversarial toward unions
		  • Excessive specialization
		
		B. *Unions*
		  • Excessive work restrictions
		  • Featherbedding
		  • Rigid job classifications
		  • Bumping rules
		  • Adversarial attitudes to management
		  • Pay greater than productivity
		
		C. *Employees*
		  • Preference for leisure
		  • Resistance to change
		  • No pride in workmanship
		  • Abuse of alcohol and drugs
		  • Inexperience (age/sex mix)
		  • Poor work ethic

SOURCE: The matrix concept was adapted from Robert H. Hayes and Steven C. Wheelwright, *Restoring Our Competitive Edge* (New York: John Wiley & Sons, 1984), p. 393.

suspect causes occurred: OPEC, high inflation, high environmental expenditures.

- Some Japanese firms acquired or built plants in the United States in the 1970s and ran them with high productivity and quality, using American workers, operating under U.S. environmental, regulatory, and tax laws.
- Finally, our personal experiences in business lead us to believe other factors were the main causes of the slowdown.

We agree that macroeconomic variables *do* influence productivity, and that they undoubtedly had some role in causing the slowdown, but we think the principle causes lie elsewhere than the traditional suspects. Economists traditionally focus on only half of the real determinants of economic change—the quantifiable factors of production—and omit the noneconomic influences. Besides, most of the slowdown suspects are proximate causes: *They do not get to the five underlying causes of the productivity problem.*

1. Lack of International Competition

For most of the postwar period, the United States operated virtually without international competition both in domestic markets and in international trade.

The United States was so far in the lead, and competitors so far behind in economic strength and technology that the United States hardly knew it was in a race. Thurow labeled it "effortless superiority." The country had no balance of payments to worry about, no comparisons on quality or price, and no competitors with technological sophistication. It did pretty much as it pleased in both the private and public sectors.

The result was that in *firms:*

- Low or medium quality was tolerated. The market had no comparison.
- Management added layers and layers of staff.
- A Kleenex philosophy typified attitudes toward people and jobs: Use and dispose of at will.
- Marginal managers weren't even perceived as marginal, as there was little basis for comparison.
- People moved often, so why train employees for competitors?
- Managers didn't feel they had to learn from overseas; as late as 1981, GM stamping processes were operating at 30–40 percent efficiency, and Japanese at 80 percent.

- Pattern bargaining was easier and less time-consuming, and subjected everybody to the same costs.

Unions also thrived in the no-competition times:

- Pay increases could be demanded without regard to productivity. The company would simply pass it on, and no comparisons existed as to what wage was "too high."
- Jobs were not threatened, so it didn't matter too much if there were high absentee rates, numerous grievances, or low quality.
- Everyone knew the adversarial bargaining game, and it became a comfortable ritual. Everyone knew the drill.

Government joined in:

- The key issue was dividing up the pie, not creating it—consumption, not productivity.
- Antitrust focused only on tests of domestic markets, not global ones.
- Imposing higher and higher costs and taxes on individuals and businesses in the private sector didn't matter.
- No need for export promotion or information on other nations' productivity and technology.

Like a fighter or football player with no competition, the United States became out of condition: fat, inefficient, apathetic. It also emerged from those years saddled with rigidities and a sense of invincibility, calling to mind images of French knights weighted down with heavy, confining armor riding confidently into battle against the English longbows at Agincourt.

H. Ross Perot, former chairman of Electronic Data Systems (EDS) scoffs at the idea that the decline in American competitiveness has been due to an "unlevel playing field." He says the real reason was that after World War II America "had no effective competition. That made us soft. The 'level playing field' means a field where you own the bats, the balls, both teams, the dugouts, the stadium and the lights. It's hard to lose that way."

2. Affluence

All through history, nations stagnate from great wealth. "Prosperity and success are their own worst enemies," said Landes. And Toynbee: "Success seems to make us lazy or self-satisfied or conceited."

An affluent society seems less eager than in its earlier years to work as hard, to make sacrifices, to work as a team with others toward a common goal, to avoid waste and frills. It's not as "hungry" any more. It clings to its wealth, and is more focused on "keeping it" rather than "making it." Established ways of doing things prevail over the pains of adjustment and change. Conservatism turns into ossification.

We don't believe that affluence must completely spoil a nation or that all challenge has to disappear automatically with wealth. Wants never end. No society will ever have "enough."

Most people at one time or another have seen the power of the reverse side of affluence, that is, the ingenuity of those who have to "do with less" resources: the single-mindedness and drive of those pulling together toward a common goal, like Japan and Germany after World War II, and the "skunk works" disregard of formality, focus on essentials, and avoidance of time-wasting procedures.

We're not advocating poverty. Pearl Bailey was right when she said, "I've been poor, and I've been rich. And, believe me, honey, rich is better."

It isn't wealth *per se* that is bad, but the habits that come with it.

3. Politics and Economics

One of the authors (Grayson) was a price controller in Washington from 1971 to 1973 and had direct experience with the difficult mix of politics and economics, two words that can often be appropriately collapsed into "polemics."

At least three problems arise in productivity improvement around the intersection of politics and economics:

• *Equity and Efficiency* was the subject of a classic book by the late economist Arthur Okun. Politics, he explained, is concerned with equity, social justice, legitimacy, and power; economics with efficiency and optimization. When the two conflict in the public sector, efficiency (productivity) usually loses. Thus, the greater the number of decisions made by government over the economy, the less the efficiency.

In the late 1960s and the 1970s, various programs and policies gave higher priority to income distribution, entitlements, regulation, and the environment than to productivity. There is nothing wrong with any of those. The problem was that the pendulum swung too far the other way. Alfred Malabre, Jr., news editor of the *Wall Street Journal,* cites statistics showing that "nearly one of every two Americans depends entirely or in large part on some variety of governmental 'transfer' payment,''—one government-dependent individual for each working citizen, compared to one in three in the early 1970s.

This relates to the rise to power of Mancur Olson's "distributional coalitions," who, in seeking their special interests, delay, change, and divert resources from productive use.

• *Time horizons* are tremendously different between the public and private sector. A politician's economic thinking is largely focused on the next election. Genuine productivity-improving activities very often involve the long term. When politics and economics mix, the long term suffers.

• *Adversarial relationships* hamper the ability of the private and public sectors to work together.

Nothing new about this. This adversarial relationship has been going on in the United States ever since the nation was founded.

The U.S. Constitutional system gives highest priority to checks and balances against authority, not to consultation, cooperation, and consensus building. Groups seeking to work together on public issues find they are hampered by laws and due process, which focus more on procedures than on relationships and results. "Animals eat one another without qualm," the Durants said, "men consume one another by due process."

Professor Joseph Bower of Harvard suggests that perhaps *this nation cannot resolve this issue.* "The calls for consensus and cooperation, for a reduction of due process, are in fact calls for a rewriting or reinterpretation of the Constitution in the interest of a more effective management of the society."

The impact on productivity is that the government is now much larger and has much more impact on resource allocation. Now that there is less growth, there are fewer resources for the politicians to divide, which leads to adversarial battles over resources and with politicians always wanting re-election, consumption always tends to win.

4. Inadequate Attention to the Human Dimension

The fourth underlying cause of the productivity slowdown is the relative neglect of the human dimension by both managers and government officials.

At the governmental level, it appears as an underinvestment in the quantity and quality of education, which we shall discuss in Part V.

In business, it means a lack of involvement of employees, treating employees completely as "variables," a neglect of training, and a much larger preoccupation with "hard" assets, like return on investment, earnings per share, cost per unit. People values are "soft"—nice, fuzzy, and warm—but not really central to "the business."

Many managers will deny that assertion, saying: "We believe people are our most important asset." Yet, if you examine what they *do* in organization structures, job design, commitment to employment security, delegation, information sharing, and involvement, the facts don't sustain what they say.

The relative neglect of the human dimension, if continued, will be a powerful detriment to a restoration of U.S. competitiveness.

5. Aging

The fifth underlying cause is one that everyone understands intuitively and personally, but it is difficult for us all to accept: *getting older*.

Simply stated, the United States has grown older.

"The economy of the United States is getting old," Charles Kindelberger, a Professor of Economics, at MIT says. Kindelberger suggested in a 1974 *Challenge* article the possibility that the United States, like England in the late nineteenth century, "might be aging, becoming sclerotic, or proceeding into its climacteric."

In the youth of a nation, it is daring, hungry, vigorous, hard-working, goal-oriented, results-minded, and relatively unencumbered with rules, habits, regulations, checkpoints, and procedures. Growth is in the air.

Then it gets older.

Security begins to become more important. Protecting what you have, distributing, and spending become more valuable than "making it." Special interest groups rise like vines to snare a larger share of the pie. Territory becomes more important—jurisdictions, job descriptions. Youthful competitors are initially regarded as insignificant upstarts, impertinent challengers, and workaholics.

Kindelberger has researched the economic histories of nations and lists in his writings some common characteristics of aging nations that prevented or hampered their ability to mount a competitive response to a challenger.

Using Kindelberger's observations, plus our own, we see six symptoms of an aging nation in the United States today:

a. REDUCED CAPACITY TO CHANGE AT NATIONAL LEVEL

- Reduced ability to shift rapidly from low- to high-productivity industries
- Budget deficits and subsidies hard to reduce (a thesis of Nobel Prize–winning economist James Buchanan)
- Increased barriers to entry in professions
- Otherwise effective macroeconomic policies not working as well as before

b. REDUCED CAPACITY TO CHANGE AT FIRM AND UNION LEVEL

- Old techniques difficult to change
- Tendency to featherbed
- Rigid job classifications and work rules
- Shark repellant barriers to mergers that block change
- Rigid wages and salaries
- Specialists preferred over generalists
- Functional compartmentalization; turf protection

c. PREOCCUPATION WITH "TERMS OF TRADE" INSTEAD OF ADJUSTMENT

- Exchange rate manipulation
- Bashing and retaliations
- Protection: quotas, tariffs, marketing orders

d. MORE FUNCTIONS DELEGATED TO GOVERNMENT

- Rising percentage of GNP allocated by government
- Increasing Congressional staffs and committees
- Increasing government intervention into economic decisions
- A higher and higher percentage of people receiving some form of government assistance

e. MORE INTEREST IN THE PRESENT AND PAST, NOT FUTURE

- More focus on short term earnings and payback
- Low investment in training
- Low savings rates; increased desire to consume, not invest
- Criticism of those who work harder as "workaholics"
- Risk aversion in investments

f. GROWING VESTED INTERESTS

- Rising number of "associations" and professional societies
- Increasing reliance on "credentialism"
- Growing number of lobbyists

Kindelberger concludes: " . . . the nation of the United States as an aging economy, increasingly arteriosclerotic, slower to adapt, to respond, to innovate fits the broad picture. . . . In this process the country is *following the path of many others,* of which Britain is only the most recent" (emphasis added).

Does that mean the United States is inevitably destined to decline as are all organisms, and that the best we can do is bundle up and draw our wheelchairs up in a circle in the sunset of our declining days? No. Societies are not organisms, and "renewal, restructuring, and revitalization" are not only possible but, if we are to maintain our lead, absolutely essential.

These aging symptoms also raise the question John Gardner posed:

Every few years the archaeologists unearth another civilization that ruled for a time and then died. The modern mind, acutely conscious of the sweep of history and chronically apprehensive, is quick to ask, "Is it our turn now?"

Is It Our Turn Now?

The United States is certainly not the first nation to lead the world and then face challenges from others. As we mentioned in Chapter 1, Toynbee characterized the rise and fall of nations as a series of successive "challenges and responses," a timeless drama enacted in a large chasm with sheer rock walls rising from a deep void below.

Scattered along the cliff walls are climbers representing civilizations at various levels, and on the ledges far below lie the inert and lifeless bodies of earlier climbers (ancient civilizations), who have hurtled to their death.

Others dangle at various levels, clinging by their fingernails to cliffs too steep for their exhausted strength to scale. Other more aged climbers move slowly along the cliff walls, laboring with every move, their strength waning. The younger challengers are climbing more rapidly, full of vigor and straining upward to reach the next ledge.

Using Toynbee's imagery, the positions of climbers on the rock face could be viewed as the *levels* of productivity, and their rates of climb as *productivity growth rates*.

The United States is now on the highest ledge. Other climbers—Germany, Canada, France, the Netherlands—have moved closer to the United States in recent years. Japan is farther behind but climbing rapidly. Korea and Taiwan are moving even faster but are much farther below.

The U.S. rate of climb has noticeably slowed.

Questions:

1. Is the United States in a creative pause, resting only to resume a vigorous climb again?
2. Or is the United States exhausted, soon to stop and be passed by more vigorous, fresh climbers?

We don't know the answer to those questions, but it is to history that we turn to get some clues.

—*Part III*—
A Historical Perspective

—7—

Lessons from History: The Leader's Perceptions

History is full of cities and nations that rose and fell: Sumeria, Babylon, Assyria, Egypt, Persia, Phoenicia, Carthage, Athens, Rome, China, India, Venice, Spain, Antwerp, Portugal, Amsterdam, the Netherlands, France. And more recently, England.

All rose to great power, commanded vast resources, were the envy of the world, felt themselves invincible—only to fall behind on Toynbee's cliffs as new challengers passed them by.

Fascinated and puzzled by those civilizations, people ask:

1. How did they rise to such power?
2. Why did they decline? What did they do wrong?
3. Did they know it was happening at the time?
4. Why didn't they do something about it if they knew?

5. What were the mistakes of the leaders? The strengths of the challengers?

We believe more knowledge of the economic history of nations can generally be useful for Americans, and specifically useful in reviving American competitiveness.

First, studying the economic histories of the rise and decline of other nations may help to remove the common American illusion of invincibility, which holds that somehow the United States is destined to rule the economic world forever.

Second, Americans can extract some valuable "lessons" that may be useful in responding to their late-twentieth-century challenge. Economics runs through all of history as one of the most powerful forces creating civilizations, even ancient ones. "Economic ambition, not the face of Helen . . . launched a thousand ships on Ilium," the Durants said. Economic decline has also led to their downfall.

Finally, economic history can help Americans escape from their almost myopic focus on Western civilizations. As we discuss in the next-to-last chapter, the next century is likely to be the "Century of the Pacific," and Americans need to understand more of the history of Asian civilizations that were in existence thousands of years before the United States came into being.

LIMITATIONS OF HISTORY

We are well aware that history as a guide to the future has limitations. No two time periods are alike. The twentieth century is not like any other time period in history. Yet there remain consistencies and trends that influence the future: The world is not all random. Sören Kierkegaard, the Danish philosopher, phrased it well: "Life can only be understood backwards but it must be lived forwards."

Also, history does not have to repeat itself in some recurring pattern. We do not agree with "historical inevitability" or the idea that "those who ignore history are bound to repeat it." Our view is the same as that of Toynbee, who concluded after an exhaustive study of civilizations that the rise and fall of nations is a matter of choice, not a locked-in repeating pattern.

Despite those limitations, we think nations can learn from the past. In this and the next two chapters, we present ten "Lessons from History," factors which caused leaders to decline and challengers to rise to take their place. Because these are lessons we think the United States could well afford to heed quickly, here, as a preview, is how we think those lessons apply to the United States today:

1. *Complacency:* Like other extremely dominant nations, the United States has become complacent following its world dominance after World War II—asleep from no competition, soft from affluence, lulled into believing itself invincible, it has underestimated competitors and engaged in defensive strategies.
2. *Copy:* The United States used to be more willing to learn from others and now wastes time complaining about others copying from it.
3. *Quality:* Relative to competitors, the quality of American products and services has declined, and less attention has been paid to customers.
4. *Education:* The U.S. educational system has deteriorated relative to its own past, and the United States stresses education far less than competitors.
5. *Protection:* The United States, like other nations that have lost, has moved toward protection at the worst possible time, further harming its competitiveness.
6. *Relative:* The United States has overlooked relative gains of its competitors until they are now right on its heels.
7. *Size:* American has underestimated much smaller Asian rivals, not believing they could ever become serious technological competitors.
8. *Slow:* Because nations decline gradually, Americans have failed to perceive the slow erosion and thus failed to react sufficiently fast or deeply.
9. *Drive:* America's earlier drive, energy, and determination have diminished, especially relative to younger and hungrier competitors.
10. *Adjust:* America, like other aged nations, has lost some of its flexibility because of laws, habits, vested interests, managerial models, and work rules that have reduced its ability to adjust.

What follows is a brief discussion of each of these factors in a historical perspective.

THE LEADER'S PERCEPTIONS: COMPLACENCY, RELATIVE, SLOW, SIZE

LESSON 1: COMPLACENCY IS THE CANCER OF LEADERSHIP

The United States has held the productivity leadership for ninety-eight years. And for twenty of those years, 1948–68, the United States almost totally dominated the world economically, politically, and militarily.

In the process, the United States has become complacent.

In our reading of history, we found five ways in which leadership and dominance cause the leading nation to grow complacent, setting the stage for replacement by a challenger.

1. *Affluence.* In civilization after civilization—Babylon, Persia, China, Egypt, Greece—we've seen the tendency of wealthy nations to succumb to some of the "softening" factors of affluence. They became too comfortable and too safe, and their focus shifted to enjoying the wealth, forgetting how they got rich in the first place. They invited challenges from hungrier mouths.

The historian Carroll Quigley described historical change in civilizations as occurring in seven stages, with the first four stages successive moves to power and affluence. Stage 5 is "The Golden Age [which] is really the glow of overripeness, and soon decline begins." Stage 6 is Decay, followed by Stage 7, which is the Stage of Invasion by "outsiders" who are younger, hungrier, and more powerful civilizations.

In Chapter 6, we listed "affluence" as one of the five underlying causes of the U.S. productivity decline, and its eroding influence appears over and over in history.

2. *Lack of competition.* Part of the reason for Rome's decline, Toynbee said, was that "a universal state is not subject to the pressures of rivals which is so potent a stimulus in the struggle for existence." The British historian E. J. Hobsbawm judged that the best explanation of the loss of dynamism in British industry was that it was as the result of the "early and long sustained start as an industrial power," and that it declined as it lived off the remnants of world monopoly.

Having no competitive forces in the Soviet Union accounts in part for its low productivity record, and, as we said in Chapter 6, we believe the lack of competition for so long after World War II was one of the underlying causes of the productivity slowdown in the United States.

The expression "dead as a dodo" refers to the extinction of a bird which, having no predatory enemies for generations, forgot how to fly and was unable to escape from new predators. Human beings and nations suffer the same fate with no competition.

3. *Belief in invincibility and immortality*. This is the "victory disease." The leader, after victory or a long period of dominance, tends to "rest on his oars" as Toynbee put it, "living in a fool's paradise where he dreams that, by having extended himself once upon a time, he has won a title to live happily ever after." He becomes both complacent and arrogant.

Rome knocked out Carthage and Macedonia, and proclaimed the Roman Empire to be eternal "just as the sum total of things is eternal." In the late nineteenth century, David Landes says, the "British basked complacently in the sunset of their economic hegemony."

The United States has to be especially attentive to this complacency trap, for there is a common belief that the nation is slow to anger and slow to act, but when aroused, it "always" wins. The complacency generated by viewing oneself as impregnable is often the last act of civilizations.

4. *New challenge, old response*. When a new challenge arises, merely to repeat what worked earlier can lead to defeat.

Toynbee stressed the theme of "challenge and response" repeatedly in his study of history. We have to rid ourselves, he said, of the illusion that what worked once will necessarily work again.

In industry, this mistake is worshiped as "back to basics." Back to basics can mean down to defeat.

5. *Disregard*. Nations receiving news of the rise of competitors often disregarded such warnings as only alarmist Doomsday reports, exaggerated threats, or familiar troubles that always go away over time.

The British were warned of the German economic threat as early as 1840, and we found repeated warnings over the next several decades, especially near the end of the nineteenth century. Despite books, articles, and speeches in Parliament, few took the threat seriously.

When England finally faced the fact that Germany was right at its heels, "it was one of the longest double takes in history," Landes said.

For a long time, the United States has ignored rising competition. A surprising number of Americans still find myths, reassuring falsehoods, and blaming the competitor more comforting than reality. Joseph Boyd, then chairman of the Harris Corporation, said in 1985: "Perhaps the most difficult thing for Americans to recognize is that we do, in fact, have a real problem. That it is a new and different problem and that 'business as usual' will not resolve it. And it won't just go away.''

Those five complacency factors—affluence, lack of competition, belief in invincibility, repetition of old responses, and disregard of the seriousness of challenges—have appeared throughout history as handmaidens of leadership.

While there is now a much greater awareness in the United States of the challenge, the United States remains too complacent.

LESSON 2: LEADERS OVERLOOK THE RELATIVE GROWTH RATES OF THEIR CHALLENGERS

Leaders focus on their own good fortune and growth rates and pay insufficient attention to relatively higher productivity growth rates of competitors, especially if the relative differences are small.

A leader growing at, say, 2 percent a year may be happy with its growth and unconcerned with a competitor growing at 3 percent. After all, the difference is only 1 percent.

That's a mistake. Even very small differences, compounded over time, are important.

As we showed in the previous chapter, England overtook the Netherlands in the eighteenth century when the difference in their average growth rates was only about .05 percent—*a half of 1 percent.*

The same lesson was repeated when England, in turn, failed to respond to the higher productivity growth rate of the United States in the late nineteenth century. England was still growing, but "they had little care for comparative rates of growth." The British author E. E. Williams tried to explain the importance of a relative difference by illustrating it in terms of relative wealth:

> A man with a thousand pounds is a rich man, as long as none of his neighbors have more than a hundred; but if *they* increase their possessions to ten thousand a-piece, *his* thousand spells poverty.

As the following table shows, England was still growing at 1.3 percent, but the United States was growing faster at 2.1 percent:

	Productivity Growth 1870–1890
United States	2.1%
England	1.3

Notice that the difference in growth rates between the United States and England was very small, only 0.8 percent, from 1870 to 1890. Yet the small difference, *compounded over time,* was enough for the United States to pass England in productivity level in the 1890s. The difference in growth rates widened to 1.1 percent from 1890 to 1913, but, as the following table shows, those small differences carried the United States from 88 percent of the English level in 1870 to 124 percent by 1913:

U.S. PRODUCTIVITY LEVEL

Year	*England = 100*
1870	88%
1880	90
1890	96
1900	106
1913	124

Today, the United States leads in productivity level, but as we pointed out in Chapter 3 other nations have been growing faster than the United States for some time, and many have now almost caught up.

The top half of Exhibit B shows what happened to England in productivity leadership as other nations grew faster. From the top of the pack in 1870, England fell to number 9 today. The bottom half of the exhibit shows what would happen to today's world productivity leader—the United States—if nations continue to grow at the 1973–86 rates. In just two decades, the United States would rank number 8.

We stress the point we made in Chapter 3: *Trends do not have to continue.* The United States can speed up. Other nations can slow down. But the arithmetic of relative rates of growth cannot be ignored. In twenty years, if these trends continue, the United States will no longer be the world productivity leader.

It is of vital importance for Americans to understand that (1) relative growth rates between nations are extremely important, (2) very small differences in growth rates eventually add up to very large numbers, and (3) if the United States does not adjust its productivity rate at least to match the growth of its strongest competitors, it will eventually and inevitably lose the lead.

Exhibit B: RELATIVE LEVELS OF PRODUCTIVITY

United Kingdom = 100			
1870[1]			1986[1]
U.K.	100	U.S.	142
Belgium	93	Canada	135
Netherlands	93	Netherlands	123
U.S.	88	France	120
Canada	76	Italy	118
Italy	55	Belgium	116
Germany	54	Germany	115
France	53	Norway	114
Norway	50	U.K.	100
Japan	21	Japan	98

United States = 100			
1986[2]		2006[3] (*if 1973–86 trends continue*)	
U.S.	100	France	118
Canada	95	Norway	117
Netherlands	86	Germany	113
France	84	Belgium	109
Italy	83	Canada	109
Belgium	81	Japan	108
Germany	81	Italy	103
Norway	80	U.S.	100
U.K.	70	Netherlands	90
Japan	69	U.K.	86

[1] The 1870 figures are GDP/hour from Angus Maddison, *Phases of Capitalist Development*, (Oxford: Oxford University Press, 1982), p. 212.
[2] The 1986 figures are GDP/employee from unpublished data from BLS, U.S. Department of Labor, August 1987.
[3] The projections to 2006 use 1973–86 trend growth rates in GDP/employee.

LESSON 3: CHANGES ARE SO SLOW THAT LEADERS FAIL TO SENSE CHALLENGERS

Though history books often record events as sudden and dramatic, economic history usually occurs in slow motion. The rise of nations to leadership and their subsequent decline can sometimes consume centuries.

That slow process makes it very difficult for a leader to sense that it is losing power and that others are gaining.

England's decline began after the 1850s, but few sensed it. Even though warnings and statistics were published throughout much of the decline, the idea that England had lost the lead didn't really sink into the British consciousness until almost 1913.

One reason is that even after the heart has gone out of a system, the system continues on automatic pilot, driven by habit, tradition, and institutions. It may continue to expand, as did England after its decline had set in, thereby masking the internal decay.

Declining nations borrow to sustain an illusion of well-being, as the United States is doing now. The challenge is felt to be only temporary, due to some transitory or unfair advantages that will dissipate. The stagnation is taken to be only a manifestation of cyclical events, certain to turn up again with the next favorable economic wind. And the leader mistakenly believes, as many do today in the United States, that challengers surely must slow down and settle in behind the leader as they converge.

One is tempted to take comfort in the Durants' observation that "history assures us that civilizations decay quite leisurely." With the rate of change in the global economy, the former leisurely decline rates may now be greatly accelerated.

For all those reasons, if the United States fails to respond until too late, the danger grows that the American frog will be boiled.

LESSON 4: INITIAL SIZE IS NOT A PREDICTOR OF WINNERS

In 390 B.C. Rome was a miserable little city on the borders of Etruria that was constantly being sacked by the marauding Gauls. A hundred years later, Rome was ruling and unifying all Italy, eventually to become the ancient world's most powerful nation.

The Dutch were the economic leaders of the eighteenth century even though they were smaller than England. Their population was about 2 million, as against Britain's 11 million.

"Half the country is under water," said the Spanish economist Ustariz in 1724 of Holland, "or is on land that can produce nothing. Holland is a barren country; it cannot feed a fifth part of its inhabitants." Yet the Dutch in the eighteenth century became a leading world economic power.

England was the birthplace of the Industrial Revolution and eventually became the world economic leader, although, as Fernand Braudel, the French historian, reports, France was larger and more imposing at the time—thirteen times the size of Holland, three or four times the size of England, with four of five times as many people.

Germany, even as late as 1870, was still an agricultural nation, with the majority of its people living on the land. Germany ranked seventh in productivity level behind England, with about 50 percent of Britain's productivity. Its industrial capital was small, its manufactures were unimportant, and its export trade was "too insignificant to merit the attention of the official statistician."

The United States in its earliest days was never considered by England or anyone else to be a potential leader of the world. When the United States challenged England, it flew a flag that said, "Don't tread on me" at a time, as Ross Perot pointed out, "when we were so small, so tiny and so ineffective, it would have been hard to find us to step on us."

In 1883, Japan was so far behind the world it was regarded as backward. Great Britain had 37 percent of world trade in manufactures, the United States had 3.4 percent, and Japan almost none—0.1 percent. As recently as 1960, Japan accounted for less than 3 percent of the world's economy, and its productivity was about 15 percent of the U.S. level.

Now Japan represents about 10 percent of the world's economy, its productivity stands at about 70 percent of the U.S. level, and it is now probably the most competitive nation on earth.

The lesson: A leader tends to overlook small challengers as insignificant at first. When they grow larger and begin to enter domestic and foreign markets, the leader tends to think the challenger must be engaged in "unfair" competition, based on "unsound or immoral principles." "If we are losing, it must be an unfair fight."

The United States should be concerned not only about Japan but about other nations that are now small in size or in GNP—especially Taiwan and South Korea—as will be discussed in Chapter 28.

The world is not a safe place for leaders.

—8—

Lessons from History: The Ways of the Challenger

LESSON 5: GAINERS HAVE DRIVE—THE "EYE OF THE TIGER"

What a challenger lacks in population, geographical size, or natural resources can often be compensated for by what historians call "elan," "push," "hunger," "hustle," "obsession," or "striving."

These noneconomic, intangible, attitudinal factors, which we call "drive," help nations not only to overcome disadvantaged starting positions but also to recover from destruction and defeat, as in the case of Germany and Japan in the post–World War II period. Nations seem to show strong drive in their early years or after devastation, only to see that drive fade in later years.

England, in its move to the top in the late eighteenth and early nineteenth centuries, showed drive, ingenuity, and a fury of innovation.

The venturesome spirit was so strong, the British created new ways of making and selling goods, even outside the accepted order. Barbers, schoolmasters, and ministers became inventors and entrepreneurs of their day. So many new things were being tried, Samuel Johnson complained, that "all business is to be done a new way, even men are to be hanged in a new way."

But England seemed to lose its drive just about the same time the Germans exhibited what Williams called "push": "It is a little word, but it conveys the meaning of perhaps the biggest part of Germany's success."

He pointed out that the Germans persisted in the face of lack of capital, lack of skill, and lack of innovation. Difficulties caused them to work harder. The great cause, Williams said, of German success is "an alert progressiveness, contrasting brilliantly with the conservative stupor of ourselves." The historian David Landes, in *The Unbound Prometheus,* agreed: "The reasons for German success in competition with England were not material, but rather social and institutional."

The United States also had that intangible characteristic in its early years. In his book about the "American invaders," F. A. McKenzie said: " 'Driving' is the rule in American industry . . . the American business man works harder and works longer than his average English competitor."

A question many American are asking today is whether the strong drive apparent in the early history of the United States still exists and, if diminished, whether it can be revived in sufficient strength to match Asian nations, which now show the drive of challengers? One American businessmen's tour group went to Japan in 1982 and in their report said, "In factory after factory, everyone inside is trying to whip us. If we don't get that attitude, we literally won't survive." Such intangible factors are almost impossible to put into productivity ratios or economic models, because they can't be quantified.

Yet, as any athlete, artist, or business manager will tell you, drive is a critical element in performance. As Rocky's trainer told him, when you face a determined challenger, "you gotta have the eye of the tiger."

Lesson 6: Challengers Stress Education

A hallmark of challengers is that they stress education more heavily than the leaders.

Germany and England

Germany started emphasizing education very early in its history, some parts of Germany even going back to the sixteenth century in compulsory elementary education. Frederick the Great made education compulsory for all of Prussia in 1763. By 1860, the proportion of children of school age attending classes was 97.5 percent, and the German educational system was famed throughout Europe.

Observers from abroad, Landes reported, were impressed not only with the almost universal attendance but also with the content and structure of their education. Schooling lasted longer. The range of subjects was greater. The children were all neat and decorous in class, leaving teachers free to concentrate on instruction, not discipline. And there was a national consensus on the importance of education.

The Germans built an extensive system of technical education and linked vocational, technical, and scientific education. Williams reported:

> There is not a subject germane to industrial, scientific or commercial training, which is not taught and taught well in a number of schools up and down the German empire.
>
> The technical education of German workers is far and away better than that of an Englishman in a similar position.
>
> Training is supplemented by visits to work, actual surveys, inspection of farms, drainage, and hydraulic works. It is severely practical.

Because the German workers had a good scientific and technical background, they could keep abreast of the greater complexity and precision of manufacturing equipment and the closer control of quality. It allowed the *average* German worker to appreciate its economic significance and to adapt it to the requirement of production.

That contrasted greatly with England.

In 1860, England had only about half of its school-age children receiving some kind of elementary instruction. It wasn't until 1870 that England created its first universal elementary education system—more than a hundred years later than Germany.

England's educational system was basically elitist, with a strong emphasis on the "public" (private) upper schools and universities for training the brightest and wealthiest. Even as late as 1897, less than 7 percent of English grammar school pupils came from the working class.

England continued to lag educationally during the early years of the twentieth century. Just prior to World War I, in 1913, England had only 9,000 university students; Germany had 60,000. While in England

and Wales "only 350 graduated in *all* branches of science, technology, and mathematics," Germany produced 3,000 graduate engineers per year.

The differences between the British and German educational systems were widely discussed in England all during the latter part of the eighteenth century. Landes reports a "long chorus of anguish" over their educational shortcomings from 1867 onward: articles, speeches, reports, and testimony before parliamentary commissions. Despite this, the English educational system did not basically change.

The English continued with their elitist and classical orientation toward education, vestiges of which still exist today. The German educational system, on the other hand, was more intense, deeper in content, and aimed at producing a widely educated citizenry with a base of scientific and technical competence.

United States

American education in colonial days languished as a national movement because of inherited European traditions, insufficient resources, and because Americans still regarded education as mostly a private matter.

As time went by, that changed. Education began to be seen as a public responsibility, as a "right" of all, and as a route to escape from poverty. Accordingly, American education evolved toward free, public, nonsectarian, and universal education.

It wasn't until the mid-nineteenth century, however, that the movement toward compulsory education really got under way with the passage of such a law in Massachusetts in 1852. Other states did not immediately follow, but over the years the movement grew, with Mississippi the last state to pass a compulsory education law in 1918.

Thus, both Germany and America opted for mass education while England still clung mostly to its elitist and classical model. It cannot be proved that this was a principal cause of the English decline, but widespread national education is now recognized (belatedly by England today) by most researchers, economists, and businessmen as a critical force in competitiveness.

Pounds and Bryner concluded in their book *The School in American Society* that "schools tend to reflect the societies in which they are found." To which we add, societies and economies also tend to reflect their educational system.

Japan

Japan has also long been committed to education. Before the Meiji Restoration in 1868, it is estimated that 40 percent of the school-age boys and 25 percent of the girls were receiving some form of elementary education in Japan. In Great Britain during the same period, only 25 percent of the boys attended, and almost no girls.

One of the first acts of the Meiji government was to make education compulsory and universal.

The government sent missions to tour Europe and the United States and imported teachers to teach them foreign ideas, methods, and technologies. Wisely or luckily, Japan avoided the elitist educational models of the European Continent and adopted the U.S. mass education model.

By 1925, 99.4 percent of all Japanese children attended school, and by 1927, 93 percent of all Japanese could read.

Today, Japan continues its strong dedication to learning, which we discuss in detail in Chapter 23.

LESSON 7: GAINERS COPY THE LEADERS

Many Americans accuse the Japanese of copying American ideas and technology, as if that were something unique. Wrong.

The record of history is clear: *All* nations copy from one another, directly and indirectly.

Ancient Civilizations

Copying in ancient civilizations was largely accomplished by force—by conquerors such as the Mongols and the Scythians, who swept down on the wealthy leading nations, such as Babylon, Egypt, and Sumeria. They secured weaponry and riches, and they also copied technologies: the wheel, irrigation systems, writing, the plow, pottery making, and so on.

Trade also promoted the diffusion of ideas through the ships of the Phoenicians, the silk caravans to Asia, and voyagers such as Marco Polo, who returned not only with goods but also with such "wild" ideas as China's using paper money instead of gold and silver.

Europe copied many ideas and techniques over the centuries from Asia: saltpeter for gunpowder ("Chinese snow"), the compass, the wheelbarrow, the crank, playing cards, paper currency, the stirrup, and paper making.

England

The British borrowed technology from China and ideas from Greece and Rome. Braudel reports that the first ''true factory'' in England was in 1716–17, a silk mill ''copied by the English after two years of industrial espionage in Italy.'' But they especially copied from the Dutch. Angus Maddison reports:

> In fact, most of British progress in the eighteenth century was a replication of the Dutch merchant capitalist model. This was true in agriculture, canal building, shipping, banking, and international specialization. In agriculture and services . . . the UK was a follower, not a leader.

In 1776 even Adam Smith, the British economist, urged emulating the Dutch institutions, technology, and use of division of labor.

Germany

Williams, in his 1890 book, cited many instances where the Germans irritated the English by the ''faculty of imitativeness'':

> The Germans have been following the English step by step, importing their machinery and tools, engaging when they could, the best men from the best shops, copying their methods of work and the organization of their industries.

The Germans even sent people to English schools: A ''third of the day pupils at the Manchester Technical School were foreigners, who after completing their studies, return to their homes and compete with the people who provided them with their training at a nominal cost.''

United States

The United States copied from Europe, especially England, in the nineteenth century, when it was in the process of overtaking England. As reported in Chapter 5, the United States in its developing years was known as a ''land of copiers.''

It didn't stop after the United States gained the lead.

The jet engine was invented in Britain but commercially developed by the United States. Britain's EMI invented the brain scanner, but it sold the technology to America's General Electric. In fact, the number of ideas and inventions copied from Europe is astounding: the automobile, the Bessemer process, sewing machines, radios, radar, nuclear electric power plants, polyesters, and penicillin. America didn't excel in science and technology until after World War II.

Japan

In 1543, storm-tossed Portuguese mariners went ashore on a Japanese island and traded a few firearms in return for food and water. Thirty years later, one of the sailors returned and found the populace armed with 20,000 guns, each an exact replica of the original weapon.

From the Chinese, much earlier, the Japanese studied and absorbed philosophy, music, cooking, dress, sports, poetry, pictographic writing, administrative methods—adapting the new ways but strongly maintaining their own spirit and character. In the end, Japan began to rival the culture and luxury of China.

The Japanese sealed themselves off from the world for 250 years beginning in the seventeenth century, and then explosively opened up again with the Meiji Restoration in 1868. They made up for lost time by openly scouring the world for ideas and technology.

Teams of Japanese went to Europe and the United States to study their industries and institutions. They copied German law, the French Army, and the British Navy. Englishmen were brought in to superintend construction of railways, telegraphs, and battleships. To the Germans was assigned the organization of medicine and public health. Italians were brought in to instruct Japanese in sculpture and painting.

In the post–World War II period, the Japanese copied many ideas from the United States. The transistor was invented by Bell Labs. As Bell could see no way to make money out of it, it offered licenses for $25,000 to outsiders. Despite resistance from the Japanese government, Sony bought a license in 1953.

RCA sold its color TV technology to the Japanese in the 1950s. In 1968, Unimation licensed Kawasaki Heavy Industries to make industrial robots. The first commercial videotape recorder was developed in America by Ampex, but Sony turned it into a successful consumer product.

Followers don't simply copy the leader's ideas; they (1) adapt them to their nation and other nations; (2) improve on them (sometimes called "creative imitation" or "improvement engineering"); and, most important, (3) put the ideas to work in the market place speedily.

As an old Japanese saying has it, "The highest compliment a student can pay his teacher is to surpass him."

—9—
Lessons from History: The Challenger Closes In

LESSON 8: QUALITY IMPROVEMENT AND CUSTOMER FOCUS ARE KEY
STRATEGIES OF CHALLENGERS

In the early nineteenth century, British manufacturers were known for neatness, attention to detail, and inventory controls. "Wedgwood was uncompromising on this point," David Landes writes. When the Great Exhibition was held in the Crystal Palace in London in 1851, England led the world in quality.

It was the Germans who were renowned for poor quality. Charles Kindelberger reports: "In Paris in 1865, German products were distinguished by being shoddy and cheap. The showing was regarded as a disaster for German exporters."

Eleven years later, at the 1876 Centennial Exhibition in Philadelphia, the German exhibits were still denounced for poor quality even by the German Commissioner. That created such a stir in Germany that German manufacturers began to pay attention to quality in products, in their manufacturing processes, and with regard to customers.

Part of the reason for the increase in German quality was German attention to manufacturing.

The German manufacturer began concentrating on superior technology and was aware of the need to keep employees and technology up to date:

> [T]he changing content of technology compelled supervisory employees and even workers to familiarize themselves with new concepts, and enhanced enormously the value of personnel trained to keep abreast of scientific novelty, appreciate its significance, and adapt it to the requirements of production.

British businessmen touring German plants came back with reports of the general efficiency and cleanliness of German plants: "British visitors to German steel plants marvelled at bins to catch oil dripping from the lubrication boxes and steam captured, condensed, and re-used. Above all, they admired the Germans' efficient use of fuel." Germans had *less* capital investment and often made their own machinery in plants.

They also commented on the neatness and general appearance of the German work force: " 'Look,'' my informant said, 'at the factory girls coming out of a printing works on the Continent—tidy, clean, smart, and neatly dressed; and compare them with the horde of girls trooping from an English printer's—frowsy, tousled, and untidy! . . . The appearance of the girls in the streets shows clearly their fashion of work inside the factory.' ''

The German manager was generally a technician, trained for his work. The British, on the other hand, recruited many of their managers from "the counting room." Even the British technical men who were elevated stuck with the established ways of doing things.

By "the end of the century, the tables had turned," Landes reported. "From slavish imitation and adulteration in the first half of the [nineteenth] century, Germanware ultimately became known for their solid quality." Near the end of the century, German products were scoring triumphs at exhibitions in Chicago in 1893 and in Paris in 1900.

At the same time they were improving product and process quality, the Germans paid attention to customers, whereas British firms ignored them.

The "last thing," Williams said, "an English firm usually considers when soliciting orders, is the tastes of its customers. 'These are our goods: take them or leave them.' "

Germans, on the other hand, designed goods for local taste, and were "always ready to comply with any hints their patrons might give them as to variations in design and quality."

In addition:

- The English trader refused to quote in terms of currency and weights and measures other than those of England.
- The English houses booked only large orders; the Germans took small orders, which grew.
- The British demanded cash in sterling against a bill of lading or at most three months of credit; Germans regularly granted four or even nine months.
- The British stayed home, wrote letters, and published catalogs in English. The Germans published catalogs in local languages, learned foreign languages, were always ready to travel to foreign lands and "endure privation and rebuff."

Germans sold directly to customers, which enabled them to work out technical improvements to the customers' satisfaction. The British manufacturer sold through merchants who stood between the producer and customer.

In short, the Germans listened and adapted to customers; the British did not.

The Americans were also more customer-oriented, McKenzie pointed out:

> Every year sees the rapid spread of American drugs in our business . . . about half the medicines I sell are American and a considerable proportion of the remainder German. . . . Why is this? . . . They provide the things wanted in such a convenient form that the older preparations stand no chance beside them.

In the twentieth century, Japan repeated the same transformation as the Germans—changing a worldwide reputation for poor quality into a reputation for the highest quality, and with close attention to the customer. "We go into the field to listen to the voices of our customers, to study our competitors models, or search for any research findings," employees of Fuji-Xerox said.

After years of neglect, some American manufacturers and service firms are increasing their emphasis on quality, as we shall report in

Chapter 13. But for many, it may be too late. Many American customers are now loyal to Japanese quality and to their customer orientation.

LESSON 9: THE PARADOX OF PROTECTION—IT HELPS CHALLENGERS;
IT HURTS LEADERS

In the early stages of growth, England, the United States, and Japan all used protection to help their "infant" industries get started and to catch up to the leader.

England

England was a very protectionist nation for much of the eighteenth century when it was catching the Netherlands.

Adam Smith in the *Wealth of Nations* (1776) was the first to argue that England should drop protection and mercantilism, that "free trade" based on comparative advantage would let everyone gain: a win–win growth world.

But Smith's idea of laissez-faire was accepted only very slowly. As Alvin Rabuskha points out, England as late as 1815 was "the antithesis of a free economy." Government regulated wages, prices, and conditions of work; a prohibitive tariff wall protected agriculture and manufacturing; a ban existed on export of machinery and emigration of skilled craftsmen; the Navigation Acts regulated colonial trade and shipping; and thousands of taxes regulated all activities of economic life.

In short, England for many of its developing years was a heavily regulated economy.

As England prospered, it removed many of those government interventions. Some argue that trade barriers and government controls *caused* England to prosper. Others say that only as England reduced protection and regulation did it become strong and dominant. No one can prove causation in either case, but it is a fact that (1) protection did exist during England's early growth, and (2) as England reduced protection, growth accelerated.

By the mid nineteenth century, England had removed almost all trade barriers, was far and away the world's most dominant economy (half of the world's manufacturing production), and had reached its "ideological apogee" as the most open economy the world has ever seen. It even welcomed dumping.

Then things changed.

Competitors around the globe grew stronger, especially Germany and the United States. News of commercial competition in all parts of the world began to appear regularly in the press. Cheaper and better-quality imports began to come into England itself. Americans began to sell telephones, machine tools, electric railways, matches, boots, books, food, drugs, and printing presses in British markets. Jobs were lost. Businesses failed. The cry went up: "England is being flooded with foreign manufactures!"

Support for free trade began to erode. The first responses were accusations of "unfair" methods. Those rose in pitch and culminated, Landes reports, in the "midsummer madness" of 1896:

> Parliamentary orators exercised their eloquence on government purchases of Bavarian pencils . . . newspapers denounced the purchase of cheap German garments. . . . No item was too small to heap on the flames of indignation: Playing cards, muscial instruments, buggy whips.

Joseph Chamberlain, a leading British Conservative of the time, deplored the "de-industrialization" of England:

> We are to lose the great industries for which this country has been celebrated, which have made it prosperous in the past. We are to deal with inferior and subsidiary industries. Sugar is gone. Let us not weep for it; jam and pickles remain!

"How many workers," he went on to ask, "have found equivalent wages and comfort in stirring up jam-pots and bottling pickles?" Shades of Walter Mondale asking in 1984, "What do we want our kids to do? Sweep up around Japanese computers!"

Cries increased for retaliation against the United States and Germany for maintaining closed markets.

Does any of this sound familiar?

But despite rising pressure, England did not give in right away to protectionist pressures. It remained for the first decade of the twentieth century fully committed to free trade. Economists like Alfred Marshall argued that the growth of Germany and the United States was natural and discounted Britain's ability to use tariffs to pry open U.S. and German markets.

But as competitive inroads continued, English support for free trade continued to erode. The "royal crown was slipping," Landes reported, "and the doctrines of economic theorists on comparative advantage and international division of labor were cold comfort."

In 1915, the British instituted import duties with the disguise of "saving shipping space." The steel industry began to rely on protection, and "the British economy as a whole tended to retire from industry to trade and finance." In 1919, the country took another protectionist step when the nations within the British Empire received "preference" in trade.

When the United States enacted the Smoot-Hawley tariffs in 1930, England joined the world in full scale protectionism.

The United States

Most people believe that the United States has always been a strong advocate of free trade and competition.

Within its borders, that is true, but internationally, not so. *The United States has been mostly a protectionist nation.*

Look at Figure 9–1.

The United States has had high tariffs for almost three quarters of its history, except for just prior to the Civil War and just after each of the two world wars.

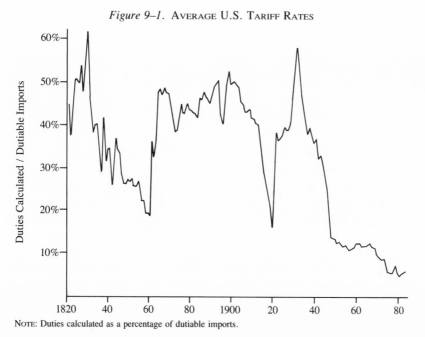

Figure 9–1. AVERAGE U.S. TARIFF RATES

NOTE: Duties calculated as a percentage of dutiable imports.

SOURCE: U.S. Bureau of the Census, *Highlights of U.S. Export and Import Trade, Historical Statistics.*

Even as the United States was overtaking England in productivity in 1890, it enacted the McKinley tariffs, raising the average rate for all goods to 50 percent, and raising it again in 1897 to 57 percent. That crippled several British industries and excluded many foreign products from U.S. markets. This infuriated British manufacturers who saw the United States gaining advantage by hiding behind "closed markets" and engaging in "unfair" competition.

U.S. protectionism reached a peak with the famed Smoot-Hawley bill. It elicited immediate retaliation from the rest of the world, raised even further worldwide trade barriers, and aggravated the Great Depression of the 1930s.

At the end of World War II, the United States reversed course and led the world in reducing tariffs with the 1947 General Agreement on Tariffs and Trade (GATT) and the creation of the Organization for European Economic Cooperation (OEEC), which in part was designed to reduce trade barriers between members.

It was the United States that led this charge, pushed hard for free trade around the world, and became the leading champion for open world markets.

But, as in England in the late nineteenth century, strong American support for free trade is now beginning to erode as competition increases. The United States could follow the path of England into protection when England lost its competitiveness.

Japan

Japan was also highly protectionist during its early growth period in the 1950s and most of the 1960s. But, beginning in the late 1960s, Japan began dismantling many of its tariff and nontariff barriers.

Estimates today are that Japan and the United States are roughly equal in their levels of protectionism.

The Japanese experience parallels that of other challengers and leaders in recent history: (1) They engage in protectionism during the growing period—the "infant industry" strategy—and then (2) they lower tariffs and other barriers when strong. If either or both nations follow the English path, they will attempt to reinstate protection when they are "attacked" by younger competitors following their own earlier strategy.

The ninth lesson of history is that after reaching maturity and facing increased competition, leading nations tend to use protection not for growth, but to reduce competition, to "save" jobs in inefficient industries, and to prevent change. That boomerangs, further weakening the leader.

The strong response is to adjust. But that's not easy for a mature nation.

LESSON 10: THE LEADER'S ABILITY TO ADJUST DIMINISHES OVER TIME

Most of the early civilizations were deliberately engineered to maintain social stability, to perpetuate religious, political, and economic patterns. Stability and tradition, however, could not forever withstand innovation.

While the Greeks, for example, respected tradition, they became fascinated by novelty. "It is always the newest song men want to hear," Telemachus tells his mother in the Odyssey. And the author of the Acts of the Apostles characterized the Athenians as men who "spend their time in nothing else but either to tell or hear some new thing."

But over the centuries, innovative spirit waned, and the Greeks became static and incapable of adapting to changes in their environment. They reached equilibrium, lived in the past, and became absorbed into a more vigorous Roman world.

When the Romans were young and aggressive, they built ditches around their camps at night to avoid surprise. The ditches had wide spaces through which the Romans could counterattack.

Later, the Romans built high earthworks through which access was only by narrow gates, and counterattack was impossible. Rome concentrated on "holding ground" by building walls, such as Hadrian's Wall on the Scottish border. By concentrating on defense only, Rome became a sitting target for invaders.

The Dutch in the early part of the eighteenth century were vigorous economic and social innovators. Then a conservative and fearful attitude gradually settled over the nation. Those who had accumulated fortunes tended to sit on them and not invest.

"The Dutch were slow to adopt new advances in shipbuilding, weaving, fishing, mapmaking and navigation," Robert Reich said. "The new ways of doing things—and the new talents, skills and organizational arrangements they required—were too threatening to the established order."

The static Dutch were replaced by the more vigorous English, who tore up their cottage industries with the machines and factories of the Industrial Revolution. Even the wrecking of machines by the displaced Luddites in the early nineteenth century didn't stop them. But, like so many other nations before them, having secured the lead, the English in turn failed to adjust to the competitive challenges from Germany and the United States.

The British manufacturer stuck by his tried and true ways of manufacturing and managing. British mining technology was rapidly surpassed by that of the Ruhr and Pittsburgh. British shipbuilding was overtaken by Scandinavian motor vessels and German diesels.

When the British were confronted with the superiority of new technology, the typical reaction, cited by McKenzie, would be something like that of the leader of a British importing and manufacturing firm:

"Well, Dick, you may be right. I won't say you are not. But why should I change? Th' owd machines were good enough for father, and they were good enough for grandfather, so I am thinking they're good enough for me."

Labor in the engineering trades was also resistant to change: strongly organized, craft-oriented, and fearful of technological unemployment. "They fought all changes in the condition of work." Master craftsmen became "vested interests," and their interest in the status quo was an obstacle to innovation.

Eventually, England did respond. But in the meantime its industries had lost ground. It was too late.

A natural question for Americans to ask at this point is whether the United States can still adjust? Or has it, with time and age, built in so many habits, traditions, laws, and vested interests that it can no longer respond?

Has the United States reached a "climacteric"?

A Turning Point: A "Climacteric"?

"Climacteric" is not a word Americans often use, but the British use it. Its dictionary meaning is a "crucial period." Used in an economic sense, it means a turning point for an economy, or as Kindelberger phrased it, "some critical stage of the economic aging process—a climacteric, change of life, or economic menopause."

We believe the United States is at such a turning point. It will never again be such a singular dominant economic power as it was in the 1950s and 1960s. Other nations have almost caught up, and U.S. manufacturing productivity and prowess have been equaled by other nations. The United States still leads, but whether it remains the leader depends on what happens in the decades around this turning point, on whether it adjusts.

A U.S. climacteric does not mean that America must decline. Its growth could turn upward, not downward, following the path of an "S" curve, accelerating, not stagnating or declining.

In order for this climacteric to turn out to be merely a "creative pause," followed by an upturn in productivity growth, American labor, business, and government have only one viable option: *Adjust.*

The United States, in framing its response, has to heed Toynbee's admonition about not responding in the *same old ways* to a new kind of challenge, the mistake made so often by nations in the past. If the United States fails to respond or responds in the same ways it used in the 1950s and 1960s, then historians in the twenty-first century may well write the history of the U.S. decline in terms of the ten lessons.

Does this mean leaders are doomed once challengers start a run at them? Not at all. Many of the challengers of the past have surged forward, leaders have responded, and the challengers have fallen back on Toynbee's cliffs of history.

What gets written into the historian's log is up to Americans, not to fate. Neither Kindelberger nor Toynbee believed that a "climacteric" *has* to mean decline. Nor do we. A climacteric is only a turning point. The outcome is not inevitable or predetermined. It is up to us.

Which is why we devote the next ten chapters to *adjustment*—to ten areas where we believe the greatest adjustments are possible and needed.

—*Part IV*—
Agenda for Adjustment: Private Sector

—10—
The Agenda for Adjustment

An old Chinese saying neatly sums up the results of many current attempts at restructuring: "Lots of noise at top of stairs, but no one coming down."

Lots of mergers, acquisitions, and plant closings and a bewildering assortment of financial and monetary maneuvers are yielding frustratingly little in terms of productivity and competitiveness.

Why? Because, as necessary as some of those defensive tactics may be, they are an inadequate substitute for real change. Worse, they have created a dangerous illusion that American business has restructured, that it is now lean and mean and ready to take on all comers. They have diverted attention and energy from the true sources of productivity and competitiveness: dramatically altering the way products and services are invented and produced, and the role of people in the process.

It would be unfair and inaccurate to imply that managers and employees have been sitting on their hands waiting for Wall Street or the currency markets to sort it out. You name it, and American companies are trying it: quality circles, two-tier pay, downsizing, quality of work life programs, outsourcing, incentive plans, employee of the month awards, automation. One manager told us recently that his people feel as though they have been through the spin cycle of an economic washing machine.

But far too many of those efforts are falling short for the same reasons they are so popular: They do not confront the management and union status quo. They do not challenge the way the work is done; the roles of managers, employees, and unions; or the traditional relationships with customers and suppliers.

There are no insurmountable historical, cultural, or technological reasons why America can't renew itself. As we shall show, options for what to do and how to do it are everywhere, for those who are ready to see them.

Fortunately, hundreds of American firms are beginning to realize that restructuring is more than a financial maneuver and that the game can still be won if they will tackle the tough issues. But getting to that state of awareness has cost precious time as managers have had to pass through a series of stages we call "working through."

WORKING THROUGH

We've seen U.S. firms reacting to the competitiveness threat in the same way as once-secure individuals react to crisis and trauma; that is, they go through a five-stage and time-consuming process which many psychologists call "working through":

1. Denial and disbelief
2. Anger and blaming
3. Buying time and testing
4. Retreat
5. Acceptance and adjustment

Figure 10-1 shows these as "stages" in a cycle of change and renewal through which firms have passed in the last five years. It has helped us understand why real change is so difficult and so slow. We'll give our current estimate of the percentage of firms at each stage.

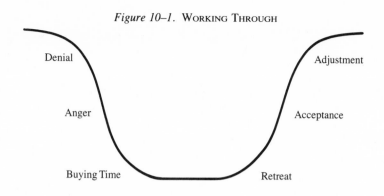

Figure 10–1. WORKING THROUGH

Denial

Anger

Buying Time

Adjustment

Acceptance

Retreat

Stage 1: Denial and Disbelief

The first reaction to the productivity and competitiveness crisis is denial and disbelief. Despite newspaper headlines, TV evening news stories, reports of Presidential commissions, and speeches by leaders, a surprisingly large number of people still don't believe they are faced with a crisis requiring them personally to change.

They rationalize:

1. The problem is temporary, caused by transient factors: exchange rates, the business cycle, women and young people entering the work force, high wages, tax laws, inflation, and so on.
2. "While some firms may be having problems, it isn't happening to my company." A survey of 512 *Fortune* 1000 CEOs in 1986 found almost 78 percent citing productivity as an issue of "great concern." But fewer than 5 percent said improving productivity or quality was one of *their* most important objectives.
3. "We have the best technology. Didn't we teach them everything they know?"
4. "These new management practices are just gimmicks, and not for serious business people."
5. "We're a great company. If we just keep doing what we know how to do best, we'll be fine."

We saw those attitudes in steel and autos, formerly two of America's most powerful industries. The steel industry failed to adopt new technology, change its operating systems, or pare down its organizations until market share had eroded tremendously. Despite flashing warning signals, in 1971 the then president of Bethlehem Steel was proclaiming, "The long-range threat of foreign steel competition seems to be diminishing.''

It was the same in the auto industry. The chairman of General Motors said in 1980, ''GM is supremely confident of its ability to meet and beat any and all overseas-based competition.'' GM has since lost 10 percent of market share, primarily to foreign imports, but some to Ford and Chrysler, who were not so supremely confident. In fact, Ford's profits in 1986 exceeded those of GM for the first time since 1924.

As we argued in the lessons from history, it is a fatal mistake of leaders to deny that a problem exists and dismiss warnings as irrelevant, misguided, or unpatriotic.

We estimate that about 20 percent of American firms are *still* denying the threat. Most of them are in the service sector. Still too many people in banking, finance, and personal and business services behave as if they are immune from foreign competition. As one investment banker cautioned, ''You never know when the Japanese may reverse engineer the investment business, too.''

Eventually, when the threat can no longer be ignored, the next stage people enter is ''anger and blaming.''

Stage 2: Anger and Blaming

When people begin to experience unpleasantness right on their own doorstep—deep loss of market share, loss of jobs, loss of union members, a large drop in wages or profits—they look around for someone other than themselves to blame. We estimate that at least 20 percent of firms are at this stage, blaming someone else or waiting for the government to rescue them.

We hear managers bitterly accuse unions of excessive wages and restrictive work rules, as if managers had nothing to do with it. Unions are indignant that established practices must change. Both groups take to the barricades, and years of good relations go down the drain.

Anger and blame are also directed toward the foreign ''enemy,'' who is accused of dumping, protecting its own markets, working too hard, saving too much, not paying its people enough, or not understanding the need for high quarterly earnings. Too many managers support the free market system and espouse the virtues of competition only until a foreigner proves to be better at it. Then companies and unions demand that the government protect them against the offending nations or industries.

It reaches the point where the mere existence of a trade surplus implies unfair practices. If that were the test, one could claim the United States has been trading unfairly for most of the postwar period.

Of course, we can cite examples of firms that have used protection to get their house in order. Harley-Davidson, protected by five years of stiff U.S. tariffs on imported motorcycles, announced in 1987, "We no longer need the special tariffs in order to compete with the Japanese." Unfortunately, Harley-Davidson is the exception. The record to date is that such protection, while providing some benefits for the industry or union in the short term, has saved very few industries or jobs, has cost consumers billions (including artificially high prices for motorcycles), and has delayed adjustment.

When denial and anger don't work, people eventually move to Stage 3.

Stage 3: Buying Time and Testing

In Stage 3, we see people bargaining and buying time, and willing to try some of this "productivity stuff." We estimate that 30 percent of firms are at this stage, and those at later stages have certainly passed through it.

Two approaches are common. We find the first in firms with union contracts. Both sides try to buy some time with "concessions," a terminology that in itself implies that the adjustment is temporary, that management "won" and labor "lost." The employees later ask for "restore and more," sounding like a creditor seeking payment from some delinquent deadbeat.

When the concession cycle starts, the cuts seem never to be enough, for the real sources of inefficiency aren't being addressed. Eastern Airlines, from 1978 to 1986, asked for wage concessions four times, with worsening labor relations each round, and the possibility of bankruptcy always at its back. Eastern's fundamental problems were never solved, and eventually the board gave up and sold it to Texas Air.

The second strategy for buying time is to start a new productivity, quality, or employee involvement program. Some of these will fortunately evolve later in Stage 5 into systemwide restructuring and renewal efforts.

Others are a stunted hodgepodge of programs-of-the-month, few of which produce significant or lasting results. Managers are under pressure to show they are "doing something," and employee involvement programs, for one, provide great material for slide presentations at quarterly meetings.

One jaded manager described the process:

Management has a two week attention span. We're great at launching programs and running a bunch of people through training. But no one every looks beneath the slide shows to see if anyone is doing anything differently. The quarterly dog-and-pony shows are a smoke-screen of activity and events, but nothing is really happening.

When the numbers keep heading south, the guys at the top say "See, we tried that and it didn't help much." The truth is nothing actually changed.

The words change, but the music is still the same; go after quarterly results, get the product out the door, and take your bonus.

As Professor Richard Hackman at Harvard Business School points out, the most popular, and least effective, approaches to productivity improvement have had three things in common. First, they do not change the core technology and operating systems used to make products or deliver services. Second, they do not alter the authority and responsibility structure of the organization. And third, they do not challenge assumptions about the role of people in the process.

No wonder most programs limp along underfunded, poorly planned, and peripheral to the real business. No wonder many American consumers have continued to prefer foreign products for quality, delivery, and service.

Since the efforts to buy time don't work for long, firms face a choice: (1) They can give up markets and leave unprofitable facilities, and/or (2) they can decide to tackle the ten tough issues, get on with real restructuring, and stay in the game.

Those that choose the first option enter the fourth stage.

Stage 4: Retreat

Firms under siege will do a lot of things to survive:

- Move operations offshore
- Close plants and offices
- Divest unprofitable businesses
- Reduce the number of product offerings
- Buy more foreign-made components
- Sell plants to foreign investors

We estimate that 15 percent of firms are currently at this stage, pruning down or selling off product lines at the same time as foreign firms are expanding theirs. Market share once lost to aggressive competitors is rarely regained. As we shall show later, Xerox stands out as one of the few firms that fought back to restore its low-cost copier market after an initial retreat in the face of foreign competition.

Some of the actions listed above may be very realistic and sound short-term business strategies, when they are part of an overall plan of adjusting to new and different competition. But in too many instances, firms prematurely close facilities and abandon markets with the explanation that it is "impossible" to operate competitively. Along come competitors—often foreign—who reopen those plants with the same workforce, restructure the way they manage, and make money. Evidently, some firms prefer retreat to the rigors of adjustment. A 1986 study of plant closings found that in *no case had attempts been made over the prior years to use employee involvement, share information openly on the situation, or develop gain-sharing to help save the operation.*

Bucking this trend is the recent encouraging return to the United States of some manufacturing operations. Lionel Trains and Rawlings moved their plants back to the United States when they found that low wages couldn't compensate for poorer quality and higher inventory and shipping costs, plus problems with suppliers, communication, and slow response time. GE announced in early 1987 that it would resume domestic production of color television sets rather than buy them from abroad, only to decide in mid-1987 to sell off its consumer electronics division.

Firms can survive Stage 4 and make fundamental changes in their operations. Others go right from Stage 3 to Stage 5: acceptance and adjustment.

Stage 5: Acceptance and Adjustment

Stage 5 firms have discovered a different route to restructuring. None of the hundreds of firms we have worked with at the American Productivity Center has ever made significant progress in productivity and competitiveness without addressing and starting to resolve creatively what we call the "Ten Tough Issues"—together they constitute our "Agenda for Adjustment." Each of the following chapters is devoted to one issue.

THE TEN TOUGH ISSUES

1. Operating systems
2. Organization structure

3. Quality
4. Employee involvement
5. Competitive compensation
6. Employment stability
7. Training and continuous learning
8. Accounting systems
9. Symbols, status, and membership
10. Labor-management relations

Our estimate is that no more than 15 percent of American firms are currently tackling the ten tough issues and making the adjustments required to be competitive over the long run. Most American firms are still using managerial methods and operating systems inherited from the Golden Era of American business supremacy and, with the help of American business schools and their own bureaucracies, have gone to sleep in noncompetitive postures.

Unlike market strategy, asset management, or financial structure, the Ten Tough Issues do not automatically catch the eye of senior management. Yet the greatest strategies conceived at the top will not bear fruit unless managers simultaneously tackle those Issues. Otherwise, they have trouble executing their strategies and leave themselves vulnerable to more sophisticated domestic and foreign competitors.

WHY ARE THESE ISSUES "TOUGH"?

Whenever we describe to managers and employees how others have addressed the Ten Tough Issues, almost to a person the initial response is either "Why should we do that?" or "We can't do that!"

Initially, they don't want to come to grips with the changes we describe, because those changes:

- Run counter to U.S. management tradition, assumptions, principles, and experience
- Are primarily "human," "soft" issues, the areas where American management systems are most deficient
- Require structural changes in decision-making and control, pay, and job and organization design that violate the old managerial control model learned in business schools or from former bosses
- Upset the traditional distribution of power and information
- Are so central to organizations that changes in one area of the

business quickly reverberate through other parts of the organization.

For exactly those reasons, adjustment is not easy, and the majority of American firms have still made only token gestures toward fundamental change. Of course it isn't easy. One manager described the process as "trying to rebuild an engine while moving down the highway at 55 miles an hour."

Fortunately, the number of firms and unions that have entered this fifth stage is growing all the time as more and more firms discover some new principles for responding to the new challenges.

1. Nothing less than a *fundamental restructuring* of traditional management systems will work. Anything else is too little and too late.
2. Real restructuring is an *ongoing process,* not an event. Change has to be initiated, managed, and sustained. Even if today's competitive threat is met, firms can expect new and different challenges from another quarter tomorrow.
3. The restructuring *will touch every aspect of the business,* from technology and the way people work and are paid to relationships with customers and suppliers.

CAN WE "ADJUST IN TIME"?

During the last ten years at the APC we have worked with and observed hundreds of firms "working through." We have seen a dramatic shift in the distribution of firms at the five stages. The table below shows our estimate of how the percentage of firms at each stage has changed over the last decade:

A DECADE OF WORKING THROUGH

	1977	1982	1987
Denial	90%	50%	20%
Anger	5	20	20
Buying time	0	20	30
Retreat	0	5	15
Adjustment	5	5	15
	100%	100%	100%

The trend is encouraging, but the number in stage 5 is still too small. Perhaps surprising to some readers, at least 20 percent of American firms, their managers and employees, still deny there is a problem!

Part of the reason more firms are not adjusting is that managers, union leaders, and employees willing to adjust aren't sure what to change or how to change it. In the next ten chapters we shall describe many successful examples of inventive ways to tackle the Ten Tough Issues on our private sector agenda for adjustment. We begin with a core issue: the design of better operating systems.

—11—
Integrated Operating Systems

The first tough issue on our Agenda for Adjustment is the redesign of a firm's operating system.

The real test of an operating system is how well it helps the firm compete in the market place. Using that criterion, conventional American operating systems are out of sync with today's market realities:

- Product life cycles are shorter, variety is greater, and volume is smaller. Yet firms are trying to compete with systems designed for long runs of standard products.
- Process technologies are more sophisticated than the old assembly line mentality of narrow jobs can accommodate.
- Demands for quality, service, and response times are too great for traditional rigid production and inspection systems and traditional decision-making.

121

- Direct labor as a percentage of operating costs is declining while information work is increasing, yet productivity is still measured by direct labor content.

The new market place calls for operating systems that are simpler, leaner, and more flexible. The most competitive systems we've seen have the following ten characteristics.

1. Small operating units with fewer, more highly skilled people per unit
2. Few management levels
3. Team structures
4. Customer-driven schedules and procedures
5. Flexible product mix potential
6. Minimal inventories
7. Faster startups
8. Flexible equipment, some designed in-house
9. Higher productivity and lower unit costs
10. Higher quality and a focus on customer–supplier relations

Unfortunately, too many American firms are holding onto older systems, either because they don't want to change or because they don't know how. Fortunately, there are plenty of examples of better alternatives.

- Procter & Gamble has eighteen plants that operate at 30 to 40 percent higher levels of productivity than P&G's more conventional operations. Those eighteen are also faster at switching product lines and production runs.
- Xerox has operations that are consistently 30 percent more productive than traditionally designed Xerox units.
- Federal Express is aiming for perfection. In 1986, a station in Texas delivered every one-day-delivery package on time for sixty days straight, remarkable considering that anything from a traffic jam to weather can slow deliveries. Breakthroughs to perfection are now happening all over the system.
- IBM's electronic typewriters and keyboards produced in Lexington, Kentucky, match Japanese quality and costs.
- The cost per gallon at the Sherwin-Williams paint plant in Richmond, Kentucky, is 45 percent lower than at sister plants, productivity is 30 percent higher, and absenteeism is 60 percent lower—with the same equipment and material.
- NUMMI, the Fremont, California, joint venture between GM

and Toyota, is producing 200,000 Novas and 50,000 Corollas annually with 2,500 UAW members. Before GM closed down its old assembly plant in Fremont, it had 7,800 workers (and almost that many grievances a year) producing fewer cars.

These American operations are achieving at least 30 percent better productivity and quality than their competition. The manufacturing operations can compete with the Japanese, whose cost and quality advantage is usually 30 percent over many of their Western competitors.

Why are these operations and many others like them more flexible, more productive, and, as we'll show, able to use technology better than most?

It is because their operating systems were consciously *designed,* in the case of startups, or *redesigned,* in the case of existing operations, using components of sociotechnical system design.

SOCIOTECHNICAL DESIGN

As academic as the term sounds, sociotechnical design is not some social experiment cooked up on campus. It is a sound way to design an operating system for committed people, high productivity, quality, and profits.

There are two parts to a sociotechnical system. First, the *technical system* refers to more than capital investment and technology. *How successful operations use technology and equipment seems to be more important than the actual equipment they select.*

The technical system includes not only "hardware" like equipment, but "software" as well: what tasks are done and by whom; job design and work flow; the layout and the way space is used; the skills, knowledge, and methods used by employees to get the job done; and training and development.

The second component, the *social system,* is critical to the success of the technical system. It is designed in conjunction with the technical system, not turned over to the personnel department after the equipment is installed. The social system includes selection and promotion; responsibility for decision-making and problem-solving; pay and reward systems; and status symbols.

In the rest of this chapter we shall describe the way sociotechnically designed operations look and function.

Let us begin with the technical system, since that is where most managers start when they think of how their company works.

The Technical System

There are *six* related characteristics of the technical system that are treated quite differently in sociotechnical design:

1. Mission and philosophy
2. Organization structure
3. Job design and the role of employees
4. Layout and space utilization
5. Training
6. Use of technology and capital

1. MISSION AND PHILOSOPHY

Successful operating systems using sociotechnical design have a clear mission and set of values or philosophy that guide their design and operation. Employees at all levels are involved in developing the mission and philosophy and are highly committed to them.

The mission is the "what"—what does the organization have to deliver in order to be successful? The philosophy is the "how"—how should people and technology be integrated to achieve the mission?

Design teams in companies like TRW and Cummins Engine have known for years that answering the "what" and the "how" questions was the right way to start designing a new operation. More recently, we've worked with companies asking "what" and "how" to guide their redesign efforts. In 1985, McDonnell Douglas Electronics Company took thirty managers offsite to hammer out a mission, then sixty people from throughout the company created the philosophy to support it. MDEC's mission places a strong emphasis on supplier–customer relations, internally and externally, which leads to very high performance standards for quality. What the philosophy says about people and technology has served as MDEC's guide in their redesign ever since.

A point of caution: Many companies have great-sounding mission and philosophy statements written by the CEO or the PR department, who, unfortunately, are the only ones committed to them. Mission and philosophy statements written by a broader set of stakeholder/employees may have the same lofty ring to them but an altogether different impact on a sociotechnical organization.

2. ORGANIZATION STRUCTURE

Traditional organizations—and that means most of them—have erected complicated, towering organizational structures. One company calls them "silos." They mean that accountants talk to accountants, engineers talk to engineers, customer service talks to customer service.

Few communicate across the boundaries in these Towers of Babel. Engineers toss product designs over the wall to manufacturing, which in turn leaves it up to marketing to explain to the customer why it isn't right or why it is too expensive.

Sociotechnical principles say, "Do it differently": Create a new team with all the pieces of the functional organization, tell its members what they need to do, give them the resources they need, let them know where they can go for help, and get out of their way.

Business, product, or process centers with performance and cost responsibility are created under the umbrella of the larger operating unit. That helps foster a "small business" mentality, with more entrepreneurship and fewer barriers between specialities. Old fiefdoms are disbanded. Engineering, manufacturing, and marketing are brought together into new, smaller organizations defined by product type or business niche.

All that has to be done over the inevitable objections: "duplication of effort," "It's more efficient to have the engineers all in one department," "We tried that and it didn't work."

Those objections were no doubt heard at Ford when it threw out the traditional process for designing a new car and created "Team Taurus." Representatives from planning, marketing, design, engineering, and manufacturing were members of the design team and were located together during the whole design process.

As a member of the design team, manufacturing was able to make design suggestions that resulted in higher productivity and better quality.

The team asked assembly line workers for advice even before the car was designed and was flooded with suggestions. Workers complained they had trouble installing car doors when body panels were formed in too many different pieces—up to eight to a side. So designers reduced the number of panels to just two. One employee suggested that all bolts have the same size head so workers wouldn't have to change wrenches.

Team Taurus also had the good sense to take a lesson from history and copy Japan's best small cars. It bought Hondas and Toyotas and tore them down, looking for good ideas.

Result? One of the hottest selling U.S. cars in years. By mid-1986, more than 130,000 of the midsize Taurus sedans and station wagons had been delivered, and there was a backlog of orders for 100,000 more.

Other companies have adopted a similar approach to speed up the time it takes to get a product to market. David Kearns, chairman of

Xerox, likes to claim it was the first American company to win back market share from the Japanese by introducing good products faster than before.

Xerox's share of the copier market had dropped from 82 to 35 percent in less than four years, partly because it had introduced only three new copiers in a decade. Xerox split the copier division into three product centers with profit and loss responsibility. The first product out the door of the "new Team Xerox" came to market in record time and sold three times as many copiers as projected in the first year.

One nice benefit of this "business-centered team management" is that fewer levels of management are needed. Goodyear Tire & Rubber Company's Lawton, Oklahoma, team plant has 35 percent fewer managers than a traditional operation and turns out twice as many tires. Companies can rely more on self-management by individuals and teams.

In contrast, conventional American organizations have many levels of management. They need them. One of the main roles of their managers is to negotiate the barriers created by their own departmental structures.

3. JOB DESIGN AND THE ROLE OF EMPLOYEES

The "small business" mentality that comes from a sociotechnical organization structure is mirrored in the way work is designed. Instead of classifying work into "jobs," the work system in sociotechnical operations is organized so that tasks and jobs become the responsibility of teams of multiskilled people. Teams are responsible for meeting production goals, the way work is organized, safety, housekeeping, training, quality, and often the selection and hiring of new team members. In short, teams take responsibility for a large chunk of the business or process.

This "chunking" or team concept approach is spreading rapidly in America: In a 1986 survey of 1,600 companies, the APC found that 8 percent were using self-managed or autonomous work teams. Why? It seems to work better than conventional job design. For instance:

- Tektronix Inc. converted its metals group from assembly line manufacturing to teams or cells of a dozen or fewer employees who are responsible for the entire production process for simple products. One cell can now turn out a product in three days instead of fourteen with half as many people as before.
- Members of the Aluminum Workers union at Rohm & Haas's Plexiglas plant in Knoxville, Tennessee, have improved productivity 60 percent in the four years since they moved to a team-based approach.

- With the breakup of AT&T, American Transtech, formerly AT&T's stock and bond division, was spun off into an independent subsidiary. Freed from the bureacratic underbrush that seems to grow up in huge organizations, American Transtech management moved its offices to Florida and converted all 2,400 employees, from executives to part-timers, to business center and team concept operations. They have achieved a 600 percent improvement in productivity from the integration of new technology with a team structure.
- The First National Bank of Chicago garnered steep increases in productivity, customer satisfaction, and staff morale when its employees in the letters of credit unit transformed their paperwork assembly line into complete jobs performed by a team of broadly trained professionals.

A team approach also makes traditional job classifications obsolete. Some of the biggest productivity gains have come from redesigning work and training people so that the number of job classifications drops from hundreds down to a handful. Most of the newer U.S. automotive assembly plants have fewer than five job classifications, compared to two hundred or more in a traditional U.S. assembly plant. The United Automobile Workers has proved that this approach can work in unionized operations. UAW members work in such a system at NUMMI: Saturn Corporation will use it, as will the new Mazda plant in Flat Rock, Michigan.

Most of these examples come from manufacturing, because the goods producing sector is under the greatest pressure from competition to change its operating systems. But even if they are still ignoring it, service providers are not immune from competition. With competitors like American Transtech and the First National Bank of Chicago integrating people and technology better, we think other service companies would be wise to examine their systems as well.

4. LAYOUT

The layout and placement of work areas and equipment in a sociotechnical system reflect the need for team members to see and talk to each other and move quickly between areas. More circular or cell arrangements are used instead of an assembly line or separate offices.

Good layout can speed quality and operating adjustments and cut down on processing and material handling time. For example, McDonnell Aircraft in St. Louis is just beginning to use "process center" production cells. In one cell in 1986, the time to machine a standard part was cut from forty days down to three days, using the same equipment and union employees. The chief difference is that machines and people are now located together instead of in various departments in remote locations.

5. TRAINING

In a sociotechnical system, training is not a personnel function. It is an integral part of a multiskilled team concept. Team members are responsible for continuously improving their operations and developing more skills. Cross-training permits people to float as needed between jobs within the team and creates a more fertile environment for innovation.

The level of training and competency also has a direct impact on organization structure. Properly educated and trained employees at all levels can operate more independently, which reduces the need for narrow spans of control and many organizational levels between line workers and top management. That is a principal reason why the Japanese can operate efficiently with a much larger span of control than is typical in America. Everybody knows his or her job, employees have the skills and flexibility to move quickly to different tasks, and very little supervision is required.

6. CAPITAL AND TECHNOLOGY

American business is not getting its money's worth from the billions invested in factory and office automation:

- Despite billions spent, white-collar productivity—output per hour—is about where it was in the late 1960s.
- The better productivity growth in manufacturing is due more to one-time cost cutting, workforce reductions, and changes in work rules and operations than in capital *per se*.

Why isn't business getting more bang for the buck from capital investment? We see five reasons.

First, most research shows that capital accounts for only about 20 percent of the improvement in U.S. productivity. Estimates are that only 20 percent of the difference between U.S. and Japanese productivity can be traced to capital investment. The *productivity* of investment is far more important than its *volume*.

The main productivity advantage of capital investment comes from its proper integration into an already well-performing operating system. If the layout is scattered and hampers communication, design is uncoupled from manufacturing, quality is poor, and uncommitted employees are not trained and given responsibility for realtime decisions, then the equipment doesn't pay off.

Second, investing capital to enhance an inefficient system is a waste of money. In 1980, Shenandoah Life Insurance Company bought a \$2 million computer system to process policies and claims at its Virginia headquarters. Not much happened. It still took thirty-two clerks in three departments twenty-seven working days to process a typical policy. So Shenandoah attacked the problem with a sociotechnical approach. It analyzed the work flow and reorganized employees into small teams with responsibility for all the functions that were once spread out over three departments. Case handling time dropped from twenty-seven days to two, and service complaints virtually disappeared. By 1986, Shenandoah was processing 50 percent more applications with 10 percent fewer employees than it was in 1980 (employment dropped through attrition). Employees are more satisfied with their jobs, and turnover has decreased.

Again and again, managers tell us the most expensive lesson they are learning is, "Clean up the system before you automate it."

The third reason for the less-than-remarkable impact of capital investment on productivity is that too much of the investment is being spent on reducing direct labor, even though direct labor counts for less than 15 percent of costs in many industries. Indirect labor, materials, and equipment utilization are far greater components of the cost structure.

Japanese flexible manufacturing systems (FMS) are simple and inexpensive by U.S. standards, because they are not usually aiming for unmanned production. They are automating tasks only where a machine can do it more reliably or with higher quality. They are trying to enhance labor, not get rid of it. And their systems work better.

In contrast, GM's new \$600 million Hamtramck assembly plant was a technocrat's dream: 260 robots doing welding and painting, fifty automated guided vehicles shuttling parts from station to station, and scores of cameras and computers controlling the manufacturing process. Hamtramck was to be GM's "Factory of the Future."

But the technocrat's dream turned into a management nightmare. Robots spray painted each other instead of the cars, the guided vehicles sat idle while software programmers tried to figure out how to direct them, and the plant manager took early retirement for health reasons.

Hamtramck was to be producing sixty cars an hour by 1986. The actual production was running closer to thirty-five. In December 1986, GM put Hamtramck employees on indefinite layoff.

Meanwhile, 2,000 miles west, GM management was stunned when NUMMI, the automaker's Fremont, California, joint venture with Toyota, started achieving Japanese-like efficiency with careful management rather than exotic automation. As a result, GM has slowed its investment in automation so the rest of the social and technical system can catch up. One GM senior manager pointed out that GM could have bought Toyota and Honda for the $33 billion it has spent on automation in the last six years.

The fourth reason capital isn't paying off is that much of new technology is so complicated that only people who have been involved in its design and installation know how to use it. When problems occur, untrained operators stand around intimidated and afraid to tinker with it, waiting for an "expert" to show up.

As John Clancy of McDonnell Douglas Information Systems Group mused, "Futurists of the 1940s and 1950s envisioned twenty-first-century industries in which robots would manage as well as produce, and people would be obsolete. Experience has shown us that just the opposite is true. We have learned that the more sophisticated we make our factories and manufacturing processes, the more dependent we become on the sophistication of the people who run them."

Finally, sometimes sophisticated and flexible technology is wasted on rigid production. Flexible manufacturing systems (FMS) are a good example. Ramchandran Jaikumar of Harvard studied half of the installed FMSs in Japan and in the United States. Each Japanese FMS produces an average of ninety-three different parts, while U.S. systems produce only ten. Each American installation averages long runs of 1,727 units of every part it makes; in Japan, the comparable number is 258. Jaikumar concludes:

> These figures and others tell a terrible tale: American companies are using computerized manufacturing for the same old-fashioned, high-volume, low-variety production they have always pursued. The difference between U.S. and Japanese performance is due not to the equipment but to how things are managed. . . . All it takes is a few machines, a small team of highly skilled engineers who design, build, operate and troubleshoot the system, and a new managerial mind-set.

These five reasons why Americans are not getting enough "bang for the buck" from capital investment support our original assertion: New technology is only as powerful as the social and technical systems allow it to be.

The Social System

When we talk about the "social system" we don't mean Friday afternoon beer busts (although we don't exclude them!). The companies we know don't redesign their social system just to "make people feel good." Their social system is designed to fit the demands of the technical system, just as the technical system ought to produce the best use of people's talents. The social system has four key components:

1. SELECTION AND PROMOTION

In an organization known to value people and technology, it is not uncommon for hundreds of people to apply for one opening. At Frito-Lay's sociotechnical plant in Kern County, California, twelve thousand applicants were interviewed for 300 jobs. Organizations like Frito-Lay get to pick the cream of the crop.

There are two criteria for selecting and promoting employees in a sociotechnical operation: (1) their technical expertise and ability to learn and (2) their interpersonal skills and values, which will allow them to operate effectively in a self-managing environment.

Promotion is also based on how well the person—manager, technician, or analyst—contributes individually and as a team member, and how well his or her behavior reflects the mission and philosophy of the operation.

Because sociotechnically designed organizations make a huge investment in selecting and training employees, they try to avoid layoffs. Turnover is usually quite low.

2. DECISION-MAKING AND PROBLEM-SOLVING

Decision-making and problem-solving in sociotechnical systems are team-based. Teams are responsible for meeting their production and quality standards and are trained in the necessary problem-solving and analytical skills. These employees are not just "involved"—they are *responsible*. The role of managers and team leaders is to provide resources and coordinate with other teams. Since the people and technology are so interdependent, the opportunity for conflict is high. People need to be selected and trained to identify and openly resolve conflict. At Frito-Lay, teams meet regularly in conference rooms that adjoin their work areas to discuss their operations. A worker says, because of their training, "we attack problems, not people. We decide what is right, not who is right."

3. REWARD SYSTEMS

In sociotechnical systems, pay is set at competitive levels to attract good candidates. Employees can also earn more money when they learn more skills. In this "pay-for-skills" system, the more tasks a team member is qualified to do, the more pay he or she earns. Pay continues to increase until the person learns all the "jobs" in all the teams within an operation.

A pay-for-skills system contributes to the flexible assignment of people within a team. But the reason for using pay for skills is even more basic to a sociotechnical system. To quote Ernesto Poza and Lynne Markus on why the Sherwin-Williams Richmond plant uses pay-for-skills:

> The team philosophy of job design views operating personnel in much the same way that most organizations view their managerial personnel: as a resource, one that makes what they are *able to do* when the need arises more important than what they are *actually doing*.

To eliminate an artificial barrier between salaried and hourly employees, some organizations using pay-for-skill systems also have all of their employees on salary, as opposed to hourly pay systems. GM's new Saturn Corporation and LTV's $135 million electrogalvanizing line decided to use all-salaried workforces. In both cases employees are still union members.

4. STATUS SYMBOLS

Sociotechnical operations are designed to have an egalitarian atmosphere and to avoid barriers between management and employees, whether those barriers are physical, like separate work areas, dining facilities, and parking, or unwritten rules about who can talk to whom. People are more open and willing to communicate up, down, and across. People eat together, park together, and work together.

These four components of the social system—selection, decision-making, reward systems, and status symbols—go far beyond quality circles or better communications. Because they strike at the heart of traditional human resources practices, they are as much a shock to the average American organization as the radically different technical system they support.

BARRIERS TO SOCIOTECHNICAL DESIGNS

We think the sociotechnical approach we have just described makes more sense and works better than traditional operating systems. Anyone who has ever spent time in one of the places described knows that watching a sociotechnical system at work is like watching a beautiful ballet choreographed by the dancers. Watching a traditional system at work is like watching a boxing match, with management trying to referee *and* box.

If sociotechnical systems are better, why isn't everybody using them?

Organizations have been slow to adopt this approach for the same reasons that the "working through" process can take so long: People have to be willing to admit that their current systems are uncompetitive and accept that alternatives do exist.

No matter how much evidence supports the superiority of this operating system, there always seem to be a lot of reasons why "it can't work here." These are some of the objections we hear most often:

- "Well, that makes sense for factories. But we are an (office/information/service) operation."
- "Our unions won't let us."
- "This stuff is a union avoidance strategy. That's why they use it in new plants in the South."
- "That only works in new operations. It would be too hard for us to change."
- "We've got too much invested in our current systems and equipment to change."
- "We aren't about to pay people for skills they aren't using. We don't get a full day's work out of them as it is."
- "We don't have time for this stuff. We have an (office/factory) to run."
- "We can't justify the ROI."

And on and on.

Those are often legitimate points of view. We *do* find a sociotechnical approach used more often in plants than in information or service organizations; traditional labor relationships *are* a barrier to better operating systems; it *is* easier in new operations, because you can start unencumbered by history or bureacratic underbrush; capital *is* important—and expensive.

We see many optimistic signs that those objections are being addressed and overcome. *The companies that aren't doing it will be left with their objections, while the competition takes their markets.*

The remainder of the Agenda for Adjustment focuses on the alternatives many firms are using to handle these tough issues.

—*12*—

Redesigning the Organization

Managers are always hunting for organizational structures that will accomplish two things: first, produce and deliver high-quality products and services at ever increasing levels of efficiency and effectiveness, and second, create and bring new products to new markets quickly.

To create structures that work for either case, managers have to overcome three hurdles:

1. Functional silos built on traditional job design
2. Unwieldy size
3. Too much staff and too many layers

THE FUNCTIONAL SILO

Traditional functional organizations are fairly good at some things:

- Their specialists are highly competent.

- They are an efficient way to organize people for routine, repetitive tasks that don't require much collaboration or fast decision-making.
- They are relatively easy to manage.

But the same functional structures have glaring weaknesses:

- Communication across the functional boundaries is difficult and slow.
- Decision-making and problem-solving are even slower. Problems follow the chain of command. To solve a cross-functional problem, first it has to be communicated within a function, get tossed over to the next function, get the data, back with the answer, and over again. Much time and much information are lost in the process.
- Often, functional specialists neither speak each other's language nor understand each other's problems.
- Management bonuses and promotions go to people who optimize their own areas, even if it leads to suboptimizing the organization.

In short, it seems to us that functional "vertical silos" are the weak link in the American organizational chain. Stronger horizontal linkages are urgently needed, especially between design, engineering and manufacturing. Those groups need each other to solve operating problems, yet they are usually geographically and functionally separate.

Eastman Kodak, plagued by slow functional decision-making, scrapped its functional organization and reorganized into twenty-four business units with profit-and-loss responsibility. Colby Chandler, Kodak's chief executive, says: "Under our old system many product decisions went all the way to the top of the company to be resolved. That deep, tall organization has really been changed now."

In another case, one large capital goods manufacturer was under severe pressure from its customer to get production back on schedule. Manufacturing was having trouble translating customer-requested design and engineering changes into the assembly process. In a last-ditch effort, management moved three hundred engineers out of their offices and onto the shop floor.

The results were enlightening. After everyone got over the shock, engineers were able to respond more rapidly to needed production changes because they could physically *see* the problems and work with the assemblers to solve them. No longer did it take a flurry of paper flying through interoffice mail to communicate. Production was back on schedule two months earlier than predicted.

Moving people out of the traditional functional organization also changes how jobs are defined.

From Job Design to Organization Design

Since the Industrial Revolution, companies have tried to organize work by assigning smaller and narrower tasks to employees. Carried to its assembly line extreme, that produced fractionated, boring jobs, poor quality and productivity, and unmotivated and resentful workers.

In the 1970s advocates of job enrichment and enlargement tried to give employees in offices and factories "larger" jobs with more variety, autonomy, meaningfulness, feedback, and sense of completion. While the approach sometimes made jobs more satisfying, it rarely had much effect on overall performance.

Why? Because *the problem cannot be solved at the level of individual jobs*. Instead of redesigning the smallest piece of the organization—the job—organizations should have been looking at the larger system—customers and markets—and working backward to design a structure that can best serve that market.

The basic building block for that kind of system is not a function or a job but a team of "cross-functional" people who are responsible for meeting an internal or external product, market, or customer need. A team structure gives people the opportunity for satisfaction and gives customers what they need in a way that traditional job design was never able to do.

Goodyear's Lawton, Oklahoma, plant has 164 work teams of from five to twenty-seven members, called business centers, responsible for their own goals, productivity, costs, waste, and all other business and performance measurements. Their actions are coordinated by four plant teams. Goodyear's chairman, Robert C. Mercer, boasts: "The Lawton-delivered tire cost will beat the cost of comparable tires from the lowest-cost foreign producers, meaning the Koreans, who think the Japanese are lazy."

The team concept is clearly a logical fit for new manufacturing assembly processes. Traditional manufacturing work centers are giving way to cellular manufacturing centers—and changing the role of employees in the process.

A work center reflects the old functional organization. All like machines are grouped together—e.g., all lathes are in one area, all presses in another, all final assembly in another. Partially completed components are carted to the next work center and sit in queues until needed. After it leaves a work center, employees never see the component again, unless it comes back for rework. Even then, rework is often handled by yet another center. That is not exactly the formula for a flexible, continuous-learning, low-inventory operation!

In contrast, cells include the full mix of machines and people that were once scattered across work centers. Each cell becomes responsible for a larger piece of the total fabrication or assembly process. A product or component is completed within the cell before it is sent on. That greatly reduces material handling and the queues of work-in-process, and it provides faster feedback on quality problems.

The employees in a cell come from a variety of specialties. In a cellular center, they now have the opportunity to broaden their skill repertoires and learn how to operate other machines. They can also see the full process. Members of the cell can achieve more autonomy, variety, feedback, and sense of completion than they did at their individual, single-machine work stations.

Since each cell is able to track its process and detect and correct problems immediately, companies have found it is more efficient and effective to have six of these multifunctional cells than six traditional work centers or departments.

The cell becomes even more efficient when the members begin to take on scheduling, material handling, and maintenance in their area. When and if the cell members are given full responsibility for meeting goals, monitoring and maintaining their own quality, and selecting and training their own members, they approach the team concept of sociotechnical operating systems described in Chapter 11.

The same principle applies to service and knowledge worker settings. One insurance company had three separate departments responsible for (1) issuing original policies, (2) handling payments, and (3) processing claims.

It restructured those functions into six teams, each with the full responsibility for handling a set of clients. Within the team, an individual was assigned to particular clients, matching the difficulty of the client work with the experience of the employee. With computer access to all information about a client, it was possible for an individual to provide much faster and more personal service to clients.

In many union settings, however, this approach runs up against job classifications and work rules. The number of job classifications in a traditional automobile assembly plant can approach two hundred. To the surprise of many manufacturing managers, the situation isn't much better in some service firms: The number of job and technical classifications in one large urban hospital is almost six hundred.

To management, job classifications and work rules represent a substantial barrier to increased flexibility, leaner staffing, and lower unit costs. But to employees and unions, they represent the way to protect seniority, skills, and jobs.

Both unions and management realize the situation must change. Negotiators on both sides have begun to come to the bargaining table willing to address restrictive work practices, not from a perspective of "concessions" but as necessary adjustments to stay competitive and keep people working. For example, one factor in Toyota's decision to engage in the Fremont, California, joint venture with GM was the UAW's agreement to allow only four assembly job classifications and only three skilled trades classifications. Bruce Lee, director of the UAW West Coast Region, said, "Job definitions were something management created and the union acceded to. I like the idea of the old millwright who could do everything."

Employees and unions fear that managers will take advantage of increased flexibility by arbitrarily assigning jobs and overtime. We have found that those fears can be overcome when workers themselves share the responsibility for assigning and organizing work in the teams.

The functional organization and traditional job design are the first challenges to overcome. The next is size.

SIZE

Economies of scale may be a useful concept in economics, but the concept ends up as a cumbersome way to make a product or deliver a service. We have found that operating systems suffer from the "diseconomies" of scale more than they benefit.

- Most people work better in small rather than large groups. There is more personal accountability, faster communication, more *esprit de corps,* and more innovation.
- Hay Associates found that the productivity of groups of less than five hundred people is 50 percent higher than groups of 4,500.
- Smaller plants and offices entail a smaller investment risk.

Tom Peters and Bob Waterman made a powerful case for small operating units in their book *In Search of Excellence.* They reported case after case of small groups of people able to achieve far more, communicate better, and learn faster than mammoth divisions. They concluded: "Regardless of industry, it seems that more than 500 or so people under one roof causes substantial and unanticipated problems."

Companies who have learned that lesson are "repackaging" existing facilities into smaller operating units and designing their new facilities accordingly:

- GE has shifted manufacturing in its aircraft engine business group from two mammoth complexes to eight smaller plants.
- S. C. Johnson & Son, the consumer goods giant, has increased manufacturing productivity by dividing its 1,200-person workforce in Racine into four smaller groups.
- TRW now has a policy against designing operating units with more than five hundred people.

The design, fabrication, and assembly of many capital goods, such as automobiles and aircraft, cannot be accomplished by only five hundred people. But they *can* be produced by several *subunits* of five hundred or fewer people.

The total number of employees a company has is not the issue. It doesn't matter than Motorola has 90,000 employees or GM has 350,000. It seems the basic building blocks of any organization are ideally small teams of fifteen to twenty people, working in operating units of about five hundred. Then those operating units can be combined in a number of ways: divisions, subsidiaries, sister plants, branch offices.

First, the operating process must be divided into logical and semi-independent units that can be given full responsibility for a definable part of the process. Then, those internal "customer–supplier" units feed each other.

Cutting across the barriers of functional structures and repackaging the organization into smaller units overcome two hurdles. The third hurdle is excessive staff and too many layers.

EXCESSIVE STAFF AND LAYERS

An A. T. Kearny study found that below-average companies in an industry (in terms of sales and earnings growth) had four more staff and managerial levels than highly successful firms.

Much staff work consists of people "taking in each other's laundry," that is, writing reports that no one reads, undertaking studies no one needs, and reviewing and commenting on each other's work.

Just as high levels of inventory and work-in-process mask errors and inefficiencies in production, high levels of management and staff mask the errors and inefficiencies of decision-making. Bureaucratic organizations can't find out what is going wrong.

As the Japanese say, "When you lower the water, you can see the rocks." Getting rid of excess management layers and staff functions cuts through all the "decisions-in-process" and gets decision-making back into real time so problems can be corrected.

Some companies do it by cutting people. One estimate is that eighty-nine of the *Fortune* 100 have cut out layers of management in the last five years. An executive search firm estimated that about 35 percent of middle management jobs have been eliminated since 1981.

- Ford and Chyrsler are producing almost as many cars today with 40 percent less staff than they had four years ago.
- Texas Air cut the number of vice presidents at Continental Airlines from fifty-three to nineteen and the number at Eastern from forty-seven to sixteen.

But just getting rid of people won't do the trick. As Tom Peters astutely observed, "The great American answer to efficiency, 150 years in the making, is still to eliminate people rather than to view them as a primary source of value added."

It makes no sense to eliminate staff and middle management if you don't also change the organizational structure—the way information flows and decisions are made. Otherwise, the boxes on organization charts, like sinkholes, soon fill up again.

Some organizational sinkholes are easy to spot. Theodore Leja, president of Bethlehem Steel's bar, rod, and wire division, found a simple way to cut through layers of management bureaucracy. "I just went down the list and eliminated every job that began with the word assistant."

A more thoughtful approach would be to leave staff and middle-management jobs vacated by attrition unfilled—either eliminate the function or allocate it to user groups—and reconfigure the structure into operating unit teams.

Summary

The research seems to support the idea that smaller, leaner, and flatter organizations are more productive. Richard Kopelman of Baruch College reviewed the last twenty years of research on the effects of organization structure on performance. He concluded that

. . . .the weight of evidence does suggest greater organizational productivity if (1) sub-units are small, (2) there are relatively few hierarchical layers, (3) administrative intensity is controlled (e.g., not too many deputy assistants or staff specialists), (4) the structure is not too complex horizontally (e.g., it has a limited number of departments), and (5) managers have relatively wide spans of control.

In sum, operating units that deliver good products or services efficiently and effectively, and get better all the time, seem to have the following traits:

- They are structured around a product, market, or customer, rather than a function.
- The *building blocks* of the operating units are small groups or teams, rather than functions or departments.
- There are few layers of management and wide spans of control.
- Everyone has broad responsibility and room to take initiative.

What about organizational designs that develop new products and get them to market fast? The characteristics are remarkably similar.

GETTING NEW PRODUCTS TO MARKET

Americans have discovered the most innovative R&D in the world is of little use if new products don't get to the market ahead of the competition. The Japanese left American consumer electronics firms in the dust when they took American technology in video-cassette recording and brought it to the market first. Biotechnology, computers and superconductors are the new battleground for product-to-market skirmishes.

The key to new product development is getting the right product designed *and* produced fast.

The traditional approach to developing new products, called phased project planning (PPP), dates from NASA in the late 1960s. PPP proceeds in steps, with the design group completing its work (theoretically) before handing off designs to manufacturing engineering. Engineering, in turn, would then turn the blueprints over to manufacturing. While that approach appears to make each function more efficient and easier to monitor and control, it often produces designs that are hard to manufacture. And all the coordination needed across functions slows down the process.

As product life cycles get shorter, companies are abandoning PPP in favor of *parallel development* done by multidisciplinary teams. Whether they are called skunkworks, entrepreneurial teams, small business units, or new venture groups, the concept is the same: Small teams of people have full responsibility for designing, manufacturing, and marketing a new product—in parallel.

Examples of this are cropping up throughout industry. Team Taurus (Ford) and Team Xerox, mentioned in the preceding chapter, threw R&D, design, manufacturing, and marketing together in the same organization and got better products to market faster. Hewlett-Packard calls its end-run around PPP (and the functional bureaucracy) "concurrent product-process development." It found it could take months off the R&D cycle by putting design and manufacturing together to invent the product *and* the production process at the same time.

Compaq Computers continues to beat the competition to market by first taking a long time to decide to create a new product, using a product definition team from engineering, marketing, manufacturing, sales, and even finance. When the decision is a "go," teams from manufacturing, marketing and engineering work under a program manager to create the entire design, production, and delivery system.

Procter & Gamble is on a headlong rush into team product development, a radical departure for a relatively turf-oriented firm long convinced that a vertically integrated functional organization was the best way to develop new products.

CONCLUSION

Though the details differ, innovative structures for both steady-state operating systems and new product development are remarkably similar:

1. They are based on small multidisciplinary teams responsible for all aspects of their business, "from beginning to end."
2. Coordination and integration occur within the team, not across functions.
3. The teams depend on members with good people skills who can be creative while still functioning as team players.

However, there are some important differences. First, new product development may bring teams together for relatively short-term assignments. When the new product enters steady-state production, the team members may disperse to form new teams. In contrast, operating systems benefit from longer-term personnel assignments.

Second, new product development thrives on breakthroughs. Operating systems thrive on continuous improvement, as we'll discuss more in the next chapter.

But neither does well in traditional organizations. To accomplish these deep changes, many companies opt to undertake them in new sites or new ventures. Others are committed to the five or more years it can take to redesign existing divisions into smaller operating units, subunits, and teams. In either case, the American organizational structure is in transition. Change is occuring in the way information flows, where decisions are made, who does the staff work, and the nature of jobs.

A reorganization is always dramatic, sometimes earthshaking, and never really finished. Campbell's Soup has reorganized twice in less than five years, first by exploding its functional chart into dozens of semiautonomous operating units, and second by aligning the marketing organization with the distribution system in order to get closer to final customers.

Restructuring as we have used the term is an ongoing issue on the Agenda for Adjustment. We see every new product, process, or market as an opportunity to break down functional silos, move to smaller, flatter team structures, and give people the opportunity for innovation and renewal.

—13—
The Quest for Quality

Quality—in process, in products, and in services—can give a firm enormous competitive advantages in the market place. Conversely, if customers decide that better quality at a reasonable price can be had elsewhere, their emotional allegiance and their dollars quickly follow. Just as Mark Spitz's winning times in the 1972 Olympics wouldn't even qualify him for the U.S. swimming team today, so quality levels that were adequate ten years ago are now woefully uncompetitive.

While managers have always said they "believe" in quality, are "for" quality, and have always strived for quality in their business, most are beginning to realize that they have settled for "the 95 percent solution"—just acceptable quality levels.

Despite the hoopla and rhetoric, quality is not yet "Job One" across America. It simply isn't yet part of the daily thinking of most CEOs, middle managers, and government officials—and certainly not of macroeconomists. Quality remains a tough issue on the Agenda for Adjustment because deep changes in operating philosophies and systems have not yet been made.

There are a growing number of exceptions. In the last five years, we have seen more and more companies learn six important lessons in the pursuit of quality:

1. Quality efforts must be integrated into the company's total business philosophy.
2. It is more cost effective to focus on improving the process than to focus on simple cost-cutting.
3. Rely on continuous improvement; don't wait for the "Big Bang" breakthrough to solve all your problems.
4. Make suppliers partners in the process, not scapegoats.
5. Train, from the top to the bottom of the company.
6. Remember that *everybody* delivers a service to some customer, internal or external.

Those were not easy lessons to learn. As a manager at Motorola quipped recently, "Everything we know, we learned the hard way."

LESSON 1: INTEGRATION

Quality improvement has to be communicated, integrated, and managed like any other full-scale organization strategy.

When there is no strategy, energy can be wasted in piecemeal efforts. We've seen companies stack up a variety of improvement programs like alphabetical houses of cards: SQC, SPC, JIT, CAD, CAM, CIM, EI, QWL, QC groups, and so forth. The number and scope of uncoordinated demands placed on the organization become staggering. Harried middle managers and employees complain that the programs are fragmented, don't have any clear direction, and are taking too much time without enough payoff.

It doesn't have to be that way. Ford, Motorola, Armco, Federal Express, Hewlett-Packard, and others have developed a coherent approach that avoids that kind of chaos. Ford's approach to quality spans its design process to its involvement systems to its advertising campaign. Armco's "Quality +" permeates its training, labor relations, and performance appraisal system.

Xerox is an example of a company that evolved from a Stage 3 "buying time" approach to quality to Stage 5 quality operating philosophy.

Xerox's total quality effort, called "Leadership Through Quality," evolved through three phases:

Phase 1. Competitive benchmarking: an analysis of the competition and the market. This is Xerox's process, started in 1979, of measuring its products, services, and internal practices against the toughest competitors in the world—in any industry, not just copiers. Every Xerox unit or department now benchmarks its performance against companies that are the best in that area.

Out of benchmarking came a goal: superiority in quality, product reliability, and costs. The goal led to intensive customer surveys, a complete overhaul of the process of designing new products, and substantial investments in automation and training.

The company realized the magnitude of the needed changes would require deep employee involvement, which led to phase 2.

Phase 2. Xerox adopted employee involvement in order to meet the targets set by competitive benchmarking. Management was trained in EI skills, and everyone in the organization now can participate in a wide variety of problem-solving and creative groups. As more and more people got involved and more changes were made, everyone realized that a coherent strategy was needed.

Phase 3. Leadership Through Quality. Chairman David Kearns and twenty-five of the company's most senior managers from around the world met repeatedly to hammer out a Xerox quality policy and a supporting set of quality principles, management actions, and tools. They went on to create an implementation schedule and checkpoint reviews. Finally, they agreed to call the long-term process *Leadership Through Quality.*

This is the Xerox quality policy:

> Quality is *the* basic business principle for Xerox. Quality means providing our external and internal customers with innovative products and services that fully satisfy their requirements. Quality improvement is the job of every Xerox employee.

As Frank Pipp, vice president of Xerox Diversified Business Group, says, "These words won't go down in history, but we understand them, and all of our employees understand them."

Management then developed a set of principles to guide the implementation of the policy.

1. Quality is the basic business principle for Xerox to continue to be a leadership company.

2. We will understand our customer's existing and latent requirements.
3. We will provide all our external and internal customers with products and services which meet their requirements.
4. Employee involvement, through participative problem solving, is essential to improve quality.
5. Error-free work is the most cost-effective way to improve quality.

To drive the implementation process, Xerox established a Corporate Quality Office, headed by a vice president who was elected a corporate officer by the Xerox Board of Directors.

In the first full two years of the program—1981 and 1982—assembly quality improved 63 percent, product reliability increased 20 percent, and overhead costs decreased by 20 percent. The rate of improvement has continued, and Xerox has since regained more than 10 points of market share.

Xerox management credits the teachings of Juran, Deming, and Crosby, and the examples set by the most competitive companies in the world. But the most critical component was management commitment and involvement in developing and living an integrated strategy.

LESSON 2: CORRECT THE PROCESS, DON'T INSPECT THE PRODUCT

World-class quality comes from simplifying and improving the process rather than inspecting the output. For example, Bob Hayes and Kim Clark studied twelve factories in three companies over several years. They found that the practices that make one factory more productive than another were: investing in new equipment, reducing waste, and cutting work-in-process inventories and the need for inspection by solving the problems that produced them in the first place.

We don't see how any company can afford the costs associated with the "inspect-it-in" mentality. The high costs include not only the cost of inspecting for defects but also the costs of correcting errors and the cost of customers lost because they're dissatisfied with a product or service.

To those costs add the massive carrying and confusion costs of work-in-process, and you have found America's *hidden* recycling center, occupied with reworking, retesting, reinspecting, and rejecting output. In many operations, it accounts for 15 to 40 percent of total productive capacity and costs 20 to 40 percent of every sales dollar.

The costs of bad service are hidden as well. The average business never hears from 96 percent of its unhappy customers. And each of those customers tells at least ten other people about their problems.

Compared with the costs of poor quality, prevention is a real bargain. Yet, as one wag remarked, "America practices the burnt toast formula. We'd rather burn the toast and hire someone to scrape it off than fix the toaster."

One way manufacturing has exposed those hidden problems is to move to a just-in-time system.

Using Just-in-Time

We see managers mistake just-in-time (JIT) for a Japanese inventory reduction technique, when in fact it is a much more comprehensive production philosophy.

The basic idea is misleadingly simple: Materials and parts should arrive at each stage of production at the exact time they are needed instead of having large batches made in advance and stored. JIT is a demand-pull system in which the ultimate customer starts the process by calling for product. That starts a hand-to-mouth process where materials and components are produced on demand when called for by the next downstream customer.

The true philosophy behind JIT is continuous improvement of everything and the elimination of all waste of time, people, effort, and materials. Hundreds of American companies are adopting the JIT philosophy, ranging from Campbells (food) and Warner Lambert (pharmaceuticals) to Motorola and Intel (semiconductors) and Harley-Davidson (motorcycles). The benefits can be dramatic. At Harley-Davidson, the system freed $22 million previously tied up in inventory at one plant alone. JIT also radically reduced reorder lead times.

JIT eliminates administrative costs. One American company making integrated circuits told its best supplier of blister packs (for shipping the circuits) that if it could deliver *exactly* the right number of perfect packs every two hours, directly to the packing stations, then it could have all of the plant's business *forever*. And the supplier would never have to submit an invoice. The customer would automatically pay him every month for the number of packs it had ordered. The result: no accounts receivable or payable paperwork on either end. No bills of lading: no incoming shipments to check, store, and keep track of. And this could go on forever, as long as the supplier continued to deliver perfect quality every two hours.

There are other benefits from the system:

- Defects are detected during the production process, eliminating the need for inspection at the end of the line.
- Problems are detected and fixed immediately, so no product is lost in bad production.
- Lean inventory levels reduce the risk of excess inventory if demand drops. And lean inventory-to-sales ratios throughout the economy help smooth the business cycle.

Managers inspired to adopt JIT have had to overcome fears about such a radically different operating system. They fear the loss of an inventory security blanket against high sales demands or missed production schedules; they fear the long distance suppliers have to travel to make daily deliveries. The Japanese have those problems, too. Once all of Toyota City production was shut down when a massive traffic jam tied up roads into the facility, and suppliers' trucks couldn't get through.

But we've seen those fears overcome through continuous improvement of the process, Lesson 3.

LESSON 3: CONTINUOUS IMPROVEMENT, NOT A BIG BANG

Breakthroughs are a legitimate goal in R&D, but continuous improvement is the key to quality leadership in the delivery of goods and services.

Yet we hear managers argue that "what we need is a major breakthrough to leapfrog over the competition." They believe in the Big Bang Theory of Improvement, the Hail Mary touchdown pass, the grand slam home run. While they're waiting for the breakthrough, the large Japanese exporting firms are killing them in the market place with daily, incremental improvements in their processes and products.

Continuous improvement is not as attractive as a "breakthrough," because it requires a shift in control and responsibility from management and end-of-the-line inspectors to the employees who actually do the work.

- At Xerox's facility in Webster, New York, which makes the 1075 Series copier, employees and management hold a one-hour defect analysis meeting every day.

- At the GM Pontiac Fiero plant, managers, supervisors, and hourly workers meet daily to correct today's quality problems and prevent them tomorrow.

Continuous improvement is not easy. First, to get continuous improvement one has to reward those who identify problems. Traditionally, neither managers nor employees want to be caught near the scene of a problem, quality or otherwise, because the response in too many companies is to find someone to blame for it, not to solve it.

A second obstacle to continuous improvement is the accounting system. As we shall discuss in Chapter 18, if quality is addressed at all in most accounting reports, it is usually as a variance item, such as "scrap and rework." Indirect savings from improving quality and cutting work-in-process inventory will eventually result in lower total costs, but they show up too late to provide much information or feedback. Big savings from money *not* spent won't show up at all, e.g., less borrowing to finance inventory or less need to expand floor space.

Firms have to create their own measures, and the simpler, the better. In manufacturing and assembly, Xerox created three simple measures: defects per million incoming parts, defects per hundred finished products, and, for customers, the percentage of defect-free installations.

Sharing responsibility for continuous improvement leads naturally to Lesson 4.

LESSON 4: CULTIVATE SUPPLIERS; DON'T MAKE THEM SCAPEGOATS

Historically, American companies have not trusted any single supplier, preferring to keep dozens of suppliers on the string and play them off against each other in the name of "competition." In turn, suppliers are unwilling to accommodate the customer's needs for fear of throwing off the production schedules of other customers.

The wave of cost-cutting in the early 1980's led firms to pressure suppliers for price cuts; it was simpler than cutting their own and suppliers' costs by changing their production systems. JIT was often used as a way to coerce suppliers to hold the customer's inventory. But if inventory just gets pushed back onto someone else in the chain, the cost of carrying it eventually gets charged to the customer.

Smart companies started bringing suppliers in on the early stages of designing new products, offering training in JIT techniques, and proposing long-term contracts to suppliers who could conform to JIT quality and delivery needs.

- Ford's Team Taurus signed long-term contracts with suppliers and invited them to participate in product planning. "We never had the supplier input we had on this car," said Veraldi, head of Team Taurus. "Now we'll never do it any other way."
- Xerox reduced its vendors from five thousand to three hundred and gave the survivors two- and three-year contracts—long-term by the standards of the industry—in return for big improvements in the quality of parts delivered. Xerox held classes in just-in-time to help suppliers train their own people and gained not only better supplier quality, but loyalty and good relations as well.

Xerox benefited from Harley-Davidson's experiences in getting a JIT system up and running. Harley knew that Japanese manufacturing techniques were yielding operating costs fully 30 percent lower than Harley's. Harley set out to get inventory out of its plants by bullying its suppliers into just-in-time. Through a painful learning process and a near revolt from suppliers, Harley has established mutual understandings with suppliers about quality and timeliness. Contracts are now two pages long instead of thirty-five. Harley also offered suppliers statistics courses to teach their workers how to chart small changes in the performance of their equipment. The operation has paid off. Harley's costs for warranty repairs, scrap, and rework are down 60 percent.

There are other ways to strengthen ties with suppliers:

- Cummins Engine and its customer, Kenworth Trucks, have joint teams of production employees who meet regularly to solve mutual quality problems.
- Ford has started giving awards to its best suppliers. Donnelly Corporation and Herman Miller (two of the earliest American companies to adopt gain sharing plans) have each earned the Ford Motor Company "Q One" award as suppliers with the highest assurance of product quality and on-time delivery.

LESSON 5: THERE'S NO SUCH THING AS TOO MUCH TRAINING

Nearly every company with a quality program says, "You can't do too much training."

We agree. We also think that an awful lot of companies could learn from Westinghouse, Motorola, Xerox, and Ford that training is more than teaching production workers statistical techniques.

1. Top managers need quality training, so they will speak the same language as subordinates and will understand how to support improvement processes.
2. Real problems encountered outside the classroom are seldom textbook simple.
3. Lower-level employees need the opportunity to use new skills.

In contrast to typical American approaches, look at the training offered to Japanese senior management embarking on a total companywide quality control program in a metal-fabricating company.

Topic	Hours
Role of top management in implementing QC	1.5
QC in product development	2.0
Statistical methods	3.5
Management of QC	3.5
QC in manufacturing	3.5
QC in purchasing and sales	3.5
Quality assurance	3.5
QC in Japan and in the world	3.5
Group discussions on promoting QC in the company	3.0
Reports of group discussions	3.0
Total	30.5

How many *senior managers* of American firms have been through this kind of training before directing someone else to implement a quality program?

Westinghouse has been very successful in integrating training with the companywide quality effort. Its Quality College services 2,000 quality circles involving 20,000 employees as well as providing other technical and management-of-quality training.

Partly as a result, Westinghouse has averaged real productivity gains of 7 percent a year for three years in a row. At that rate, Westinghouse could double its output every ten years without adding any resources.

Motorola, facing accelerating change and competition in electronic communications and semiconductors, began training all of its employees in statistical process control and problem-solving. About 30,000 employee a year receive a total of 2 million to 3 million hours of training. The company estimates that its rate of return is about thirty times the dollars invested.

Motorola is also training suppliers' employees in advanced computer-aided design and defect control.

Training is equally important in services. Services, in general, focus too much training on how to handle the cash register and not enough on how to handle the customer. There are notable exceptions. L. L. Bean, the huge outdoor clothing and supplies mail order company, fills orders accurately 99.8 percent of the time. The 3,600 full-time and part-time Bean employees receive forty hours of training before they deal with their first customer.

LESSON 6: EVERYONE DELIVERS A SERVICE TO A CUSTOMER

The Economist recently defined "services" as "things which can be bought and sold, but which you can't drop on your foot." Services may be "intangible," but many of the techniques and concepts of quality enhancement in manufacturing apply to service organizations. It is making the translation and overcoming the "we are different" attitude in services that is tough.

People render services as well as products to two kinds of customers: external and internal.

External Customer Satisfaction

It pays to have happy and loyal customers. For instance, a brand-loyal car buyer represents a lifetime revenue of at least $140,000 to an automaker. Appliance manufacturers estimate that brand loyalty is worth $2,800 over twenty years.

Judging the quality of a service is more subjective than determining the quality of a product. The American Society for Quality Control in 1985 asked consumers to rate a variety of services on a scale of 1 to 10. Unfortunately, the percentage of customers rating a service 8 or better are: for banks, 52 percent; for hospitals, 44 percent; for hotels, 41 percent; and for insurance, 34 percent.

It is unbelievable but true that many companies have no system for tracking customer satisfaction. In contrast, at a Quality in Services conference sponsored by the APC, every company making a presentation, from Averitt Express (trucking), to General Telephone Company of the Southwest (telecommunications) tracked and used customer satisfaction as a principal indicator of quality.

- Domino's Pizza measures customer satisfaction every week and posts the results clearly in every shop.
- At Sewell Village Cadillac, a dealership in Dallas, Texas, the performance of service personnel is measured through customer questionaires that focus on friendliness, professionalism, and time-liness, among other things. Their scores are published in books placed on the showroom floor for customers to see.

Internal Customers

People in manufacturing and in the "back rooms" of service organizations can forget that they too provide products and services to a "customer."

For example, when Corning implemented its total quality program with an "everybody-has-a-customer" theme, the reaction from the non-manufacturing areas varied. Engineers, who deal with prevention daily, and purchasing agents, who saw an opportunity to improve relations with suppliers, had no problem. But scientists felt that measuring quality was irrelevant in their "creative" work, and data processing thought it only meant getting the numbers right, which they already did.

Corning had every nonmanufacturing group gather feedback from its internal customers. As a result, the scientists discovered that one of their primary services was to run experiments and translate the results so that other people could use them. Quality for their customers was understandable results, not necessarily positive findings.

The Corning data processing group decided to find out what happened to all the reports they sent out every month. They found that some locations hadn't used the reports in years. One year's worth of eliminated reports made a pile two stories high.

THE PAYOFF

The health of the American automobile industry still serves as a psycholog-ical bellwether for many people. To the extent that these six lessons have been learned in the automobile industry, they point to reasons for optimism about quality in America.

- Ford has gone from the worst in quality to the best of the U.S. manufacturers in just five years. A Maritz survey of owners of 1985 cars showed that Ford averaged only 2.1 minor things wrong with a car, Chrysler had 2.8, and GM, 2.6. (The Japanese averaged 1.3.)
- Complaints about Ford engines dropped from sixty per hundred cars in 1982 to twenty-four in 1986.
- GM is also making strides. False starts and design problems initially hurt the Fiero, but the unwavering dedication by the Fiero people to producing a fine car is paying off. Customer satisfaction has jumped from 74 out of 100 on a consumer satisfaction index to 91 out of 100.
- Chrysler concentrated on its K-cars and produced quality high enough to keep warranty claims at half the level Chrysler expected under its new extended warranty.

A lot of the turnaround can be attributed to new production systems so precise that they produce very few mistakes. It takes cooperation among design and manufacturing engineers, training, automation, an openness to new ideas, and constant attention to detail.

None of that is possible without people who feel a sense of involvement and a stake in the outcome. In the next chapters, we address some of the ways that commitment can be achieved.

—14—
Competitive Compensation

Most American companies' compensation systems are inflexible, demotivating, and unrelated to productivity. Developed in an environment of fast growth, pattern bargaining, and little competition, they seldom promote continuous learning or improvement and do little to encourage a sense of common fate or purpose in organizations.

Before we propose some alternatives for tackling this tough issue, it is worth reviewing five reasons why American compensation systems must change.

1. Pay Has Risen Faster than Productivity

There is a fundamental law of cost competitiveness:

$$\begin{bmatrix} \text{Pay} \\ \text{increases} \end{bmatrix} - \begin{bmatrix} \text{Productivity} \\ \text{increases} \end{bmatrix} = \begin{bmatrix} \text{Increases in} \\ \text{unit labor costs} \end{bmatrix}$$

If pay rises faster than productivity, the unit labor costs of our products and services also rise. That is just what has happened in the United States.

RISE IN UNIT LABOR COSTS[*]

	Compensation per Hour		Output per Hour		Unit Labor Costs
1947–68	5.1%	–	2.6%	=	2.5%
1968–73	6.9	–	1.6	=	5.3
1973–82	9.0	–	.7	=	8.6
1982–85	4.0	–	1.5	=	2.3

[*] Average annual rates of change in the nonfarm business sector.
SOURCE: Bureau of Labor Statistics, unpublished tables, January 1987.

From 1947 to 1968, pay and productivity growth tracked fairly closely in the nonfarm business economy. But about 1968, compensation began to grow far faster than productivity. The result was a dramatic rise in unit labor costs as the two diverged from 1968 to 1982.

The rise was particularly harmful in manufacturing. From 1973 to 1985, *manufacturing* unit labor costs in the United States grew at an average annual rate of 5.8 percent, while Japan's grew at 2.8 percent. U.S. goods became less price competitive at the rate of 3 percent a year.

Several external factors having little to do with firm-level productivity were fueling the rise: skyrocketing fringe benefit costs, including a tenfold increase in health care costs; cost of living adjustments (COLA); pattern bargaining; and spreading use of wage and salary surveys to set pay levels.

Compensation growth has slowed greatly since 1983 because of declining inflation and rising foreign competition. But if inflation heats up again, pressure to raise pay regardless of productivity will grow, hurting competitiveness without adding anything to Americans' real earnings.

2. LABOR COSTS ARE FAR LOWER IN SOME NATIONS

Americans should compete on the basis of high productivity and quality, not low pay. But we cannot ignore the fact that some of our trading partners have compensation costs far lower than ours. (See the accompanying table.)

1985 HOURLY COMPENSATION COSTS, PRODUCTION WORKERS IN MANUFACTURING

	Total Compensation*	Index (U.S. = 100)
West Germany	$15.68	122
Switzerland	15.54	121
United States	12.82	100
Sweden	12.80	96
France	11.52	90
Italy	11.37	89
Canada	10.89	85
Japan	10.26	80
United Kingdom	7.28	57
Hong Kong	1.75	14
Taiwan	1.68	13
South Korea	1.44	11
Mexico	.57	4

* Total compensation includes fringe benefits, social security, pensions, and other nonwage employment costs.
SOURCE: Bureau of Labor Statistics data of January 1987, converted to U.S. dollars using February 1987 exchange rates. Figures do not reflect whatever 1986 pay increases may have occurred.

However, the "cheap foreign labor" threat does not apply to most of our competitors. Japan is clearly not a "low-wage country." Japanese wage rates, which were about 50 percent of the U.S. level before the dollar's decline, are now about 80 percent of the U.S. level. German and Swiss production workers now earn more than U.S. workers.

But Taiwan, Hong Kong, and South Korea have much lower wage rates and relatively high productivity and quality. If American firms want to continue to produce at home and pay more than the competition, they will have to be more productive.

Tables like this one frequently prompt senior managers to push for cuts in hourly workers' pay. But to our knowledge, no American firm has ever compared the salaries of its executives and middle managers to those in equally successful and productive firms in Japan, Korea, or Hong Kong—and then cut executive pay.

It is important to remember that *very productive companies can afford to pay people a great deal of money,* as Nucor Steel and Lincoln Electric have proved. But those firms tie pay to productivity and performance, which is not true for most American firms.

3. PAY IS NOT RELATED TO PERFORMANCE

Most American employees, blue-collar and white-collar, correctly believe there is little connection between their pay and productivity or quality. Most pay increases are based on other factors: tradition, current profitability (which may be very temporary), collective bargaining strength, time of the year, threats, and national wage and salary surveys. Many so-called merit pay systems are really only salaried COLA plans that foster dissatisfaction, competition among employees, and a focus on short-term results.

Despite the millions of dollars and hours spent every year administering performance appraisal and "merit" pay systems, surveys done by the Public Agenda Foundation, as well as the Harris and Gallup organizations, find that:

- Forty-five percent of the work force believe there is no link between pay and performance. Only 22 percent see a close link.
- Only 13 percent believe they would personally benefit from producing more effectively; 48 percent believe any benefit would go to their employer.

In contrast, a 1982 survey of Japanese workers found 93 percent believe they will benefit from improvements in their employers' performance. That is not the result of blind loyalty. Consider that in 1986 less than 0.9 percent of Americans' earnings were in the form of flexible bonuses; in Japan it was 28 percent. From 1982 to 1984, twice-yearly bonuses averaged 26 percent of base pay a year in small Japanese firms; 41 percent in the largest companies.

Flexible compensation would give Americans a clear financial stake in productivity and quality improvement, but that is rarely the case in the United States now.

4. U.S. WAGES AND SALARIES ARE NOT FLEXIBLE

U.S. pay systems are one instance where what goes up almost never comes down. For the vast majority of Americans, fixed compensation is 100 percent of the paycheck. There is little or no leeway for adjusting pay to changing company performance. Therefore, most firms cut people before they cut pay, though they may well end up doing both. The costs in severance pay, lost talent, personal pain, and ill will are high.

Making a portion of compensation *flexible* by using profit sharing or gain sharing allows a firm's wage bill to vary with market conditions as well as internal performance, reducing the need to resort to layoffs and cuts in base pay. For example, the three most successful companies in the steel industry—Nucor, Worthington Industries, and Chaparral Steel—all have profit sharing and/or gain sharing plans, have highly paid and productive employees, and don't have layoffs.

5. PRESENT COMPENSATION SYSTEMS DO NOT SUPPORT
A FEELING OF "COMMON FATE"

Most compensation systems reinforce the idea that top-level executives, blue-collar workers, and white-collar workers are very different stakeholders in the corporation—citizens without a common fate.

Executive bonuses and perquisites, golden parachutes, and senior-level-only incentive plans are prime examples. Employees perceive them as "unfair," especially when the firm is in trouble. For example:

- Wages in the steel industry rose 16 percent over the last ten years, but executive pay rose 52 percent.
- In Japan, the ratio of after-tax income between a company president and a first-year employee is about 8 to 1. In the United States it is typically 20 to 1. In the auto industry it is 36 to 1.
- Senior-level executives complain when employees want more job security, saying, "We pay them a fair day's pay," then turn around and vote themselves golden parachutes to "ensure the continued conscientious effort and commitment by key executives to the shareholders' interests."

U.S. executives stoutly defend their system by saying they are only following "the market" or offering other defenses that don't carry much weight with lower-level employees. GM has been criticized for giving its executives generous bonuses while the company is losing market share and cutting employment. Recently, young executives at GM have begun pressing for pay cuts in the spirit of "equality of sacrifice."

For those five reasons, the U.S. compensation system cannot remain as it is—if the United States is to remain a leading economic power. But change will not be easy.

CHANGING COMPENSATION SYSTEMS

Changing a compensation system is about as easy as moving a cemetery.

First, no one—but no one—at any level of the organization, ever wants to take a cut in pay, unless the ship is sinking. And even then, many seem to prefer drowning.

Two, if changes are to be made, how? Should everyone take a percentage cut? Different percentages at different levels? Should the directors and officers take the first hit, as they do in Japan?

Suppose there is no cut, but the firm wants to create a system for linking productivity, quality, and pay. What system should be used? What formula? Should everybody be on the same formula? Should it be based on profits? Productivity? Both?

Three, changing systems is sometimes delayed up to two or three years by the bargaining calendar. Some firms and unions have agreed to "reopen" the contract before expiration date, but the wolf had to be almost inside the door before they acted.

Unionized firms have been trying a variety of alternatives. Over half of the contracts ratified in 1984–86 included such concessions as delays of COLA, wage freezes, two-tier plans, or lump sum bonuses instead of base wage increases.

While we agree that concession bargaining is often essential to survival, it is only a temporary adjustment by those buying time before they accept the need for deeper, more permanent changes. Two-tier plans and such other devices as pay cuts and freezes don't do anything to tie pay to performance, increase employee commitment, or encourage continuous improvement.

In contrast, flexible compensation plans such as profit sharing and gain sharing can make a substantial contribution to commitment and to long-term competitiveness.

Flexible Compensation

PROFIT SHARING

More than 350,000 U.S. firms have profit sharing plans, usually as part of a retirement or executive pay package. Most of the profit sharing plans are used to build pension funds and may not be highly related to profitability. There is a growing use of annual cash profit sharing, rather than deferred compensation, as a flexible pay/shared risk–reward strategy.

Cash profit sharing, based on return on sales, has long been used in Japan, where auto workers, management and nonmanagement, earn up to 50 percent of their total compensation in twice-annual negotiated bonuses. For example, the base pay of an auto worker at Toyota is about $15,600, but bonuses bring it up to $23,500.

With the devaluation of the dollar in 1986–87, Japanese auto workers agreed to a 10 percent reduction in their bonus in order to reduce the costs of production, keep volume and market share high, and maintain employment stability. Through a long history of "mutual growth," Japanese employees are more willing to place part of their compensation at risk in the short term, in return for long-term gains.

In the U.S. auto industry, in 1982 and 1984 Ford and General Motors negotiated profit sharing plans with the United Auto Workers to replace the traditional auto industry 3 percent "annual improvement factor" pay increase.

For UAW members at Ford it turned out to be a good deal. Ford workers received about $400 for 1982, $400 for 1983, about $2,000 for 1984, $1,200 for 1985, and $2,100 for 1986, for a total of $6,100. Profit sharing has been less lucrative at GM. GM workers earned about $600 in 1983, $550 in 1984, about $350 in 1985, and nothing in 1986, for a total of $1,500.

Ironically, Chrysler's UAW members gave up their 1979 profit sharing plan just before it started to pay off. If they had kept their plan instead of taking a dollar an hour increase in 1982 (to reach parity with other UAW workers at GM and Ford), the average UAW worker at Chrysler would have received about $2,600 in 1983 and almost $5,000 in 1984. In late 1985 they agreed to a new profit sharing plan, one less lucrative than the crisis-induced plan for which they had originally bargained.

As the Chrysler example illustrates, employees may be reluctant to put part of their compensation at risk. While profit sharing is a valuable and effective approach to flexible compensation and is spreading in the United States, it has some limitations:

1. It is influenced by external factors over which employees (except at senior levels) have little control.
2. It is difficult for an employee in a large firm to see what he or she did that influenced corporate profits a year later.
3. It does not provide much feedback on the performance of the operating systems.

To overcome those limitations, many firms are turning toward operating unit gain sharing plans.

GAIN SHARING

Gain sharing is what the term implies: sharing gains from productivity. However, the term covers a wide variety of bonus systems in which some portion of an employee's compensation varies with the performance of the business unit of which he or she is a member.

Gain sharing plans are based on improvement in the performance of a *group*—it might be a plant, department, or company—where *everyone* is rewarded, not just a select few "key employees."

Unlike profit sharing, most gain sharing formulas reward directly for factors that employees can greatly influence: productivity, quality, payroll and material costs, yields, customer satisfaction, safety, schedules.

The four principal types are (1) the Scanlon plan, (2) the Rucker® Plan, (3) Improshare® and (4) "custom" plans, which vary widely. There are an infinite number of variations in how the plans work, ranging from plant and group productivity gain sharing plans used by firms like McDonnell Douglas, Motorola, Dana, General Electric, Firestone, and TRW to companywide plans at Chaparral and Herman Miller.

Though the details vary, we find several key elements that are part of successful plans.

First, a gain sharing plan needs an involvement system that allows employees the opportunity to participate in making improvements. Gain sharing is not just a way to pay people, it's a new way to manage and make improvements.

Second, the formula should be based on measures employees can influence. In a 1986 APC national survey of firms using profit sharing and gain sharing, firms reported that profit sharing had a very positive impact on attracting and retaining employees. But it had less impact than gain sharing on productivity, cost reduction, quality, scrap and rework, and employee involvement. The positive impact on labor relations, communications and pay were similar. (See the accompanying table.)

PERCENT OF FIRMS[*] REPORTING POSITIVE IMPACT OF PLANS

	Profit Sharing	Gain Sharing
Productivity	65%	93%
Cost reduction	56	81
Quality	70	80
Scrap and rework	39	61
Labor relations	73	74
Employee involvement	70	81
Communications	77	78
Pay	77	77

[*] Sample size = 200.

A third success factor is giving employees a role in designing the gain sharing plan. Instead of a plan designed by a few human resource people, industrial engineers, or managers, employees should join with these groups, working together to design the system. The key to the success of a plan is not just the formula, but who was involved in the design and whether employees trust it as an accurate and fair system.

Examples and Results of Gain Sharing Plans

Firms with gain sharing and profit sharing plans report a variety of positive results:

- At Steelcase, about 38 percent of pay comes from gain sharing and profit sharing. In a good year, the amount can be 50 percent.
- At Herman Miller, another high-quality and high-productivity office furniture company, gain sharing provides 7 to 23 percent bonuses above base pay annually. When sales slumped in 1986, employees suggested ways to trim an extra $12 million from costs.
- Nucor, a successful steel company, bases one-third of employee pay on gain sharing production bonuses and profit sharing. Nucor

produces twice as much steel per employee as the large steel companies. Its labor costs are $55 a ton, as against $140 a ton for big steel. Some Nucor mill workers earn $40,000 a year.

- More than 90 percent of Motorola's U.S. employees are covered by a gain sharing plan in which it is possible to earn bonuses up to 42 percent of base pay. In a typical Motorola location, gain sharing has helped cut scrap by two-thirds and has cut both work-in-process inventory and employee turnover by one-half. Productivity gains of 20 to 30 percent are not uncommon.

From APC surveys, we estimate that about 13 percent of American firms are using some kind of gain sharing in one or more locations.

- More than 90 percent of the two hundred gain sharing plans in our sample were implemented in the last five years, though many firms have successfully used gain sharing far longer.
- Gain sharing bonuses averaged 9 percent of base pay, but the range was far greater. In most cases, the firms' share of the gains was equal to, or greater than, that paid out to employees.
- Pay and productivity are not the only things that improve with effective plans. APC research indicates that employee involvement and information-sharing are almost twice as high in firms with gain sharing than in firms without it.

A Competitive Compensation Strategy

We have said what we think is wrong with current compensation systems. What do we propose as an alternative? What we propose is a far deeper and ultimately more positive approach based on flexible compensation, requiring a profound change in the basic philosophy about how and why people are paid.

1. It's time to start tying compensation to productivity and performance. Employees will then have a real stake in improvement, and unit costs will stay competitive.
2. A portion of pay should be flexible; that is, it should vary with productivity and profitability. All employees should have the chance to earn more or less compensation based on the performance of their firm or work unit. Bonuses are not just for executives.
3. Companies and unions need to avoid using factors external to the firm, such as industry patterns and cost of living, as a basis for permanent pay increases.

4. Compensation should be driven by a philosophy of mutual commitment between employees and the firm; it should foster cooperation rather than conflict, among all employees.

What we are proposing is a long term "competitive compensation strategy" as an alternative to traditional compensation.

Our proposal has five parts. The first two apply to *fixed compensation*—base pay and pay increases. The other three refer to *flexible compensation*—pay for performance and cost of living. These components are general guidelines. The details and timing would vary greatly across organizations.

Fixed Compensation

1. BASE PAY

Wages/salaries/benefits ought to be determined by the need to attract and retain good employees, but should contribute no more than 70–90 percent of an employee's potential earnings.

We are not, of course, talking about cutting pay 10 to 30 percent, or putting everyone on individual incentives. We are talking about phasing in flexible compensation so that fixed pay becomes a relatively smaller portion of the growth in total compensation.

2. BASE PAY INCREASES

Increases that will become a permanent part of base pay ought to be related to and justified by clear and permanent productivity improvement at the work group or organization level. Pay increases have to be tied to productivity, which is internal to the firm, not to external factors, such as industry patterns or inflation.

The "merit" pool for pay raises could be replaced by a "productivity pool." Firms that think their performance appraisal system is worth keeping could allocate base pay increases from the pool to individuals, using merit as the criterion.

Flexible Compensation

3. PROFIT SHARING

Profit sharing (of which there are many varieties) should apply to all employees and be based on company or business unit profitability.

There are two points to keep in mind with profit sharing. One, profits are a short-term measure of market success and are not necessarily a good basis for allocating base pay increases. Second, profit sharing is a "risk-sharing" strategy, since many market place factors outside employee control affect profits.

Therefore, if employees are going to share the risk with the company and shareholders, the potential returns from profit sharing need to match the risk.

4. GAIN SHARING

Since gain sharing is a bonus and involvement system that rewards employees for the performance of their operating unit (plant, branch office, and so on), ideally all employees should be eligible for gain sharing in their group.

A small company might need only profit sharing *or* gain sharing. Big firms need both: companywide or divisionwide profit sharing, and gain sharing for operating units and small business units.

Experience and survey data on profit sharing and gain sharing plans indicate that such flexible compensation can significantly increase employee pay. *Gain sharing firms pay more and get more for it than their competitors.* In highly productive firms such as Lincoln Electric, pay can rise to twice the industry level without increasing the price of the product. Again, productive firms can afford to pay people a lot of money.

However, let us suppose the United States enters another era of double-digit inflation. What if the combination of fixed and flexible pay is not enough to keep up with a rapid increase in the cost of living? That brings us to the fifth component of our proposal, cost of living adjustments.

Obviously, in setting pay, firms cannot ignore the cost of living (COL), just as they cannot ignore the labor market, but we're suggesting it no longer be the main determinant of fixed increases in compensation.

5. COST OF LIVING

Cost of living adjustments (COLA) would not be a part of base pay. They would be "extra one-time compensation bonuses" triggered by extraordinary inflation levels. The "inflation adjustments" could be made annually in a lump sum bonus or as add-on quarterly or monthly pay. They do not become part of base pay, which, as we said earlier, rises only as productivity rises.

Impact on Collective Bargaining

For years, both management and unions have attempted to make wages the same across all firms in an industry. But pattern bargaining has almost disappeared in the face of competitive pressures.

Union leaders are facing a difficult dilemma. If they let base wages vary widely between firms, they violate a union tradition of wage parity and "equal pay for equal work." But if wages don't adjust and firms go out of business, the human toll is high, and dwindling union membership will decline even further.

Flexible compensation can provide a win–win alternative, one that is beginning to emerge in the steel and auto industries. Firms and unions can

- Adopt relatively uniform, but lower, base wages within an industry or within product lines
- Develop guidelines for gain sharing and profit sharing formulas across firms
- Ensure that union members earn similar base pay, but vary flexible compensation with productivity improvement
- Through gain sharing, make multiyear contracts responsive to changes in the business cycle without sacrificing the stabilizing advantages of long-term contracts

Other Nontraditional Reward Systems

We have focused on flexible compensation—profit sharing and gain sharing—because the concept is so consistent with common fate and continuous improvement in organizations.

There are additional pay strategies firms should explore in their search for better compensation and reward systems. They are also consistent with the model presented above.

Pay-for-skills or pay-for-knowledge plans, described in Chapter 11, are ways of encouraging continuous learning and increased employee expertise and flexibility. Our data indicate that about 8 percent of manufacturing firms are using pay-for-skills in some of their team-structured locations. When the majority of employees have learned all the skills and are being paid at the top rate, many of those facilities adopt gain sharing plans to reward for continuous improvement.

All-salaried plans, which eliminate the hourly–salaried barrier in organizations, are an alternative to traditional hourly pay plans. Many new plants are designed to use all-salaried work forces. The GM Saturn project will have an all-salaried union work force, with gain sharing introduced after the subsidiary is fully operational.

Employee stock ownership plans (ESOP) have spread rapidly, partly because of their tax and "antitakeover" appeal, but also as a way to give employees an ownership stake in their companies.

A variety of *noncash, nonfinancial rewards* are being successfully used, ranging from special merchandise and travel awards for money-saving ideas to earned time off for high performance. This can be a useful approach to motivation and rewards because of its trophy value and because the gift never gets lost in the paycheck.

SUMMARY

It is clear to us that the solution is to change not just the compensation system but the *philosophy* behind the system. It's the shared responsibility, flexibility, and mutual benefit they imply that make gain sharing and other approaches more successful than the current system.

Whatever compensation method is used, it is clear that the philosophy that drives it will affect the rest of the Agenda for Adjustment, especially employment stability, the subject of the next chapter.

—15—
Employment Stability and Flexibility

There are no guarantees. The best we can do is try to be productive and successful, stay in business, and grow. That's the only way people can really have employment security.
[That is what a computer company executive told us recently. Sounds reasonable. So does this, from a union leader:]

I'm not going to tell my people to come up with cost-cutting ideas that are gonna cost jobs. Do they think we're crazy? Until we get some guarantees around here, they know where they can stick their employee involvement program.

   [Recently a works manager at a steel plant gave us yet another side of the story:]
   We need to close this plant. It will never be competitive. But the cost to close it is too great—we don't have the cash for the early retirement and massive severance penalties we agreed to.

> *So we keep it open, lose megabucks and market share*
> *every day. We'll be bankrupt soon, and nobody will have a*
> *job.*
> *Great system, huh?*

Those comments are evidence of why employment security is one of the most controversial issues on the Agenda for Adjustment. Some managers don't want even to bring up the subject in an era of downsizing. Yet our experience says that if management expects employees and unions to be flexible, embrace new technology and operating systems, and accept more responsibility for improving productivity and quality, management had better address employee fears of job loss. As Lowell Mayone, Hallmark's vice president for personnel puts it: "If we have too many people, we consider it a management problem, not an employee problem."

We also think greater employment security can make companies more profitable and competitive, *if they use the strategy of stable employment as a vehicle for creating greater job flexibility, greater employee commitment, and a more skilled workforce.*

We want to stress that employment security will *not* achieve these results if it:

- Locks in inefficient job classifications
- Is equated with "lifetime employment"
- Causes long-term underemployment of people's skills
- Causes complacency and excuses poor performance
- Discourages new technology

Too many managers automatically associate those negatives with increased employment security. As we shall show, *they do not have to occur.* Employment security can make good human sense and good business sense. A few years ago, when we made that argument to managers, we were typically rewarded with stony silence, derisive smiles, or raised eyebrows that questioned our allegiance to the free enterprise system. Now we get a flurry of questions about whether employment security is "really" worth the price, and if so, how to do it.

WHY IS EMPLOYMENT SECURITY A BIG ISSUE NOW?

There are six principal reasons for the increased interest and demand for greater employment security.

1. Fear of Being Laid Off

No one likes being laid off. While layoffs have always occurred to some degree in the dynamic U.S. economy, the recession of the late 1970s and early 1980s saw waves of layoffs, firings, and early retirements greater than any since the Great Depression. The Bureau of Labor Statistics (BLS) has estimated that 11.5 million workers over the age of twenty lost their jobs in the 1979–83 period because of plant closings, employers going out of business, or layoffs from which they had not been recalled.

But it isn't just blue-collar workers. BLS also estimates that between 1981 and 1986, almost 500,000 executive, administrative, and managerial personnel lost jobs they had held for at least three years. Ford and Chrysler alone cut more than 50,000 white-collar jobs. The pattern was repeated in companies like AT&T, Bank of America, Kodak, Polaroid, and Exxon, where such moves historically had been inconceivable.

Most American corporations, we are happy to say—about 60 percent by some estimates—have made a strong effort to ease the dislocation costs by providing severance and retirement benefits; advance warnings of six months to a year; joint labor—management outplacement committees; job search training; new skill training; and extended health care benefits.

But the result is still fear—for those who wonder if it could happen to them and for those who have been through it.

2. The Japanese Example

By now many people are aware that: (1) "lifetime" employment in Japan is a misnomer—security lasts only until age 55–60; (2) such security applies to only 25–30 percent of the Japanese workers in the largest enterprises; (3) under extreme financial pressure, Japanese firms *will* dismiss employees; (4) the agreement is implicit and is not written down anywhere; and (5) security is only one piece of a total human resource system based on extensive employee involvement, training, seniority pay, and flexible compensation.

With those caveats, it is still fair to say that the stability afforded many Japanese employees has been one of the cornerstones of Japanese productivity and quality, resulting in flexibility in work assignments, loyalty and common fate, lower turnover costs, and continuous learning through horizontal career development.

3. American Examples

Pressure is also mounting as word spreads of the strong commitment to employment security in successful American firms.

- IBM, by an unwritten policy, has not laid off an employee for economic reasons for thirty-five years. They have frozen hiring, stepped up retraining and relocation, offered early retirement, and even assigned 9,000 staff people to sales offices to maintain a high degree of employment stability.
- Delta Airlines has not furloughed an employee for twenty-five years.
- Hewlett-Packard has a manpower planning policy that puts a high priority on stability in hiring. It has turned down some government contracts that would have required hiring employees and then firing them at the end of the contract.

Materials Research Corporation, Nucor, National Steel, Pacific Bell, DEC, and many others have human resources strategies to avoid layoffs. Given that it works in those firms and a growing number of others, employees in other firms ask, "Why can't we do the same?"

4. Fear of Automation

Workers' fears of being replaced by machines have existed since the early days of the Industrial Revolution, when Luddites smashed mechanical weaving looms to protect jobs.

Resistance today does not take the form of machine smashing; it happens in battles over work rules and resistance to new technology, transfers, and training. Employees have a point: "You expect me to cooperate in introducing new technology so that you can fire me?" If automation is viewed mainly as a "labor-replacing device," its adoption will be delayed until firms work out ways of retraining and of redeploying workers.

5. Turnover Is Expensive

Managers have learned that turnover can be very expensive, and skilled experienced employees are hard to replace. For instance, the boom-and-bust cycle of aerospace and defense has contributed to high costs as the industry gears up for each new weapons system. A recent study of sixty-four aerospace companies estimated that the average cost to replace an entry-level manager or engineer was $57,000. In the production ranks, the costs and confusion that accompany bumping and training add millions to the cost of defense.

6. Resentment About Golden Parachutes

Employees who are denied any employment stability complain of the "golden parachutes" being provided for senior-level managers in 30 percent of the *Fortune* 1000 companies. Almost none provide any protection for lower-level employees.

In a creative twist, Herman Miller Inc., a gain sharing firm mentioned in the preceding chapter, implemented a "Silver Parachute Plan" in early 1987, designed to give each of Herman Miller's 3,500 employees general severance pay and benefits if a hostile takeover threatens their jobs. Primarily a "poison pill" tactic, it is consistent with Herman Miller's common fate philosophy. In most companies, parachutes still reinforce the image of a double standard for managers as against lower level employees.

For those six reasons, the pressure for some security is greater than ever and will increase.

How are firms responding?

THE APC SURVEY

In mid-1986, APC conducted a survey of almost 1,600 firms, asking them about their employment security policies and practices. A surprising number are moving in the direction of greater stability.

- More than 650 facilities reported that they had formal or informal employment security practices—41 percent of the sample total. Of these, 310 had formal written policies for employment security, retraining, or relocation.
- Flexible assignment and cross-utilization of employees were the most frequently used tactics to support employment stability, followed by retraining, recalling subcontracted work, and worksharing.
- Only forty-seven had a "no-layoff" policy; thirty had guaranteed employees a minimum number of hours or days of work. Only nine promised permanent, lifetime employment.

The results were encouraging. Seventy-eight percent of the firms reported their employment security practices had a positive impact on employee relations and morale, 62 percent reported a positive impact on flexibility and employee motivation, and 55 percent reported a positive impact on long-term productivity.

Despite the spreading use of a range of employment security options and the positive results reported, there are many valid concerns about employment security.

Management Fears

Many managers have an almost instinctive negative reaction to the whole idea of employment security. They fear opening a Pandora's box of undesirable consequences:

- Guaranteed employment for life
- People frozen into obsolete job descriptions and manning levels
- Higher fixed employment costs
- Reduced flexibility of the level of workforce in the event of an economic downturn
- Permanent inefficiencies and featherbedding
- An erosion of management's prerogative, the "right to fire"
- A host of other management nightmares

Union Fears

Most unions favor greater employment stability, but have a residual fear of total management control over job assignments if they trade work rules for stability. A few wonder privately: If employees don't fear job loss, have greater involvement in their work areas, and have their compensation tied to the firm's productivity, where is the role for the union?

Misconceptions

To address those concerns, Americans must clear up some of their misconceptions about employment security.

First, start by cleaning up the terminology. "Job security" and "employment security" can be misleading. The correct term is *employment stability*—a human resource planning policy and supporting tactics that increase the stability of the workforce.

Second, employment stability does *not* mean maintaining outmoded job descriptions. It is silly to guarantee someone a "job" for life. Job requirements are constantly changing. Narrow job classifications are inconsistent with flexible operating systems and long-term stability. For example, Hallmark maintains employment through continuous retraining. Hallmark employees can cite numerous skills and jobs: a cutting machine operator becomes a custom card imprinter, painter, or modular office assembler as needed. Hallmark's Mayone says: "Foil-stamped cards may have been popular last year but not this year, so you've got a skilled crew of foil-stamp operators you may not need this year, but maybe next year."

Third, no firm can absolutely guarantee "lifetime" employment. After all, the firm itself may not survive. But continuous improvement and a flexible workforce do improve the odds.

The fourth misconception about employment stability is that it equates with long-term "income security." No firm can afford to pay people for long periods for doing nothing. Americans should avoid the European mistake of creating a large cadre of the permanently unemployed, supported on the "dole" by the state or by firms.

American firms should provide severance help, bonuses, and higher-than-average pensions in order to close a nonproductive facility and increase the movement of employees into more productive facilities and jobs. But if the costs of closings become too high (as they inevitably will if legislation is enacted), then American firms, like the Europeans, will avoid hiring people because they can't afford to fire them.

Finally, the role of unions will change as society changes. Unions that work with management to provide greater employment stability through flexible jobs and pay will be rewarded with increased loyalty and respect from their members.

By clearing up these misconceptions and addressing these concerns, American firms can develop creative solutions and increase commitment to employment stability.

WHAT ARE THE OPTIONS?

The commitment to greater employment stability may take many forms. We divide the options into two broad categories, response to crisis and long-term strategies.

1. Response to Crisis

The dramatic shift of workers out of the manufacturing sector is beginning to look like the exodus out of the agricultural sector earlier in this century. It has taken many firms and unions by surprise, thrown them into a panic, and rendered them unable to think rationally about other adjustment strategies. Norman Augustine, president of Martin Marietta, has quipped, "The seventh month of pregnancy is a strange time to start family planning." For the more farsighted members of the manufacturing sector, it is, however, a good time to consider strategies for preventing a worse crisis in the future.

For example, Ford, GM, and the UAW agreed to employment stability measures in 1984. They include protection and retraining commitments when any of four layoff-inducing events occur: (1) the movement of production offshore, (2) transfers and consolidation of manufacturing facilities, (3) introduction of new technology, or (4) negotiated productivity improvements.

Ford committed $280 million and GM $1 billion for training programs to teach laid-off workers new skills and to upgrade the skills of active workers. Some locations have gone farther:

- GM and Local 717 of the International Union of Electrical Workers (IUE) agreed to guaranteed jobs with full pay until retirement for all 8,900 hourly workers hired before January 1, 1982, in exchange for a two-tier wage agreement for new hires. Both parties credited their prior cooperative and employee involvement efforts for the agreement.
- In Mansfield, Ohio, the UAW acepted work rule changes that eliminated 145 jobs at GM. But because the UAW's contract says that such changes cannot result in layoffs, the company donated fifty-two workers to local social service agencies while keeping them on the GM payroll.

Since 1983, 70 percent of the collective bargaining agreements have included some form of employment stability provisions, usually in conjunction with needed labor force reduction, wage and benefit concessions, and work rule changes.

Although those agreements were negotiated in a period of crisis, they provide a basis for moving to what should be a "long-term employment stability strategy."

2. Long-Term Employment Stability

We found, in the APC survey cited earlier, many firms developing two kinds of manpower planning and business strategies to maintain employment stability across the business cycle: peak demand strategies and downturn strategies.

PEAK DEMAND STRATEGY

The objective of peak demand strategies is to avoid unnecessary hiring to cover cyclical demand.

1. *Operate lean.* Even in boom times, stable firms try to operate lean. The most radical examples of lean staffing are in high-technology firms. Motorola staffs at 80–85 percent of normal demand. IBM Office Products staffs at 85 percent. Control Data staffs even leaner—70 percent of projected needs.
2. *Use buffers.* During peak periods, extra staffing needs are met by using four kinds of buffers:

   - Subcontractors
   - Overtime (IBM requires employees to work up to twenty-two Saturdays overtime a year during peak demand periods.)
   - Reassignment of employees to peak demand areas
   - Buffer work forces—temporary and part-time employees

3. *Diversify the business.* A company committed to employment stability needs a product mix that follows different demand cycles. Some products are relatively stable across a business cycle. Others alternate in demand—new high-growth products and seasonal products and services.

Those three tactics are used by IBM, Delta, Hewlett-Packard, Motorola, and other American firms.

But what goes up must eventually come down. Firms with high employment stability have a downturn strategy in place before they need it.

DOWNTURN STRATEGIES

It is during a downturn that all the peak period strategies pay off. The engines are reversed. Overtime gets cut first; then temporary and part-time employees are let go; then hiring is frozen; subcontracted work is brought back in; and employees take holiday and vacation leaves.

Companies also find other work for employees to do during lulls in business. For instance:

- IBM produces for inventory, even though this increases carrying costs.
- Lincoln Electric and Control Data intensify their sales efforts and send nonsales employees into the field.
- Firms use slack business periods for training and retraining employees.
- McDonnell Douglas lends employees to other divisions.
- Many firms have employees do maintenance work that they normally would not have time for. Worthington Industries, a steel company that hasn't had a layoff since 1961, does all of its construction, maintenance, and installation of new technology during downturns.
- In severe but temporary downturns some companies have the option of worksharing programs. Twelve states, including California, Washington, Texas, Florida, Missouri, Oregon, Arizona, and Illinois have laws allowing firms to have employees work four days a week and collect unemployment compensation for fifth day. That has the effect of reducing the work force 20 percent without actually losing any employees or seriously hurting their income. Motorola has used worksharing arrangements for up to twenty weeks. Fifteen thousand of its employees have participated since 1982. But few other companies are aware of the worksharing option.

CONCERNS

These strategies aren't simple to implement and raise sensitive issues. For instance:

- A company can recall subcontracted work only if the workers and facility are capable of producing that product or service.
- Worksharing requires changes in production planning and increases unemployment insurance costs.
- Hiring freezes can leave the company short of skills in critical areas.

In addition, the workforce "buffers" required by employment stability strategies raise concern about corporate obligations to temporary workers and subcontractors.

Temporary Workers. Temporary and part-time workers are a growing segment of the workforce. It offers an alternative for workers who prefer nontraditional work arrangements.

But many people are rightly concerned that the use of temporary and part-time employes will create a contingent work force of "second-class" citizens with low stability, low pay, and no benefits.

Many part-time and temporary workers are underpaid and unprotected, and would prefer full-time employment. But many contingent workers are not victims of the two-tier society.

- A large number of new temporary and part-time employees are (1) retired persons reentering the workforce, (2) former company employees who, for personal reasons (e.g., education, children, avocations) prefer not to work full-time, (3) self-employed professionals, and (4) students.
- The fastest growth in temporary workers includes not only the traditional administrative and clerical "temps" but also doctors, lawyers, engineers, and a variety of specialists who prefer more flexible work arrangements.
- Temporary employees are often paid a premium by companies, and leasing agencies are providing benefits to their employees. Retail firms, which are very dependent on part-time workers, extend benefit packages to those workers.
- Temporary and part-time employment also serves as a testing period for the employee and the company to decide if they want to make the relationship permanent.

Firms that regularly use temporary workers to buffer their core work force will have to develop personnel and pay policies that will overcome the divisions it can produce.

Suppliers and Subcontractors. A company doesn't build a loyal relationship with suppliers by farming out its unemployment to them. IBM tries to avoid undue damage when it recalls subcontracted work by using contractors who are widely separated geographically to avoid a serious negative impact on any one community. IBM also avoids being too large a percentage of any one supplier's business.

Unions strongly object to subcontracting under normal circumstances. They argue that the company is "taking away work from our people." That may be one of the tradeoffs unions may have to accept if they want to protect the employment of their members. One union leader suggested that his union ought to organize the subcontractors.

THE RELATIONSHIP OF GAIN SHARING AND EMPLOYMENT STABILITY

As we pointed out in the last chapter, flexible compensation can contribute to employment stability. Most gain sharing plans, for instance, have formulas that are sensitive to volume or profit changes. When orders or profits are down, the gain sharing bonus will decline, reducing a firm's total compensation costs without layoffs.

Because of that automatic "compensation buffering," many firms with employment stability also have gain sharing:

- McDonnell Douglas Electronics and the International Association of Machinists and Aerospace Workers jointly designed a gain sharing plan to support their employment stability agreement.
- Lincoln Electric's extensive flexible compensation system is matched by a two-year employment guarantee.
- Sherwin-Williams's plant in Richmond, Kentucky, has a gain sharing plan and a commitment to employment stability. In 1985, employees surprised the company with a "refund" of their gain sharing bonus, expressing gratitude that the company kept them working even though business and profits were way down.

We suggest that firms include temporary and part-time employees in their gain sharing plans to increase commitment and pay.

REQUIREMENTS AND TRADEOFFS

If a company wants employees to share its commitment to productivity improvement, a strategy for employment stability has to be developed. As we have shown, a strategy will almost inevitably require major changes and tradeoffs for management, employees, and unions.

For Management

1. Managers will have to plan as if employees are an asset, not a variable cost.
2. Manpower planning will become a central issue in business planning, making new product development and market share as critical as immediate profits.
3. Selection and orientation must become more sophisticated, since employees are now being screened to become long-term members of the enterprise.
4. Career planning and development won't be just for managers any more. With less turnover, horizontal career development will become a primary focus. Training will become an investment expense.

5. Firms may have to accept lower profit margins in lean periods. Then when business turns up, they will be ready for it with their work force intact.

6. Both management and employees will have to think longer term. Short-term discomforts like overtime will have to be tolerated. With a long-term perspective and less fear of job loss, neither group has any incentive to avoid or delay the systematic rejection of old equipment and practices when necessary.

For Unions and Employees

Employees at all levels, while initially enthusiastic about the prospect of greater stability, must also be aware that productivity growth and flexibility are the only permanent solutions. To that end, the firm may have to use (1) temporary and part-time workers, (2) subcontracting, (3) frequent transfers and job reassignments, (4) shifting pay scales and flexible compensation, and (5) more overtime during peak periods.

For Shareholders

As we will show in the chapter on accounting systems, American shareholders are cheating themselves with a short-sighted emphasis on stock performance. Having a skilled and committed workforce is worth a lot of money, but one would never know it by the reaction of Wall Street. For example, IBM, faced with two years of declining earnings, has tried to be flexible without breaking faith with employees. This just irritates the Wall Street analysts, who would much prefer IBM layoff people. But if IBM is to overcome its current woes, it will need an intact and committed organization. Companies that listen to Wall Street to manage their people will end up with short-term gains and long-term losses.

SOME FINAL ADVICE

We don't have a magic prescription for employment stability, but we do offer a few final words of advice on the process of discovering a solution:

1. Don't lose sight of the objective. The overall goals are increased flexibility, continuous improvement and learning, common fate, and better

productivity and quality. If an employment stability strategy isn't consistent with that, then it isn't the right strategy.

2. The strategies need to be jointly developed by management, unions, and employees. Everyone is going to have to accept some tradeoffs.

3. Integrate the strategy with the rest of the business and human resource systems. An employment stability strategy for a highly cyclical, high-risk industry will be very different from one for a slow-growth industry.

4. Consider making flexible compensation systems a part of the employment stability strategy. It is much more desirable in the long run to have a little lower pay during a downturn than to have a high-paying, inflexible system that leads to unemployment. After all, as one auto worker said recently, "You can have the best pay and benefits in the world, but if you don't have a job, it doesn't much matter, does it?"

—16—
Expanding Employee Involvement

Companies following the Agenda for Adjustment are moving employee involvement (EI) from the small group problem-solving arena and onto center stage.

To understand the significance of the shift, a little history is in order. It has been fourteen years since a team of Lockheed managers first brought the concept of quality circles back from Japan. It is estimated that about 300,000 quality circles (QC) are now operating in the United States.

- EI groups are found everywhere: from manufacturing and financial services to inmates in a Missouri prison.
- Half of the 1,600 companies in a 1986 American Productivity Center national survey have some form of EI, from suggestion systems to quality circles to autonomous work teams. Most have two or more EI activities.

- The Department of Labor estimates that more than seven hundred firms use joint labor–management approaches to EI, up from about one hundred in 1980.

As quality circle programs and small problem-solving groups gained favor, they became synonymous with EI. Managers came to believe that employee involvement was something that happened when employees were given problem-solving training and met for an hour once a week.

As valuable as that approach has been in many firms, we think it underutilizes the potential power of involvement. We shall provide some examples of how employee involvement can become part of the way a business is run, not a limited add-on activity.

THE LIMITATIONS OF TRADITIONAL EI GROUPS

Traditional EI programs have suffered from some built-in limitations. First, only a small number of employees are involved. American Productivity Center surveys have found that in most companies with EI programs less than 15 percent of employees are active participants. Most firms with quality circles have fewer than 10 percent of employees involved.

Second, most of those who *are* involved are shop floor and office personnel with no organizational clout. They have to accept current operating systems as a given, because they have little power to change them.

Third, traditional EI groups tend to be process-driven rather than business-driven. It is not uncommon to ask for EI volunteers, train them in structured problem-solving, then say "work on whatever you think is important."

Perhaps the biggest flaw in traditional EI is the way the process is divorced from day-to-day operations. Groups meet once a week, and the rest of the time it's business as usual.

These limitations do not mean that quality circles and other EI groups are not useful. They are. They have awakened many managers to the talents and potential of the workforce. They provide employees with much-needed training and education in structured problem-solving and group processes. EI groups also appear on the surface to be a low-risk, low-threat way to get something started. They are easy to sell to top management; they often produce measurable improvements.

In short, small EI problem-solving groups meet the criteria for widespread popularity: They do some good without affecting the basic management or operating system.

But, because of the limitations of their structure, membership, authority, and scope, traditional EI programs are blocked from making substantial organizational improvements. Some firms are breaking out of the
limitations of traditional EI.

EXPANDING EI BEYOND THE TRADITIONAL LIMITS

There seem to be two preconditions for expanded EI. First is a *willingness*
to give employees a role in helping with real business problems, either
because of prior success with EI groups or because managers think employees can help solve one of management's pressing problems.

The second is a compelling *need*. Three of the most common are:

1. A crisis, problem, or opportunity needing immediate attention
2. A major overhaul of the operating system or organization structure
3. The design of such new human resource approaches as gain sharing
   plans, employment stability strategies, problem-solving systems,
   and quality programs

1. Immediate Crisis or Problem

The Xerox facility in Webster, New York, faced a grim choice. In
1981, a corporate study team concluded that if $3.2 million couldn't
be cut from the cost structure in the Webster facility, the manufacture
of many components would have to be sent out to subcontractors, resulting
in the layoff of 180 Xerox employees.

Webster had been successful with quality circles and joint labor–
management committees, so both management and the union were open
to the suggestion by their consultant that they create a labor–management
Study-Action Team to see if it was possible to save $3.2 million. Corporate
gave them six months to try.

Six hourly employees, plus an engineer and a manager, were released
from their regular jobs to develop proposals to cut costs. When their
time was up, they had documented cost-saving proposals amounting to
$3.7 million.

The team had consulted with people throughout the Webster workforce
to develop the proposals, which included: redesigning work flow and
floor layout; process improvements to reduce scrap; and involving employees in purchasing new equipment and in determining appropriate uses

for automated equipment. In a break with EI tradition, some proposals affected collective bargaining issues, such as the number and length of breaks, consolidation of minor maintenance jobs, and the hiring of temporary workers for peak periods.

The success of that first study team led to the development of four new teams in other problem areas of the plant. In 1983, the new collective bargaining contract formalized the use of Study-Action Teams.

Tony Costanza, president of the Rochester Joint Board of the ACTWU, said, "It's a very powerful process. We are changing things that before we were afraid to tamper with."

In response to another company's immediate need, a dramatic downturn in business due to the 1981 recession, Lincoln Electric took employees out of the shop, gave them sales training, and sent them on the road to meet with potential customers. After four months, they had received so many new orders that the "auxillary sales force" was needed back in the plant.

2. A Major Overhaul

Some organizations embark on expanded EI when they need a major overhaul of the operating system.

For one Rockwell division a crisis and the need for an overhaul were one and the same. In 1984, Rockwell's Graphic Systems Division in Reading, Pennsylvania, was faced with either reducing costs 30 percent or being shut down.

Discussions with the union led to the decision to try to meet the 30 percent goal by restructuring the entire operating system within three years. It would require the consolidation of 173 job classifications into thirty. Operations that previously had been scattered across seven buildings would be moved under one roof.

The undertaking was so massive that it simply could not be designed or implemented by management alone.

A layout committee, including both hourly and salaried personnel, was established in each department. Its task was to develop a plan for the department's most efficient layout. That plan was submitted to a plant layout design approval committee, also composed of salaried and hourly personnel. The plant committee reviewed each department design for compatibility with overall plant layout, material flow, and social architecture. By mid-1986, enough progress had been made for the division to be sure it would complete consolidation on schedule, by October 1987.

In another example of EI in the design of a major overhaul, FMC's Northern Ordnance Division management decided in 1985 to pursue aggressively repair and rework business from the Department of Defense. Success would require dramatic improvements in cost and delivery. Current business was hampered by volumes of paperwork, poor communication between departments, excessive material movements and delays, and 108 job classifications—not uncommon problems.

Again, a mixed study team of salaried and hourly personnel, under the guidance of senior management and the United Auto Workers, recommended that a new plant be built *inside* the walls of the existing facility. The new facility would be dedicated to repair and rework and have all functions—engineering, quality, program management, and manufacturing—co-located and organized into teams. (Notice that this design effort resulted in the kind of integrated operating unit we described in Chapters 11 and 12.)

Listen to what the employees say about the new operating system they helped design:

- A machinist: "I can see where the parts I make go. Before, you just made the part and it was off on its own."
- An engineer: "I like the controlled freedom. . . . If you have a new idea you can use it. You don't have to conform to the policies that have been followed here for twenty years."
- A supervisor: "They've pretty much given us the freedom to establish our own procedures and guidelines . . . and we are all equally responsible."

These are not the comments one hears from the vast majority of traditional EI efforts.

Using expanded EI to redesign operations is just as powerful in so-called white-collar service and knowledge worker settings. For four years, more than a dozen companies working with the APC have used expanded EI to redesign services in settings from engineering and R&D to human resources and accounting. Teams of exempt and nonexempt employees work together to:

1. Identify their services and internal customers
2. Participatively develop a mission based on what their customers say they need
3. Evaluate their current delivery of services and develop a plan to improve services

4. Develop a measurement system to track their performance
5. Implement the plan

The return on investment (that is, savings compared to the costs to implement) have ranged from 2 to 1 to 8 to 1. In one location, information system errors dropped to half in less than one year. In another, engineering labor hours per project dropped from 249 to 144, and the number of late proposals dropped from 77 to 33.

3. Designing New Human Resource Systems

If a company wants "high-involvement" cultures and systems, then it makes sense to use a high degree of involvement in the design of those systems.

For example, companies designing a gain sharing plan, an employee stability strategy, or even an involvement process itself should give a cross-section of employees a role in the design process. Not only will the plan have more credibility, it will be a better plan, and those involved in designing it will have gained invaluable experience they can apply to further design efforts.

GAIN SHARING
Gain sharing (discussed in Chapter 14) is a perfect opportunity for a joint study/design effort by a diagonal slice of managers and employees from all levels:

- Since gain sharing will affect the earnings of everyone in the unit, every group has a stake in the design.
- Usually no one is an "expert," so all will be learning together.
- In a union situation, gain sharing is often seen as part of the collective bargaining process, so it is a natural topic for joint exploration.

Clark Equipment, Xerox, and McDonnell Douglas Electronics Company (MDEC) each assigned cross-sectional teams of employees to full-time exploration and/or design of a gain sharing plan. Many other companies have used part-time assignments.

EMPLOYMENT STABILITY
As with gain sharing, designing employment stability strategies benefits from intense involvement of different levels of employees in the exploration and adoption of options. Packard Electric, Xerox, and MDEC

all used mixed-level, high-involvement study teams to develop their employment stability strategies. In union situations, it is mandatory that the union and representatives from the membership be involved, since many of the strategies will affect collective bargaining.

ONGOING INVOLVEMENT SYSTEMS

A logical time to use EI is in design of the EI system itself. At MDEC, employee involvement became more central to the business after the company and the union had jointly designed a gain sharing plan and an employment stability strategy.

MDEC had several years of experience with quality circles, other voluntary problem-solving groups, and a suggestion system. Those efforts had been worthwhile, but only a few of the 1,300 MDEC employees had been active participants.

Working together to design a gain sharing plan made it clear to MDEC's management and employees that they needed an improvement process involving the entire workforce. The MDEC position is that if everyone is going to share the gains generated by employee involvement, then everyone should be active in it.

To support the gain-sharing plan, employees representing all MDEC departments designed a new "Idea Handling System," which has three rather unusual features:

1. Participation is not voluntary: *All* employees are members of an idea handling group.
2. Groups are made up of natural work teams or departments in all areas of the business, from engineering to production to marketing.
3. All ideas have to be approved for further study or rejected within ten days, and authority for implementation rests within a work group unless it involves a significant capital expenditure or requires coordination with another group.

During a typical nine-month period under MDEC's old suggestion system, an average of seventy-five suggestions were submitted, and 20 percent of them were approved. In the first nine months with the Idea Handling system, about 1,000 suggestions were processed and 40 percent were approved.

Intensive information-sharing and involvement at MDEC have led to a much higher level of employee concern about business issues. According to Charlie Mercer, who holds the rather unorthodox title Project Manager for Cultural Change, and Larry Duke, Gain Sharing Administrator, MDEC now has 1,300 Monday-morning quarterbacks, each watching how company money is spent as if it were their own.

OTHER INVOLVEMENT OPPORTUNITIES

Once one's eyes are opened to the possibilities, opportunities to use an intensive EI process in the business itself seem to be everywhere.

New Line Startups

When employees were allowed to decide how a new line would be staffed at a GE facility, productivity immediately rose 4 percent, and absenteeism fell 33 percent.

Customer Relations and Feedback

Customers are a powerful source of information in improvements. Instead of having relations with customers confined to sales or customer service, some companies have expanded employee involvement into the area of customer relations.

General Motors has taken this approach in one location. Fifty GM production workers at the Fiero plant in Pontiac, Michigan, each voluntarily follow five buyers for a year, surveying them with phone calls every three months. The information they get is fed back directly to the plant where problems may have originated.

Bidding on Work

EI can expand into holding or gaining business. Armco employees suggested a plan to boost production in flat-rolled steel to avoid having the company purchase foreign steel slabs.

Another task force at a different company found that it was getting only 10 percent of the jobs it bid because the contracts department continually overestimated the need for expensive new equipment. An hourly task force worked for three weeks and won an important bid for 10 percent less than the competition and 15 percent less than the original industrial engineering estimates. The bid was accurate, and the product is now 15 percent of sales. Workers went back to their own jobs, but now use those skills in solving smaller problems.

ISSUES IN EXPANDED EI

As we have shown, companies are expanding the EI process when faced with a compelling need, when an overhaul of the operating system is in order, and when designing new human resource strategies.

But expanded EI does raise difficult organizational issues, just as does traditional EI.

Power and Control

Concerns about expanded employee involvement can come from managers, technical experts, unions, and employees themselves. At stake are the time-honored ways of making decisions, sharing information, status symbols, and relationships. Organizational structure—job descriptions, reporting relationships, flow of information, control—will be affected by expanded EI far more than with traditional EI.

Since expanded EI oftens deals with system problems, it can mean asking managers who have a great deal of power to give up some vested interests and some comfortable ways of working with their peers. Those managers have made tacit agreements with each other not to "mess in each other's sandbox," but in order to solve system problems, sandboxes *will* get messed with.

It takes courage and personal strength for senior managers to share responsibility with lower-level managers and nonmanagement employees. As long as involvement was confined to the shop floor or the back office, it was far away from the real sources of power and less risky. As one division vice-president told us,

> Don't let anyone tell you [expanded EI] makes your job easier. It is anxiety-provoking as hell and frustrating to boot. This thing could get out of hand, and I'm not sure we could turn back without really alienating a lot of people at a lot of levels.

That is why it often takes a crisis or a deep need to break through this structural rigidity and create expanded EI.

Union Concerns

Unions often have problems with the idea of employees' deciding their own job responsibilities and work schedules, especially if the union has not been normally involved in the process. For example, the International Brotherhood of Du Pont Workers objected to not being brought in on such topics, complaining that the program restricts promotional opportunities, requires more work without higher pay, and causes dissension in the rank-and-file.

RECOMMENDATIONS

Based on the experiences of companies we have worked with, we have some guidelines for those companies that have been successful with traditional EI and want to expand that process into core business issues.

1. *The first thing to change is the change process.* The typical process of change in organizations is for a group of specialists to diagnose the situation, prescribe a solution, then inflict it on the people who have to live with it. One of the biggest reasons people resist change is that it is done *to* them, not *through* them.

A better process is to give more people, at more levels, the chance to identify problems, figure out how to solve them, and then make their solutions work. This is messier and takes longer, but it produces better results in the end.

Robert Hayes, professor at Harvard, has said: "Top management's role is less to spot and solve problems than to create an organization that can spot and solve its own problems."

2. *Link existing small group problem-solving with business objectives.* Few organizations can afford to let groups operate without any idea of what the business should focus on, and few employees want to waste their time on superficial change. Managers are far more willing to support EI groups that are working on substantive issues. Involvement is a line activity, not a staff function.

3. *Bring the union, if present, in as a full partner.*

4. *Tie EI to an organizational change,* such as the implementation of just-in-time, better customer service, or the startup of a new product line.

5. *Educate employees about the business* as you ask them to take on activities to support the business.

THE SHIFT TO CREATING BETTER SYSTEMS

Traditional EI groups have been and will continue to be an important educational and improvement strategy and a place for many companies to start their EI efforts. But in most cases the quality circle and EI group format is not capable of producing the large-scale changes that may be needed for long-term competitiveness.

Whether involvement is confined to traditional EI groups or expands in form and substance to address issues central to the business depends on management's response to a basic question: *Do you want to make the existing system run better, or do you want to create a better system?*

—17—
Training and Continuous Learning

If you think education is expensive, try ignorance.
Derek Bok,
President of Harvard

The United States has three strikes against it in the global battle for productivity leadership through people.

First, in the 1890s, when the United States passed Britain as the most productive nation on earth, America had the more skilled and better-educated workforce. Today, Japan probably has the best-educated and most skilled workforce in the world.

- Ninety percent of Japanese youth finish high school as against about 75 percent in the United States.
- Today 27 million Americans, or more, are functionally illiterate,

195

more than the entire population of Canada; 15 million of the functionally illiterate are at work.

- A bank in the Midwest found that half the high school graduates it hired could not pass a simple math test.
- At GM, about 15 percent of hourly employees, and as high as 30 percent in some plants, are functionally illiterate.

The price America pays for illiteracy and inadequate skills at the low end of the human capital continuum is high; the price for underutilization of talent at the high end may be even greater.

The second strike against global competitiveness is the American tendency to overemphasis specialized knowledge and skills. American professionals—engineers, accountants, scientists—specialize in a narrow body of knowledge, for which the largest market exists outside the firm. This encourages people to move from company to company with great market place labor mobility but lousy intrafirm flexibility.

Further, specialization slows down the product development process as specialists are hampered by lack of knowledge of other disciplines. The authors of a study of the new product development process in Japanese firms concluded:

> In the United States, product development is undertaken by a highly competent and innovative group of specialists. Most of the learning is done by an elite group of technical people, largely on an individual basis, within a narrow area of specialization. Thus an accumulation of knowledge based on "learning in depth" takes place.

The process in Japan looks far different.

> Product development in Japan is often undertaken by a team of nonexperts who are encouraged to become generalists by interacting with each other throughout the development process. Learning also takes place across all phases of management and across functional boundaries. In this sense, new product development is the particular device that fosters corporatewide learning.

Top executives in the fifty largest American firms have worked in fewer than two functions on their way up the corporate ladder. Most U.S. firms focus on intrafunctional and vertical career development for managers and professionals, which means accountants, for example, are provided with learning opportunities to help them move up in the accounting function.

Rotation out of one's speciality, such as putting an accountant into manufacturing, is considered heresy, yet it may be the best way to develop the broad understanding and personal ties necessary for future managers.

The Japanese strongly believe that a good manager specializes more in the company than in a particular discipline. While climbing the seniority ladder, an employee might hold widely different positions in different functions, with each posting usually lasting no more than three years. For instance, it is not unusual for a sales executive to rotate with a purchasing agent.

- Honda has a training program in which all department managers are asked to select a functional area in which they have never worked and spend one week there.
- NEC transfers technical people from its R&D centers to its operating divisions. American firms have also found that the rate of innovations in American R&D organizations is twice as high in groups that have been together less than three years than those together more than five years.
- Many Japanese executives once served as union officials early in their careers.

As a result of those practices, a Japanese manager ends up with somewhat less specialized knowledge (which would be obsolete in five years anyway) and a much more integrated and personal knowledge of the organization.

The third strike against American firms is their tendency to pay more attention to the maintenance of physical capital than the continuous enhancement of human capital. While hard assets *are* critical, the relative neglect of "soft assets" is putting America behind the competitiveness curve. Yet selection, training, and continuous learning are neglected stepchildren in most organizations.

1. Many managers believe that training is a cost, not an investment, that it takes people away from their "real" work.
2. Accounting theory does not put human assets on the balance sheet.
3. The tax code does not encourage or permit capitalization of personnel acquisition or development costs.
4. Managers forget that true "training" starts at the time of recruitment and orientation.
5. Many managers fear that once employees are trained they will leave for higher-paying jobs with the competition.
6. Most managers and employees believe that "training" is something the training department does in a classroom.

7. Managers think training is for someone else, not for themselves (except, of course for executive courses at Harvard or MIT).

This narrow and traditional view must change, beginning with the selection process.

THE SELECTION PROCESS

If companies are to make a massive investment in the education and career development of employees, they need to be careful how and whom they hire. "Warm bodies" are not enough.

An organization with a desire for teamwork, flexibility, and continuous learning needs to select people who will fit and thrive in that culture. Traditional selection tends to focus too much on specialized skills, which will rapidly become obsolete, and not enough on selecting for lifelong learners. For example, Nissan's plant in Smyrna, Tennessee, has productivity and quality to rival its Japanese counterparts, even though less than 20 percent of employees hired had any prior experience building automobiles. That lack of experience was offset by careful selection for learning skills and tremendous training—about $60 million worth before startup. And it didn't hurt that those people had no preconceptions about how assembly plants were "supposed" to operate.

As the nature of work changes, so do the criteria for selection and hiring.

- Mazda is currently sifting through 96,000 applications to fill 3,100 hourly positions in its new plant in Flat Rock, Michigan. Mazda is looking for employees who can work in teams, rotate through various jobs, understand how their task fits into the entire process, spot problems in production, articulate the problem to others, and write detailed charts and memos.

- At NUMMI, hiring was not by seniority, which is a radical departure from traditional UAW procedures. Instead, potential hires went through a four-day assessment of their ability to function in semi-autonomous teams, including interviews by future co-workers.

- An electronics company formed a recruitment, selection, and orientation task force to develop job posting and hiring procedures. Selection criteria were defined by an interviewing team comprising the area supervisor, the shop steward, an HR staff member, and the lead person or most senior person in that classification in that area.

After hiring, traditional orientation is often too little and too late, focuses too much on a narrow job and not enough on culture and direction of the firm, and is usually assigned to the personnel department or a lower-level employee.

A new employee needs to be carefully nurtured and enfolded into the organization. With effective socialization into the company's culture and mission, an organization can get by with fewer bureaucratic procedures and manuals and can let social and personal control take over.

Selection and orientation are only part of the answer. The traditional approach to training has to change.

TRADITIONAL APPROACH TO TRAINING

American business's historically low regard for training has been a serious drag on productivity and quality improvement. Relatively few American firms are doing the *amount* or *kind* of training for employees at all levels that will be required to compete in a global economy, cope with the retraining needed in basic industries, or create the organizational skills that managers and other employees must have to run flexible, innovative organizations.

Amount of Training

U.S. firms with more than fifty employees spent about $29 billion on training in 1986 to provide training to 36.5 million American workers. While that may sound like a lot of money, it is no more than firms spent six years ago, before the trade deficit, inflation, massive job loss in the early 1980s, and growing awareness of Japanese strength. In fact, the number of employees trained and the number of hours of training in 1986 were down by more than 14 percent from 1985.

The Japanese spend *three to four times* the U.S. annual amount per employee. In Japan, continuing education is part of the work process, absorbing on the average *eight hours per week for every employee,* with half on company time and the other half on the employee's time.

The Japanese company-based training system revolves around the concept of the flexible worker. The aim is to select and prepare employees for not one job, but at least two or possibly three, and then to continue to provide learning experiences throughout their working lives.

Most U.S. firms are not contemplating spending anywhere near the amount of training dollars necessary for real productivity and quality gains. There are exceptions. IBM spent $750 million in 1986 for employee training and education. Motorola's CEO, Robert Galvin, commissioned a five-year training plan to determine training needs—the first-five year plan for training of which we are aware. As a result, Motorola now sets aside about 2.6 percent of payroll, close to 1 percent of sales, for training. In addition, Motorola opened a new $8.5 million state-of-the-art training center in 1986. Motorola's 100,000 employees received more than a million hours of training in 1986.

As an order of magnitude, our estimate is that most firms should consider doubling or tripling allocations of time and money for training, but not by allocating more funds to their existing training departments alone. It is not only *more* training that is needed, but also a *different kind* of training.

Kind of Training

The principal ingredient missing from most training programs is relevancy. Surveys indicate that only 12 percent of people found any formal classroom training useful in acquiring or maintaining their current job skills: they learned what they know on the job. Skills and knowledge learned and problems solved in the work setting are directly relevant since there is no problem of transference of the training from the classroom to the work situation.

People need "soft" skill training as well. For example, most employees would like to have more ability to identify and solve problems, and then have the interpersonal and political skills to cross territorial lines to get the problem solved. The need for interpersonal skill training is not confined to lower-level employees. Honeywell gives its engineers an intensive, practice-based eight-day course in interpersonal skills to help them better use their technical skills.

Another ingredient missing from most training programs is economic education. The vast majority of employees have virtually no understanding of the economic system, of how productivity, quality, and competitiveness affect their own standard of living and employment security. In an unusual GM/UAW program, local union officials can take a paid education leave to spend four weeks with experts from government and academia learning macro- and microeconomics affecting the automotive industry.

Training for Whom?

The vast majority of training dollars spent on middle managers is for classroom training on "management style" (which seldom has much impact on behavior), not on senior managers for "quality" training or lower-level employees for cross-training.

Westinghouse is an exception. It has made productivity and quality companywide goals, with training as a key tactical move. At its Defense Center, it has trained hundreds of its professional and management employees in value analysis; it has instituted programs to retrain veteran engineers in computer-aided design and manufacturing; employees have taken numerous study trips to Japan; management quality seminars help executives make quality a visible part of their strategic planning and appraisal process; and management, professional, and production employees receive in-house training in the statistical design of experiments.

ALTERNATIVES TO THE TRADITIONAL TRAINING MODEL

If continuous learning is to become a key feature of American organizations, then some fundamental principles of training and learning will have to be recaptured.

1. People learn best when directly involved in real problems and issues.
2. One-shot classroom training doesn't change behavior. Practice and feedback work far better.
3. The best learning is active, not passive. In an organization, active problem-solving works extremely well in cross-functional groups and in unfamiliar situations.
4. Learning by example—seeing it done—is more effective than hearing about it. That is why visits and trips to other companies are such a powerful learning and change tool.
5. Management has to believe in learning, provide time for it, reward for it, and engage in it itself if continuous learning is to take place at work.

The approach that best incorporates these principles is action learning.

Action Learning

Action learning assumes that people learn most effectively with and from each other by working on problems and reflecting on their own experience. Designers of training programs often forget that learning is largely a do-it-yourself project. Our school system has confused many people into thinking that formal classroom instruction is essential to learning when, in fact, exploration, nosing around, apprenticeship, reading and group discussion may be better learning experiences in the work context.

Action learning avoids the problem of transfer of learning, produces results in the process of learning itself, and leads to intense commitment and involvement. This kind of self-driven learning is more lasting, satisfying, innovative, and productive in both the short and the long term.

Just as the opportunities for employee involvement are everywhere once one is ready to see them, so are the opportunities for managerial and employee development through action learning. The following are a few examples.

TEAM LEARNING

Japanese companies seem to have discovered that learning plays a key role in enabling speedy and flexible product development and delivery. Multidiscipline product development teams learn from exposure to each other's diverse points of view, multiple information inputs from the market place, and especially the trial-and-error process that accompanies the parallel product development process described in Chapter 12.

Action learning is also the basis of Japanese small group activities like quality circles, which were originally designed by workers and foremen themselves as self-study groups. Deming and Juran insisted that upper-level managers receive training in quality control before passing it down to foremen and workers, who were then encouraged to train themselves through small groups, foremen's periodicals and handbooks, and quality circles. The example and encouragement of senior management provided much of the impetus for self-training.

Expanded employee involvement efforts, including involvement in designing new systems, are American examples of the process. Tremendous learning takes place when project teams are charged with solving system problems or finding out about new forms of work, pay, or involvement structures. Cross-functional teams or task forces first have to figure out where to go to find out what they need to know (that is, they learn how to learn). They devour reading materials. They learn how to design and implement real systems. As one foreman said, "Helping to design the employee involvement program has been one of my best learning experiences of my twenty-four years with Ford."

Study trips to other companies and countries are a eye-opener and a great action learning vehicle for people at all levels. Since NUMMI opened in 1984, GM has sent more than 2,000 GM managers to Fremont,

California, to study the work systems used there. NUMMI, in turn, has sent managers and union leaders to Japan.

ROLE OF THE MANAGER

Action learning provides a critical new role for supervisors and managers. They are in the best position to recognize learning opportunities and deliver the training themselves. Andrew Grove, president of Intel Corporation, argues that managers should design and deliver training themselves, with help from training specialists on process, not content. "For training to be effective, it has to be closely tied to how things are actually done in your organization."

Retraining

Retraining is taking two forms in the United States: remedial training in basic math and verbal skills, and continuous retraining for shifting technology.

REMEDIAL TRAINING

When the Ford Motor Company plant in Ypsilanti, Michigan, started training programs in statistical process control in 1983, it found that half of the workers could not absorb the material because of poor reading or math skills. Ford has since developed remedial programs for their employees.

Dozens of companies have become the educators of last resort. Ford, GM, BlueCross/Blue Shield of Massachusetts, Prudential, Polaroid, and Pratt & Whitney all provide courses in basic literacy skills. Ford and GM run the largest programs, since layoffs have left them with a workforce with high seniority, hired during an era when literacy skills were not deemed so critical. Ford, with basic reading programs at twenty-five out of ninety plants, can cite hundreds of stories of people's lives transformed by learning to read and write. More companies will find themselves doing the job that the school system was unable to perform.

RETRAINING

The Industrial Revolution took two centuries to transform society completely. The knowledge and computer revolution may take only two decades. Half of the knowledge of an electrical engineer or computer scientist graduating from a university in 1987 will be obsolete by 1992. Four out of five people in the developed world will have their jobs significantly changed by the information revolution within another five years.

The growth of high technology will carry high costs in terms of skills obsolescence, raising the need to retrain and relocate workers. One estimate is that for the rest of this decade at least 400,000 workers a year will require retraining. The price for retraining could easily average $10,000 per employee.

Still, it is often far cheaper to retrain someone than to replace him or her. In one division, GE discovered that retraining an engineer could be accomplished for less than one-third the cost of hiring a new one. And the odds that a retrained person will stay with a company are substantially better than those with a new hire. One authority, Herbert Striner of the American University, has observed

> Contrary to the perennial pessimists who, since the industrial revolution of the mid-1800s, have been cautioning that new technology must increase unemployment and provide no new alternative forms of work, actual history has proven the opposite. The real experience has been that an advanced technological society has an increasing need for new, advanced skills. The problem is that there must be a mechanism for a continuous upgrading of the skills of the labor force as we move from one matrix of skills to another.

The search for that mechanism has led to political debates and government programs. The debate is not whether retraining is necessary, but who should pay for and deliver it. Under the five-year-old federal Job Training Partnership Act (JTPA), the Labor Department annually distributes $200 million to states for retraining of displaced workers. President Reagan has proposed to increase that budget to $980 million.

The aims of past programs are commendable, but the results have not been uniformly encouraging. For example, from 1977 to 1984, 1.2 million workers received basic trade readjustment financial benefits. Only 70,000 of those began retraining, 28,000 completed their courses, and only 4,500 found jobs that used their new skills.

A 1987 report of the General Accounting Office found that JTPA results were better. Though only 7 percent of laid-off workers were eligible, 69 percent of the participants found new jobs at higher wages than other government programs. The GAO also found that programs run by employers or labor unions were three times more likely to have above-average placement success than those run by state agencies and other organizations.

All adjustment processes have their social costs, but successful industrial societies are those that find ways to ease the burden on the people most directly affected. Given the political pressure to provide retraining funds, it seems that the best use of funds will be for programs designed and administered in the private sector. Ford, GM, and the UAW are leading the way in this arena.

- GM and the UAW founded the largest privately funded education center in the world with a student body of 400,000—the entire GM hourly workforce—to retrain people for the twenty-first century.
- Ford and the UAW have established a National Development and Training Center with four objectives:

  1. Provide training, retraining, and developmental opportunities for active employees
  2. Arrange for retraining and assistance for employees displaced by new technologies, production techniques, shifts in products, and facility closings
  3. Sustain and support local and national employee involvement efforts.
  4. Provide opportunities for the exchange of ideas and innovations with respect to employee development and training needs

Pat Choate of TRW suggests a broader, long-range alternative might be the creation of "Individual Training Accounts," similar to individual retirement accounts, funded by employees and employers, that people could draw on as they need retraining throughout their working lives.

Regardless of the mechanisms Americans development, the process of continuous lifelong learning is the fountain of youth for individuals and for society and a prerequisite for continuous improvement. Investment in this process is needed for a flexible workforce that can make a real contribution to competitiveness.

—18—
Accounting Systems

Traditional financial and cost accounting systems are changing more slowly than the organizations they are supposed to track. Most financial and cost accounting systems were designed for an earlier era of labor-intensive manufacturing and cannot handle today's decisions regarding capital-intensive flexible manufacturing systems, the greater emphasis on human capital, and the rise of the service sector.

Trying to make twentieth-century decisions based on eighteenth-century accounting principles is like driving a car with the emergency brake on. You can do it, but there is a lot of smoke and screeching.

The problem is not a shortage of accounting information *per se.* Accounting is one of the greatest growth industries in the United States. From 1978 to 1985, total business output increased 15 percent, but the number of accountants rose by 30 percent, from 1 million to 1.3 million. The United States now has forty accountants for every 10,000 citizens, compared to three per 10,000 in Japan.

The difficulty lies with the systems themselves. Most accounting systems are hybrids of

- Century-old concepts of financial transactions
- Security and Exchange Commission requirements
- Generally accepted accounting principles
- Nineteenth-century manufacturing reporting methods

The main deficiencies in financial and cost accounting systems are of two kinds. The first is in the accounting systems themselves and the second lies in how the systems are used. We have found that most managers and accountants readily acknowledge the shortcomings in the systems but find them difficult to change.

PROBLEMS WITH ACCOUNTING SYSTEMS

Impact on Investment

The first problem with the systems is that they are slowing the introduction of new technology desperately needed to meet foreign competition. Standard accounting procedures do not capture such intangibles as improved quality, greater flexibility, shorter lead times, lower inventories, and better use of space, making it hard to justify an investment in advanced production technology using the yardsticks of traditional accounting and financial formulas.

Managers are left to make investments based on faith and persuasive anecdotes that the new technology will pay off in increased quality, throughput, floor space, and inventory, all factors that the current system doesn't measure. For example, Allen-Bradley found it could not employ traditional return-on-investment calculations to justify its decisions to invest $8 million in a totally automated assembly line. But the appeal to survival won the day. "If you're not going to be among the survivors," Larry Yost, a vice president who led the automation efforts, says, "ROI doesn't mean a damn."

Discounted Cash Flow

The second problem in current accounting and measurement systems lies with the discounted cash flow (DCF) technique, which measures the equivalent value today of payments to be received at a later date.

The technique tends to minimize the long-range benefits of flexible manu-facturing technology, causing decisions that "sell the future short." That is because many companies set return on investment hurdle rates too high, at 15 to 20 percent, to account for unknown risks. Those rates are well in excess of the real cost of capital and may be overstating the risk.

Moreover, using a "risk-adjusted discount rate" may lead to errors. The mathematics of discounting makes the assignment of risk per year equal to the discounting curve formula. But the risks in the real world may not be the same as the curve. Risk could be high in early years and low later, or vice versa. But the discounting formula assigns the same risk-shaped curve for all investments.

Managers tend to be far more aware of the risks associated with investing in new technology than they are with the risks of not investing. DCF usually compares the possible return in the future with the "status quo," making the assumption that even without new technology, market share, costs, and selling price will remain the same. In fact, *not* investing and effectively utilizing the technology leaves the firm at the mercy of competitors who do.

Finally, the current system can't readily measure the expected value of new flexibility and shorter lead times. According to Robert Kaplan, professor at Harvard, "It is fairly easy to get a ballpark estimate for percentage reductions in costs already being incurred. It is much harder to quantify the magnitude of revenue enhancement expected from features that are not already in place." For example, how many more orders would the firm get if it could promise delivery sooner? If it could cut product development time in half?

Direct Versus Indirect

The third problem with traditional accounting systems is the continued use of the antiquated distinction between direct and indirect labor. Tradi-tional cost accounting procedures collect data on direct labor hours per product or work order, then allocate all other indirect or overhead costs as a percentage of direct labor. This approach was developed for a manufacturing environment where direct labor was the dominant portion of manufacturing cost.

Today, production labor can be as low as 10 percent of costs in automated plants, with knowledge work an ever increasing cost compo-nent. Yet the lion's share of energy for measurement and control is focused on direct labor. Using direct labor as the yardstick for performance in such an environment is an instance of the tail wagging the dog.

Carried to its extreme, the system produces some strange numbers. When a production process is highly automated, overhead rates of 1,000 percent are not unusual. And how would one allocate indirect and overhead costs in an unmanned factory?

Traditional accounting systems often evaluate investments in terms of how many direct laborers the investment would eliminate. Investments are just as often desirable because they are *labor-enhancing* rather than *labor-replacing,* but they can't be justified using traditional cost-benefit analyses.

Productivity Measures

The fourth problem with traditional management accounting systems is the kind of information they *don't* contain on productivity, quality, and the performance of competitors.

For years, the APC has advocated more comprehensive productivity measurement and reporting in firms. Employees and managers need far better information on productivity and quality than current systems provide.

There are six serious problems with most productivity measures in organizations:

1. Existing measures focus on direct labor and pay far less attention to important inputs such as material, capital, and knowledge.
2. There is a tendency to rely on one measure, such as output per employee hour, and not a family of measures that would more completely reflect the operating system.
3. Too often the measures used are based on dollar values and not physical data, which would be more meaningful.
4. Companies often fail to deflate their financial measures to eliminate the distortion caused by inflation.
5. Often productivity measures are reported at too aggregate a level and too late to be useful for real-time decision-making.
6. Most data are actually gathered for financial reporting reasons and not to track and improve the operating system.

Organizations urgently need global and widely understood measures of productivity that consider all the factors of production (labor, capital, materials, and energy) and link directly with their financial planning, budgeting, and management incentive systems. Unfortunately, the accounting profession, as outside auditors, has no interest in creating generally accepted principles for productivity reporting.

Human Resource Accounting

The fifth problem with current financial accounting systems is that they do not treat investments in people as an "investment" for the future. A desk is considered an asset, but the person sitting behind it is reported as an expense. Recruiting and training costs are treated as expenses, not as capital investments that depreciate over time and must be renewed.

One of the authors worked with a task force trying to evaluate the financial impact of an employment stability system under consideration. The task force collected data on the costs of turnover, recruiting and hiring, and attrition rates, and forecasted skill needs. It came to the conclusion that an employment stability strategy would be a good business decision.

But the members were nervous about claiming the policy could be justified from a business perspective. They said, "When management hears the word 'justified,' they look for 'expected value,' 'discounted cash flow,' etc. Our accounting and management systems don't give us any way to reflect the increasing value of employees, or the value of greater flexibility."

Being unable to measure and justify the value of investments in human capital discourages such investments—a dangerous situation in the Information Age.

All five of these problems are a direct result of the original intention of most financial accounting systems: to allow shareholders to monitor how their physical assets are being managed. The interests of shareholders and institutional investors have come to dominate management thinking—paradoxically, not necessarily to the benefit of the firm or the investors.

For example, Japanese firms are ostensibly far less interested in their shareholders. They do not pay large dividends. Over the last five years, the return as a percent of share price has averaged only 1.8 percent in Japan. Toyota has paid dividends of only 1.3 percent, while GM has averaged 7.1 percent; Hitachi has paid 1.7 percent as against GE's 4.7 percent; NEC has paid 1.1 percent to Texas Instruments' 4.6 percent. Yet, because of capital appreciation, *Japanese investors have had a return on a pretax basis four times better than their American counterparts.*

Of course, the Japanese have to report to government regulatory bodies, shareholders, and the investment community. Japanese managers are strongly oriented toward results, but the key operating numbers they manage by and on which they make investment decisions are more likely to be up on the bulletin board than in the annual report. In the end, shareholders in Japanese firms benefit the most when the management focuses on the long-run interests of customers and employees.

PROBLEMS WITH HOW ACCOUNTING SYSTEMS ARE USED

The second set of problems is caused by how the financial and cost accounting systems are used internally.

Performance Evaluation

Management bonuses are based on financial measures of performance that (1) usually emphasize short-term (quarterly or annual) performance, (2) omit total factor productivity measures, and (3) neglect comparisons to the performance of competitors.

Managers are usually evaluated on the basis of the financial system, not the one they use to track operating performance. Managers complain that they are being evaluated on the basis of systems that do not report the right things. Few organizations use comparative benchmarking to competitor's performance as a basis for management evaluation.

The weaknesses in the accounting system really show up when trying to design a gain sharing plan based on productivity improvement. The accounting staff knows it doesn't have good productivity figures. Most employees know little or nothing about the accounting system and have a very hard time seeing what the data presented by the accounting department have to do with their jobs. When we have worked with large organizations to design gain sharing formulas, we have had to dramatically clarify the numbers coming out of the accounting and financial reports.

Information Is Not Widely Shared

According to some recent estimates, 66 percent of employees surveyed said that their main source of information about their companies was the grapevine. It is neither reassuring nor surprising to hear that employees are basing decisions affecting billions of dollars on rumor.

Because the systems are complicated and don't measure factors most people relate to, *a large number of people in organizations are completely ignorant of the accounting system and how it affects decisions that, in turn, affect them.* Accountants and managers tend to keep data under tight control, even though much of the research data say that feedback and information about the operating environment produces performance improvement.

One reason accounting systems need to be made more relevant is that bringing financial information down to the shop floor is a giant step in bridging the gap between management and labor. More than any other action, it makes the goals explicit and the nature of the partnership visible.

Obstacles to Change

Companies who want to change their systems have a hard time finding role models. Most universities continue to teach sophisticated financial and tax accounting courses with little emphasis on innovative cost accounting and productivity measurement systems. Centralized, computer-based accounting systems are not very flexible. Even minor changes or additions to the software tend to ricochet through the system, creating a nightmare of debugging problems.

Financial and cost accounting systems are extremely difficult to change. Generally accepted accounting principles (GAAP) have been developed and codified over a century of use. They are the *lingua franca* of the financial community, investment analysts, and management compensation systems. No amount of rhetoric about the need to think "long term" is going to keep American investors and analysts from looking for short-term results.

Despite all that, organizations do have a choice. They need not let the accounting system hold them hostage. They have at least four options:

1. Create supplemental or parallel measurement systems that include measures of productivity and quality and are more sensitive to operating needs.
2. Adopt approaches to human resource accounting that support operating decisions.
3. Provide employees with access to operating and financial data that will help them improve performance.

4. Charge for information and accounting services. This creates an internal market for accounting, a sure way to motivate the accountants to provide information the organization really needs.

SUPPLEMENTAL SYSTEMS

Corporations, accountants, and the Financial Accounting Standards Board (FASB) are attempting to overcome some of the deficiencies in the financial and cost accounting systems related to automated environments.

For example, Computer Aided Manufacturing International (CAM-I) of Arlington, Texas, is heading a consortium of thirty-five organizations, including government bodies, corporations, universities, and major accounting firms. The purpose is to develop an accounting basis for (1) investment justification; (2) accounting models, depreciation, and location of costs; and (3) quantification of nonfinancial and intangible factors in automated environments.

At the firm level, companies are trying to develop supplemental measurement systems that provide operational feedback. It is almost impossible to design a single system that will simultaneously provide information for (1) internal decision-making, (2) operating control and feedback, and (3) external reporting. Companies will usually do better to put efforts into special analyses for decision-making than to take on the mammoth task of revamping the entire system.

One example of this kind of effort is white-collar or knowledge worker measurement. The APC led a two-year study of white-collar productivity in which ninety-two groups from eighteen companies participated. Most of the white-collar groups (including accounting, R&D, and human resources) succeeded in developing measurement systems that tracked performance and service effectiveness and provided data feedback for problem-solving and service improvement.

HUMAN RESOURCE ACCOUNTING

Human capital—more than plants, equipment, and inventory—is the cornerstone of competitiveness, growth, and productivity. It is time that business began to measure the value of that wealth.

The act of measuring will itself encourage management to treat human resources as an asset to be deployed instead of simply a cost to be managed. For example, at Upjohn, management estimates the investment it makes in hiring an employee amounts to 160 times starting salary. An employee starting at $25,000 per year will cost the company $4,000,000 over the course of his or her work career, given probable increases in base salary, fringe benefits, and direct support services.

Therefore, on a "present value" basis, the decision to hire is a million-dollar decision. If a machine were involved, such a decision would require senior management approval, and questions would be asked about the costs of supporting and maintaining that machine over time. Few such questions are asked now about new hires.

Furthermore, any two managers producing the same short-term financial results will receive the same performance evaluations, even though one may be depleting human assets by not providing any training and the another is developing people.

The technology for human resource (HR) accounting has been explored for two decades, but only recently have many companies tried to calculate the costs of HR development.

Since there are not universally accepted accounting procedures for estimating the cost of HR development, managers and the human resource departments must collect and estimate their own costs. Xerox requires line managers to provide a human resource impact statement along with all business proposals. The impact statement includes (1) estimates of changes in headcount, (2) changes in employee compensation costs, (3) costs for relocation of people or facilities, (4) conformance to industrial relations principles, and (5) impact on other operations in the company.

INFORMATION SHARING

Information is a powerful tool for improvement. APC worked with a paper mill to design a feedback system for sharing production and business information with employees, including market pricing for certain product lines, chemical costs, scrap, and quality specifications from customers. Within six months of putting the feedback system into effect, eight production records were broken, some of twenty years' standing, with no change in personnel or equipment. Return on investment hit 33 percent, far in excess of the 17 percent budgeted.

New team-based operating systems cause firms to share information more widely with employees at all levels. At a Chevrolet plant in Detroit, employee teams know things about the state of the operation even foremen didn't know a few years ago: scrap costs, total labor costs, and the monthly bottom line.

The key is to get information into the hands of people who can use it, in a form they can understand. The surest way to do that is to have the users involved in the design of the system and the collection of the data. Managers will also have to stop using information primarily as a means to punish or reward and start letting people use it to solve problems.

For example, in APC's white-collar project mentioned earlier, professional employees initially resisted having the effectiveness of their operations measured. Every measurement system they had ever heard of was passed up the organization and used for discipline and control. The project reduced their concerns by having them develop measures themselves to support their own work.

Some managers hesitate to share information with employees, fearing it will be used against them at the bargaining table if it is good or will demoralize people if it is bad. Without that information, employees cannot appropriately respond to the need for improvement. But organizations need to train people in what the information means and how to use it.

Internal Information Markets

Information and accounting systems have become an internal commodity without an effective market pricing mechanism. This inevitably leads to inefficiencies. To avoid creating more information than they need or can afford, internal functions such as data-processing should charge for services and operate within their income. Users then become customers who pay for those services out of their own budgets. That forces the "customers" to decide how much value they are getting for their money.

In 1985, when Weyerhaeuser converted from a matrix to a product–group matrix organization, it also instituted a charge-back system that forced service departments such as corporate accounting and data-processing to bill their costs to specific users in the company. The users were then free to purchase those services outside the company if the internal charges seemed too high. Now managers can control the use of resources that cause corporate overhead costs and be held responsible for results.

Summary

When organizations change, the last component to change is the accounting system. But we don't think firms have to let deficiencies in the current accounting systems limit their improvement efforts. In sum,

1. Firms should allow users to create supplemental systems to meet their information and decision needs. The widespread availability, power, and affordability of personal computers makes this a more viable option than it would have been even five years ago.
2. Most firms have the personnel information needed to do cost-benefit analyses on hiring and training decisions.
3. Usable information has to be shared more widely in organizations. Most operating information is currently collected to be aggregated for senior management monitoring. More information must be disaggregated and pushed down in the organization for people who can use it.
4. Finally, information is not free. Organizations are paying for more information than they use. Creating an internal market for information would help make sure that users are getting the kinds and quality of information they need.

—19—
Symbols, Status, and Membership

When H. Ross Perot joined GM's Board of Directors in 1984, he got his first good look at the problems facing the American auto industry. He suggested that if GM really wanted to beat the Japanese it must, among other things, rely less on capital and more on people, and break through the barriers between labor and management.

> In my opinion, we need to do a number of symbolic things to signal a new day at GM. For example, I'd get rid of the 14th floor; I'd get rid of the executive dining rooms.

Perot thought managers and workers ought to eat lunch in the same cafeteria and park in the same lots, as they do at EDS headquarters in Dallas. The *coup de grâce* may have been his proposal that GM pay hourly and salaried workers annual bonuses based on the same formula.

As Perot found out, those things "just aren't done" at GM corporate headquarters. The GM Board was willing to pay $700 million for Perot's stock to get him to stop suggesting to the press that they should be.

THE POWER OF SYMBOLS

There were undoubtedly other frictions between Perot and GM management, but this example highlights the importance of something ignored or resisted by managers when discussing productivity—the influence of symbols, status, and membership.

We have found that many managers take great offense at the suggestion that the symbols of rank and status in organizations may be counterproductive to the very goals managers say they want to achieve.

Managers *say* they want teamwork, that they want other employees to feel the same commitment to making the company a success as they do. But it is difficult to convince employees that "we are all in this boat together" if language, modes of dress, dining, parking, and location of offices all send a *different* message.

The distinction between management and nonmanagement has long been pervasive in American industry. Reserved parking spaces, separate dining areas, different entrances, different dress codes, carpeted floors instead of concrete, time clocks, salaries instead of hourly wages, different fringe benefits, discretionary time instead of fixed breaks—all convey the message that managers are to be trusted, that they are the organization's "in-group," and that other employees are hired hands.

There is nothing inherently wrong with status symbols, unless they get in the way of communication, teamwork, or job performance. Andrew Grove, President of Intel, is convinced that, at least in his business, they do.

> A journalist puzzled by our management style once asked me, "Mr. Grove, isn't your company's emphasis on visible signs of egalitarianism such as informal dress, partitions instead of offices, and the absence of other obvious perks like reserved parking spaces, just so much affectation?" My answer was that this is not affectation but a matter of survival. In our business we have to mix knowledge-power people with position-power people daily, and together they make decisions that could affect us for years to come. If we don't link our engineers with our managers in such a way as to get good decisions, we can't succeed in our industry. Now, status symbols most certainly do not promote the flow of ideas, facts and points of view. What appears to be a matter of style really is a matter of necessity.

But many other senior managers don't understand what all the fuss is about. They bristle when we suggest that, perhaps, executive dining rooms and reserved parking spots rub employees the wrong way and hamper effective communication and innovation. "We fought and worked to get here. We deserve it." "It's only a few thousand a year." "Putting a name on a parking space is cheaper than a raise." "The cost of the dining room wouldn't show up on the balance sheet if you took it out to four decimal places." The point, of course, is not the cost in dollars or whether they "deserve" it (many of them probably do). The point is that restrictive use of these symbols and perquisites are out of sync with the kind of changes needed to create a feeling of common fate across the organization—"We are all in this together." Instead of assuming management has to give up "the good life," managers ought to consider spreading it around.

Every organization has its own set of symbols. We shall only discuss four of the most common: executive dining rooms, reserved parking, dress and insignia, and spaces.

Executive Dining Rooms

Few status symbols arouse more heat than the executive dining room. Those who have them defend them vigorously and can't imagine doing without them. They argue that senior executives' time is just too valuable to waste standing in a cafeteria line.

Yet the cafeteria line is at least one place to keep in touch with what is going on in the company. Since most people aren't interested in following the Japanese habit of drinking in bars to all hours with the troops, breakfast or lunch might be a good time to get in touch with day-to-day goings on.

There are some executives who value this opportunity. Richard Rogers, the president of Syntex, the pharmaceutical corporation, eats breakfast every morning with employees in the Palo Alto headquarters cafeteria. Syntex seems not to have lost much business as a result.

Others insist that executive dining rooms are a must for doing business with customers and clients or that confidential matters need the privacy of separate spaces. In response, McDonnell Douglas Electronics Company converted its executive dining room into a "guest dining room." *Anyone* can reserve the room for privacy, to meet with visitors, or to feed people in an all-day meeting. Otherwise, everyone eats in a very attractive cafeteria.

Reserved Parking

On a cold day in Detroit, with a 40-mph wind blowing down from Canada, employees who arrive early have a hard time understanding why the spots nearest the door are reserved for senior managers.

The rationale for reserved parking is similar to that advanced for separate dining: "Our senior managers' time is too valuable to spend circling the parking lot."

Many firms are doing away with this symbol. Firms that make parking first come, first serve have found that employees appreciate the gesture, and most younger managers feel more comfortable with the arrangement. In a recent APC survey, we found that over 12 percent of the firms sampled had eliminated reserved parking in the last five years.

It is hard to engage in a rational conversation on the appropriate uses of special dining and parking areas. If a group of managers and employees want to have a quiet and private business lunch, there ought to be a place they can reserve. Of course, reserved parking spots are needed for visitors, handicapped employees, security, material and information couriers, and others. The difference is that those spots are a reflection of tasks, hours, and responsibilities, not just privilege or position.

Dress and Insignia

The Department of Labor stopped using "blue-collar" and "white-collar" to designate types of jobs in 1982. As more and more work became knowledge and service work, the distinction just didn't make sense any more. After all, AT&T technicians now wear suits and ties and carry their tools in a briefcase. Are they bluecollar workers?

Although the way people dress has become less an issue in office settings, the issue is still alive and well in factories. At the Chrysler Jefferson Avenue assembly plant, the UAW agreed to combine ninety job categories into ten if Chrysler would renovate the facility and, at the request of the union, *supervisors would stop wearing ties.*

Clothing has long served as a status symbol that distinguishes managers from workers, and some managers are loath to give it up. Ken Iverson, CEO of Nucor Steel, tells the story of when his company made all the hard hats the same color.

> The hat idea came from me. And after we announced it, I got about four letters from foremen who said something like, "It's my recognition. I put it in the back of my car so everyone can see it. All of my

neighbors know I am a foreman.'' And I wrote back and was sympathetic, but said that the recognition has to come from your leadership ability and not from the color hard hat you wear.

Where hard hats aren't worn, the insignia of rank come in different badge colors. One company we know still gets complaints from managers four years after making all name badges the same color: ''I used to know who I was talking to by the color of stripes on his badge.'' The reply was, ''We don't expect you to treat someone differently just because he's a vice president.''

The Japanese are famous for all dressing alike at work. As Frank Gibney observed during his stint as head of *Encyclopaedia Britannica, Japan*, ''High executives, who don't touch a tool all day, sport the company work jacket. The troops like to see the general in combat gear. At the same time the Japanese sense of hierarchy is so thoroughly hammered into the corporate mind that Japanese executives don't need ostentatious signs of success.''

The practice has been exported to America. Marvin Runyon, the American president of Nissan Motor Manufacturing, dresses in blue pants and shirt, like many of the 2,600 employees in his plant. Honda employees and managers in Marysville, Ohio, all wear the same uniforms. The Koreans have adopted the same practice.

For all these practices, from dining rooms to dress codes, the object isn't to eliminate authority, but to stop making an issue of it. As American organizations become flatter, with fewer opportunities for promotion, organizations would be wise not to rub it in that the vast majority of people will never be senior managers. Other means will have to found to recognize high achievers and provide people with challenge and growth. Some options are broader jobs, special project assignments, lateral promotions and rotation, and more autonomy to select one's own projects.

We believe that removing the psychological separation caused by status symbols can pay off in greater interaction among employees and make it easier to move to team-based operations. The payoffs for overcoming the *physical separation* that occurs between factories and offices will be even more substantial.

THE DISTANCE BETWEEN THE FACTORY AND THE OFFICE

Physical separation in working spaces is a serious impediment to rapid communication and problem-solving and helps perpetuate a ''we–they'' mentality.

Studies have shown that the likelihood of face-to-face communication drops to about 10 percent when people are separated by only 40 feet. And it drops to near zero when it hits the cultural abyss between the factory and the office.

Factory workers grow to resent the people hidden behind the office walls: "Those guys sit on their butts in there all day, then tell me to work harder." Managers and administrators, in turn, think of the people in the factory as a different class of faceless citizens.

Neither side really believes the other to be that incompetent or unimportant, but the lack of interaction caused by physical separation breeds distrust and misunderstanding. In an attempt to overcome that problem, employees at Ford participated in "A Day in the Life" experiment to build empathy and understanding between the two groups. About sixty-eight production workers, professionals, and managers switched jobs for a day. A vinyl plant manager spent the day pouring 50-pound bags of filler into hoppers. An hourly quality control inspector said that attending managers' meetings helped him see they "really care about quality" and that "management isn't a piece of cake either."

There would be less need for this kind of program if people were not separated by opaque walls and long distances.

A huge industry has grown up to design "open offices" and make sure that *office* communication and activity patterns are supported by the layout. But much less attention has been paid to designing manufacturing settings for interaction. If factories are going to be structured around teams, facilities will have to be designed to bring people together around the flow of work.

For example, the amenities taken for granted in the office—private space and conference rooms—need to be provided in factories as well. As one employee said, "It's the little things that drive me crazy. We don't have any meeting rooms out here, and no place to store flip charts and team materials. The guys who designed this place evidently never expected workers to sit down and talk together." And if engineers are to move willingly from their offices to the factory floor, the factory floor is going to have to become cleaner, safer, quieter, and more attractive than it is now.

Companies where people are conscious of the power of symbols tend to avoid the "fight-for-the-corner-office-with-the-thickest-carpet" syndrome by making all furnishings equally attractive—or plain. For example, in the new Saturn headquarters being built in Troy, Michigan, the Saturn design team had a running battle with the office design firm it had hired to furnish the facility.

Saturn managers wanted all the offices to have the same grade of furnishing and decorations. But the design company ordered more expensive furniture for the eight top Saturn executives. Saturn management canceled the special order and saved the company more than $1 million.

OPPORTUNITIES TO CHANGE THE SPACES AND SYMBOLS

Changing existing spaces and symbols is difficult. Egos, the territorial imperative, and just plain habit make it a slow process. It is much easier in a new operation or office building.

Designers of many new plants and offices have taken the opportunity to minimize status differences in a number of ways. They have designed all-salaried pay plans, similar benefit packages, no assigned parking, attractive working and dining facilities, and meeting rooms for employees, and they have encouraged similar modes of dress.

NUMMI is a hybrid, a new system in an old space. Ironically, the kind of "symbolic" changes that got H. Ross Perot in trouble at GM are used at NUMMI, GM's joint venture with Toyota in Fremont, California. Everybody at NUMMI, including the president, Mr. Toyoda, eats in the same cafeteria, all employees are offered business cards, and there is no reserved parking. Managers' desks are out in the open, and the old offices have been converted into dozens of meeting and conference rooms.

Open parking and lots of meeting rooms alone didn't give NUMMI the highest quality and the lowest cost per vehicle in GM, but they reflect a consistent philosophy that "everyone has an important contribution to make to the success of the enterprise."

Symbols can be, and are being, changed in even the heartland of the American industrial caste system. At the Cadillac Engine plant in Livonia, Michigan, business teams of ten to twenty workers in fifteen departments are responsible for production. No one wears ties, and some supervisors wear jeans; they share the cafeteria and compete for parking. There is no evidence that anarchy has resulted, and managers have as much authority as ever, or more—but the authority is based on their expertise as well as on their position.

Similarly, despite the absence of explicit bureaucratic rules and status symbols, Japanese firms are nonetheless highly disciplined, closely managed, and clearly hierarchical. Yet a Japanese employee in one of the large firms knows that he is a valued member of a select community.

We are not holding up the Japanese as models to be adopted wholesale.

Most Americans would rebel at the lack of privacy and autonomy of employees in Japanese firms. Japan also excludes women, minorities, and foreigners from the "inner circle" of corporate decision-making.

But American managers can learn something from the Japanese about more closely integrated spaces and reduction of symbols.

SUMMARY

We have come to four conclusions about the use—and abuse—of status symbols in companies:

1. Bureaucracies tend to be more concerned about status symbols and less about results.
2. The greater the number of distinctions in dress, perquisites, and physical surroundings, the greater the mistrust and the worse the communication and teamwork among managers and employees.
3. The physical separation of offices and factories, engineering and manufacturing, front office and back room operations slows communication, hampers problem-solving and breeds mistrust.
4. A company that changes the symbols without changing the substance of management behavior ends up with a lot of cynical employees.

Finally, a lack of American managerial elitism used to be the envy of Europeans, hampered as Europeans were by a history of rigid class distinctions. But with increasing affluence, bureaucracy, industrial strife, and specialization, American managers have been infected with a more subtle form of the same disease.

We echo the advice of Servan–Schreiber to the Europeans in *The American Challenge:*

> There can be no progress without surrendering acquired privileges, without discarding outdated machinery, ideas and skills.

One of the strengths of Americans is their desire to band together for a common purpose, to share a vision that feeds the spirit as well as pays the rent. If managers are not careful, traditional status symbols will sabotage that strength.

—20—
A Labor–Management Partnership

Competition has backed organized labor and management into a shotgun wedding.

Given the adversarial tradition of labor relations in this country, it is an uneasy partnership: Companies have sought to protect their right to manage without interference, and unions have sought to represent and protect their members. It is against this backdrop of sometimes bitter conflict that the current quest for cooperation is being enacted.

Many of the partners are making the relationship a success. Others are ending up in economic divorce court on "grounds of noncompetitiveness."

PRESSURES FOR CHANGE

Union leaders know the labor movement is in trouble; Membership rolls are down, political clout is slipping, the unions' public image is tarnished.

Thirty years ago, unions represented one-third of the labor force. Now, less than 17 percent of the private sector workers are union members. In 1950 unions won three-quarters of all NLRB representation elections; now they win only two-fifths of the time.

Management has little reason to be gleeful at the problems faced by some unions. The problems are a direct reflection of the stiff competition facing basic industries in which unions have been historically the strongest: steel, autos, rubber, mining, transportation, and construction.

Those industries are losing out to foreign competition and to nonunion facilities. Nonunion companies are thriving in even the most troubled industries. In steel, nonunion Nucor and Chapparal and mostly nonunion Worthington Industries are innovative and profitable firms. Their nonunion plants tend to be newer, have lower benefit and pension costs, use more advanced technology and more innovative operating systems, and have more employee involvement.

The challenge to unions and management is to match the performance of nonunion firms while accepting the legitimacy of each other's concerns. We see the parties responding to the challenge in two ways; one is traditional confrontation, and the other is constructive problem-solving. We call the first the ''scorched earth'' strategy and the second ''partnership.''

SCORCHED EARTH

When a group of people is under severe pressure from an external threat, it has a choice. The members can either join together to meet the threat or turn on each other.

The nation has watched in disbelief as Eastern Airlines and its unions, and Hormel and the Meatpackers tore each other to shreds. USX and the United Steelworkers battled it out for months at great cost to both sides and little to show for it.

Those battles leave a scorched earth in their wake. For years, nothing grows there. We don't believe that either unions or management thinks this kind of confrontation and destruction is the way to meet the competitive challenge. As one manager observed, ''Pushing the union to the wall every time you have the leverage to do it is no way to form a long-term problem-solving relationship. It always comes back to bite you.''

The Alternative: A Competitive Partnership

If firms and union don't want to follow the scorched earth strategy, we believe management should take the first steps and perhaps go more than halfway in changing the relationship.

We know this is hard for some managers to swallow, but we are convinced it is necessary. With some notable exceptions (the United Auto Workers, the United Steelworkers, and the Communication Workers of America), unions are waiting for management to change before they do.

As one Goodyear vice president put it, "You don't talk yourself out of a bad relationship you behaved yourself into."

What Management Has to Do

First, we don't see unions becoming enthusiastic partners in the Agenda for Adjustment until the following three conditions are met:

1. Management acknowledges the right of unions to exist and represent employees.
2. Unions and their members are brought in as partners in the process of change.
3. The interests of the unions and their members, such as employment stability and involvement, are legitimate objectives of the change process.

1. UNION LEGITIMACY

Most managers wish unions would just go away, and most union leaders know that. Union leaders do not support productivity improvement when they constantly have to protect the union as an institution. William Winpisinger, president of the International Association of Machinists and Aerospace Workers, put the position to us bluntly: "Management talks participation eight hours a day, then spends the other sixteen supporting right-to-work laws and trying to get us decertified."

In unionized firms, management has to accept that their employees chose to be represented by a union and the union has a legitimate right to be at the table.

2. PARTNERS IN THE CHANGE PROCESS

Productivity, involvement, or restructuring programs that don't involve the union or gain its support from the beginning are usually doomed to failure.

One company we know absolutely refused to allow the local union to participate and jointly sponsor an employee involvement program, even though we warned it of the consequences. The union responded by asking employees not to participate. The program was stalemated for months. A truce was finally reached, but the ill will never dissipated and the program faded away.

Ironically, in that firm the plant manager had been perfectly willing to accept the union as co-partners in the process, but corporate industrial relations was adamantly opposed. Its position was, "We'll be [damned] if we'll let the union get some of the credit for this."

Managers who have been more successful at building a good relationship with the union see it differently. John Wolf, a vice president with McDonnell Aircraft, says that union support is a distinct advantage in the change process: "Employees often don't trust management. They do trust union leaders. So they will often listen to them before they listen to us."

3. ACCEPT UNION AND EMPLOYEE INTERESTS AS LEGITIMATE

In our experience, companies with the worst labor relationships are those in which employees' interests and ideas go unheard, unheeded, and unanswered; where management and union insist on focusing on the letter of the contract, rather than solving problems; and where management takes the position that the purchase of labor is the same as buying a shipment of steel.

Unions and employees have legitimate concerns. They worry about jobs, a reasonable standard of living, and being protected from capricious decisions. The union leadership does not want to be eased out of the picture by participation. And the union is especially concerned that it not be seen as "getting in bed" with management and abandoning its members.

Managers have to be willing to listen and respond to those concerns. If management wants to influence the union and its members to share management concerns, it will have to convince union leaders that management is responsive to union issues.

When those preconditions are met, unions and companies have shown they can create effective partnerships. The partnerships have two aspects; one is economic and the other deals with joint responsibility for change.

Economic Partnerships

In the face of adversity, unions have begun to ask for an economic and investor stake in enterprises to which they grant substantial wage concessions. Unions have sought and won seats on boards of directors, stock ownership, deferred compensation for wage and benefit cuts, and a voice in investment decisions.

- GM and Ford joined with the UAW to set up "new ventures" funds for jointly developing and launching innovative businesses to provide jobs for auto workers.
- Union leaders are board members at Chrysler and Pan Am.
- At Bethlehem and LTV Steel, the United Steelworkers granted concessions in 1986 in exchange for stock and a pledge by the companies to reinvest savings in steel operations. [A similar deal was negotiated with National Steel in return for employment security provisions.] The pact called for Bethlehem to repay in cash 10 percent of its first $100 million in earnings and 20 percent of any earnings above that amount. If Bethlehem isn't profitable, the concessions will be repaid in a convertible preferred stock, paying a 5 percent annual dividend.

Those agreements are setting the stage for a major change in the role of some unions. They still aren't comfortable thinking about ownership questions, but the new role is born of necessity. The new ownership role for unions, however, doesn't translate into increased competitiveness unless it is translated into operating unit cooperation and change.

Operating Unit Cooperation

We have found that the best way to embark on a joint effort is to have the partners develop a "safety net" to protect themselves from mishaps and keep the collaborative process alive during disagreements.

Why a safety net?

Because cooperation is a high-stakes game, and both sides have much to lose. Each side fears that if it allows the other to gain too much influence, its own side will be the loser.

Unions are especially unwilling to walk into cooperation without some protection. For instance, management occasionally gets "employee involvement religion" and tries to force the union into a cooperative mode by starting meetings with employees. The intentions are right, but if the union is suspicious and feels threatened by the unexpected turnaround, the result is often months of stalemating and no progress, as the union keeps waiting for the wolf to come out of the sheep's clothing. As a friend who is a shop steward told us, "We've hated each other for thirty years. Last month management decided we're going to have a love-in from now on. Well, I don't think so."

The safety net can provide a set of agreements that protect both parties' interests. It evolves over a series of meetings with senior leaders of both groups, includes guidelines for how they will work together and resolve problems, and sets preconditions for participation by both parties.

And, like a prenuptial agreement, the safety net spells out how the parties will terminate the collaborative process if either side wants out. That is far easier to do before a problem erupts than in the heat of the battle. Sometimes it even prevents the breakup by providing a cooling-off period.

These are some of the topics typically included in safety net discussions:

1. How to clear up grievance procedure problems that are blocking progress
2. Agreements about how the cooperative effort will be announced and publicized
3. How often meetings will be held, and how the agenda is created
4. Ground rules about consensus decision-making and interpersonal behaviors
5. Cooling-off and bailout procedures that minimize damage to the relationship if either side wants out
6. How consultants and other third parties will be selected and used

Once the safety net is in place, the parties can begin to explore the mutual goals and objectives that make the collaboration worthwhile. This is often one of the most rewarding first steps, as people discover how similar their values are and that labor and management can and do have mutual goals. Then the real work of identifying opportunities and problems that must be solved begins.

At this point, every labor–management project takes its own unique turn. Some begin by developing employee involvement groups, while others are ready to move to expanded EI and changes in the operating system. Usually significant changes in work rules, organization and job design, innovative pay systems, and other significant changes take three to five years to materialize.

It can happen faster in a crisis. Before LTV entered bankruptcy, it joined with the Steelworkers in an important experiment in workplace restructuring as radical in its own way as the Saturn agreement between GM and the UAW.

At LTV's Cleveland works, the company invested $135 million in a new electro-galvanizing line (EGL). All the steelworkers were put on salary, and, instead of traditional job classifications, workers formed cross-skilled teams of ten to fifteen members. Workers have a voice in important decisions, including hiring, firing, and procedures for handling grievances. There is a twice-yearly performance bonus that could add up to as much as 25 percent of pay.

LTV and the Steelworkers were able to develop this system because, for three years, they had been active in labor–management participation teams. So far, the process has been a success.

We have found that it takes three conditions for labor–management projects such as the LTV EGL line to become long-term successes:

1. The union is an active joint partner in designing and managing the change effort.
2. The process produces tangible improvements in productivity and performance and increases employment stability.
3. Both sides see the process as part of their longer-term strategies.

Nevertheless, to be successful, joint projects have many hurdles to overcome.

Problems in Labor–Management Projects

Most people are familiar with the usual set of problems encountered by labor–management projects, such as (1) resistance by managers, supervisors, or shop stewards who fear losing control; (2) lack of resources and skills at joint problem-solving; (3) wasting time on trivial issues; and (4) creating too much bureaucracy in programs.

Those are the standard problems and pitfalls. With enough dedication and insight, they all have been and can be overcome.

But a new set of "advanced problems" is emerging in those industries that have been engaged in problem-solving the longest and are attempting the kind of innovative changes we have recommended throughout the Agenda.

One case is the GM–UAW Saturn Project, which has run into some very interesting opposition (which may be an indication of its potential to change car making in this country). For instance, some UAW members have strongly objected to the project because of its innovative gain sharing arrangement: Once the subsidiary is fully operational, Saturn UAW employees, who will all be salaried, will earn 80 percent of the standard UAW rate paid in other GM locations. They will have the opportunity to make up the 20 percent and more through a gain sharing plan based on Saturn performance.

Not everyone in the UAW is in favor of the idea. "The agreement reinstitutes 'piecework,' endangers hard-won benefits, and encourages workers to be informers," the president of a UAW local complains.

Not only is the UAW getting criticism, but GM is under attack for recognizing the UAW as the collective bargaining body for Saturn employees. Right-to-work committees have brought suit, claiming Saturn should not have given premature recognition of the union in Tennessee, a right-to-work state.

Personal pressures are also high for unions and managers engaged in cooperative problem-solving. For example, being an innovative local union president can be a thankless job. Union officials hate to recommend anything different to their members because, in the words of one path-breaking local president, "if anything goes wrong, I'm the one they're gonna dump on. They'll say 'Hey, you told us this would be good.' " They are constantly harassed with hostile questions at union meetings. They get very little credit and lots of abuse.

If management wants to build allies among its labor peers, it is in its best interests to share credit with the union leaders and help them deal with those pressures. We know this isn't easy, since historically management has looked good to *its* peers by making the union look bad.

UNION RESPONSIBILITIES

We have concentrated a great deal on what management must do to make a problem-solving relationship with the union possible. The adjustments for unions may be even more difficult.

The union movement is doing a lot of soul-searching, looking for an appropriate role in a changing economy. We think innovative work systems and joint problem-solving hold the greatest promise for building a union's strength and membership and making a key contribution to the competitiveness of the United States. But it will take a radical shift in the role of unions. As a bargaining committee chairman for the IAM said to us,

> For forty years my union has been saying that we should have a voice in what goes on around here. Now management says okay, we want you to be on this committee that is going to decide how this place ought to be run.
>
> What am I supposed to say? "No, thanks. We were just kidding all those years about wanting to have some influence. You guys keep running the place and we'll just keep complaining"?
>
> I'm not gonna do that. I'm gonna serve on this committee because it's good for the union and its good for our members.

The speaker is often under fire from other union leaders and even his own membership.

It is much easier to stand outside the fortress and throw rocks than to come inside and design new fortifications. But if unions are to become joint partners in the process, they have to accept responsibility for making tradeoffs and occasionally painful decisions.

In that spirit, we offer ten observations and suggestions to union leaders at the national and local levels:

1. *We strongly suggest that unions consider a hybrid model of pattern bargaining.* As we described in Chapter 14, this could include national guidelines for types of agreements such as gain sharing, then freedom granted to locals to bargain specific wage and benefit packages for local conditions.
2. *Continue your own studies of innovative work systems.* Be ready to propose alternatives to management on how to restructure work systems while maintaining employee protection against speedup and unsafe conditions.
3. *Join with management to develop strategies to avoid layoffs.* Reexamine historically unattractive alternatives such as overtime, subcontracting, and temporary and part-time employees. Consider provisions for making those employees dues-paying and protected members of the union. Work on guidelines for plant closings and job placement when necessary.
4. *Insist that productivity and quality improvement be considered a measure of union success.* Bargain on the basis of the union's contribution to competitiveness.
5. *Lobby line managers to "reeducate" labor relations executives* who block the cooperative problem-solving process by treating

every disagreement and grievance as an opportunity to go to the barricades.

6. *Keep reminding management and your members that the competition is the enemy.*

7. *Make upgrading members' multiple skills and marketability through continuous training a key union objective.* Employment in manufacturing will continue to require more and more sophisticated skills, as production work becomes a profession, not a job.

8. *Educate your members about gain sharing, new operating systems, and companywide quality control.*

9. *Insist that problem-solving involvement and training for supervisors and stewards be jointly designed and run.* Train stewards how to lead teams.

10. *Educate managers about union political issues.* Otherwise, they might inadvertantly take actions that you must oppose.

INNOVATIONS FOR THE FUTURE

The United Auto Workers, the United Steelworkers, and the Communication Workers of America (CWA) are not the only unions engaging in innovative change efforts, but their experiences are convincing other union leaders—and managers—that functional change is possible.

Retraining and employment security are key areas of union leadership. After an unfortunate twenty-six-day strike in June 1986, AT&T and the CWA negotiated a major breakthrough in the telecommunications industry. Similar to prior agreements in the auto industry, the CWA and AT&T will run a school to train workers for new jobs when their skills are obsolete. Assured of some measure of employment stability and reemployment, the 155,000 CWA members agreed to give AT&T greater flexibility to structure certain job categories.

In another arena, the prestige of the UAW was on the line when Toyota and GM launched New United Motor Manufacturing Inc. (NUMMI), their joint venture in Fremont, California. The UAW has proved that American unions can participate in the design of world-class operating systems. The success at NUMMI in large part persuaded Mazda to recognize the UAW as the bargaining agent for its assembly plant under construction in Flat Rock, Michigan.

The NUMMI team structure and joint problem-solving process for resolving labor differences has changed the way workers feel about their jobs and the company. Most of the NUMMI employees had worked at the old GM assembly plant before they were rehired for NUMMI. According to one forty-four-year-old team leader, "At the old GM, no one cared what you thought. Here you are included in everything. Used to be, even if you passed out on the line, they dragged the body out and kept the line moving. Now employees can stop the line to correct defects."

The Saturn Project is another example. Both a car and an operating system, Saturn was jointly designed by GM and the UAW. Ninety-nine people from GM and the UAW set out in the summer of 1983 with a clean sheet of paper to design a new American operating system based on the best practices from around the world. Team members traveled more than 2 million miles and visited two hundred sites to gather ideas.

What resulted in the Saturn agreement is a living document that the parties will constantly improve.

SATURN ORGANIZATION STRUCTURE

Instead of a pyramid, Saturn designers describe the organization structure as a set of concentric rings. In the middle are the *work teams* of ten to fifteen multiskilled people. Work teams are coordinated and supported by a *business unit* team of union and managers. Business units are supported by the next ring, *manufacturing advisory committees,* which coordinate the entire production process and relations with suppliers. The outermost ring is a joint labor–management committee, the *Strategic Advisory Committee,* which sets the direction for the entire Saturn organization.

THE SATURN SOCIAL SYSTEM

All employees will be selected from GM and UAW members and offered permanent job security; there will be no layoffs unless there is a catastrophe. Consensus decision-making will be used from the shop floor to the corporate level. No decision can be made without the concurrence of both parties. All employees will be on salary. There will be no time clocks, separate cafeterias, parking lots, or entrances, and everyone will get the same option to purchase cars at employee prices. All employees will be referred to as "members."

GM's financial and operating problems have thrown the dates for the opening of the Saturn Springhill, Tennessee, plant into doubt. But there is no doubt that the Saturn design process and operating and decision-making systems are the wave of the future.

CONCLUSION

Labor and management are faced with a choice. They can either start treating each other's concerns as legitimate and become partners in the adjustment process or be cordoned off into the weakest parts of the economy.

There are enough successes to show it can be done. The choice is theirs. The question is, Can they adjust in time?

Summary: The Litmus Test

We have reached five general conclusions rom watching managers wrestle with the ten tough issues on the Agenda for Adjustment.

First, we know of no "silver bullets" for handling the issues. Every company arrives at its own solutions.

Second, the process of creating solutions has as much to do with how it turns out as the specific solutions. People tend to support those changes they help create.

Third, the solutions must be integrated and held together by a shared vision and a set of guiding principles. Employees are frightened by the changes around them: management restructures, jobs change, programs come and go, customers are fickle, managers are now supposed to be coaches. "What does it all mean?" they ask. "Do these guys at the top know what they are doing?"

This naturally leads to our fourth conclusion: While every employee has a role to play, it is ultimately up to managers to make it happen and give it meaning. Managers can't do it alone, but without their intense daily involvement and leadership it can't be done at all.

Finally, it can be and is being done. It takes commitment and will. It does not necessarily take a crisis to create adjustment and renewal, but it helps.

Beyond those general conclusions, are there any commonalities in successful efforts at adjustment and renewal? We think so. Changing organizations is not like investing in the stock market, where a random walk may be as good a strategy as any. We have concluded that, while there is no one "right" way to manage or a perfect strategy for change, there are five criteria for selecting adjustment strategies that enhance the probability of gaining greater productivity, quality, and competitiveness. We call these five criteria our Litmus Test:

1. Drive
2. Flexibility
3. Continuous improvement
4. Continuous learning
5. A shared sense of purpose

We have developed the litmus test after studying successes and failures—Japanese, European, American, and historical. Those criteria emerge again and again as predictors of long-term success. Readers will recognize them as criteria that guided our selection of examples.

DRIVE: THE EYE OF THE TIGER

Drive is what is missing in too many American companies. Without a sense of urgency and determination actually to change the way they operate, "competitiveness" strategies are only so much blue smoke and mirrors.

If at least one, and preferably more, of the following three drive-producing conditions are not present, drive is usually not sufficient and change is rarely successful.

1. *Competitive Crisis.* There is nothing like a clear and present danger to make people open to change. Without competition the managers and union leaders in the automotive, steel, machine tool, airline, and banking industries would not have made the changes they have. Xerox would never have restructured its copier business had it not been for competition from Canon, Sharp, Ricoh, Toshiba, and others. Without crisis, Ford

would not have more than doubled its quality, developed the Taurus, or managed to earn more profits than GM for the first time in fifty years.

2. *A new business opportunity.* People in new organizations do not have tradition and past practice to drain them of energy. The chance to start over, to do it right this time, almost always produces committed and driven people. It does not require new buildings or new people to start over. Every new product, service, or technology is an opportunity to take out a clean sheet of paper and do it better this time. The sense of drive and purpose has to be sustained over the long haul. Firms must *select for it, reward for it,* and *get out of the way:* Select and promote people who have a drive to win; reward people, as individuals and groups, for success; and design operating systems that are small and flexible enough not to kill initiative.

3. *Champions.* We have seen organizations not driven by an external threat embark on and persist in massive adjustment strategies. Why? Because a key executive had a vision and the power to sell and force change and was unwilling to let the ship start sinking before manning the pumps.

For instance, Sanford McDonnell, chairman, and John McDonnell, president of McDonnell Douglas (MDC) are leading their company in a massive self-assessment and self-renewal process. John McDonnell stated in a report to MDC executives in 1986:

> The Japanese have spearheaded an industrial organizational revolution which is in the process of superseding the hierarchal, machine-like approach to organization that powered industry since early in this century.
>
> We in MDC are lucky. Our businesses do not have direct competition from the Japanese [but] it is only a matter of time before all of our businesses will be face to face with companies that are substantially more productive than they are today.
>
> So we need to ask ourselves whether the risk is greater in trying to transform our organizations to a new culture. I can tell you my answer—the status quo never wins in the long run.

What if the top executives aren't leading the charge? Usually, somewhere down in the organization, there are a few innovators trying a few things: JIT, employee involvement, gain sharing. Peters and Waterman call them "champions." Kantor calls them "innovators." They are line managers running a division, plant, or branch office, driven by a powerful personal conviction that there is a better way to work. They are stubborn and persistent, they inspire the people who work for them, and their efforts, if successful, will eventually draw attention. When senior management is ready, their experience will give the company the data it needs to move forward.

When embarking on a change process, we ask ourselves and the companies with whom we work if there is enough drive to warrant the effort. These are some questions we have found useful:

- Where is the energy coming from to drive the change?
- Is this just a social experiment, or are the stakes and payoffs high enough to get management, union, and employee attention?
- What kind of barriers, obstacles, and opposition is the new way of doing things likely to encounter?
- Are there men and women who want this so bad they can taste it? Who are they, and how much power do they have?

People with enough drive can make almost anything work. Without it, the most elegant change strategy turns to dust. While drive alone can't prevail over everything, we believe history and experience say that in a global economy where technological advantages are short-lived, it is one margin of difference between winners and losers.

FLEXIBILITY: ADAPTABILITY AND SELF-RENEWAL

Flexibility and adaptability have defined leaders throughout history, and they are what make the Japanese such formidable competitors.

The biggest challenge facing U.S. corporations is to regain the flexibility that was lost as they grew and aged. We have walked into many corporate offices where we can literally feel the loss of vitality and flexibility. Not a physical decay, certainly, but an aura of stodginess and allegiance to standard operating procedures exudes from the heavy pile carpets, the mahogany walls, and the shelves of policy manuals. We are also convinced there is an inverse correlation between the size of a department or operating unit and the average level of motivation of its members and flexibility of its systems.

We have described change strategies that will increase flexibility. Briefly, they are:

- Small and simple operating systems instead of complex ones
- A workforce of cross-trained people with specialists' skills and generalists' mentality
- A minimum of bureaucratic rules, procedures, and symbols

- A practical commitment to employment stability
- Fewer management layers and functional territories
- Flexible compensation systems that give employees a piece of the productivity action

Flexibility is an important litmus test of the change process as well. It is important that well-intentioned senior managers not try to "micromanage" the change process. By that we mean that every unit in the organization must have the freedom to develop its own solutions to its own opportunities. A shared mission and philosophy should keep those efforts consistent, but not block creativity or initiative.

Managers and employees are constantly inventing new routes to flexibility. Here are some questions we suggest people ask themselves when seeking greater flexibility:

- Is this new technology or human resource system going to make us more responsive to the market?
- Are we going to get locked into yet another rigid and expensive system, or is it flexible enough so that we can change it later?
- What options are we cutting off by going this route?
- Is this system going to be dependent on specialists?
- Is it going to help break down departmental and functional silos?
- Am I personally willing to give up some preconceived notions and comfortable ways of behaving?

Continuous Improvement: "Pursuing the Last Grain of Rice"

The third component of the Litmus Test is continuous improvement. It is not enough to make modest productivity gains in one quarter, in one year, or even for several years. The international productivity race is a marathon, not a sprint. We think the success of many international competitors is not genius or technology, but attention to detail and the "daily hunt" for improvement.

The two-minute warning has sounded. A lot of companies, especially in manufacturing, are going to have to sustain productivity improvement at the rate of about *ten to fifteen percent a year* for the next few years if they want to catch up and stay in the international game. For them, improvement is a long-term process, not a event.

There is no improvement too small to make, no employee who can sit on the sidelines. Improvement strategies had better be geared toward harnessing everyone's energies every day. These questions are ways of detecting whether that is the case:

- Are people working toward preset standards that once achieved will permit them to relax and declare victory?
- Is there a common understanding that nothing less than perfection is good enough, and that the standards for perfection keep getting higher?
- Can the organization respond to the ideas people have? Can they get the resources to implement the ideas themselves?
- Have we broken out of preconceived limits on what can be changed?
- Do people have ways to measure and track improvement over time, against their own past and against their competitors?

Continuous Learning

Continuous improvement does not happen without continuous learning, the fourth component of our Litmus Test. The key is action learning, working together, and solving problems. From executives on down there is a need for employees to learn how to identify and solve problems in a way that makes it easier the next time. Firms must reward problem-solving rather than blaming, must share information widely and well, and must recruit people who want to learn. Ask yourself:

- Are jobs and assignments structured so that learning takes place constantly?
- Do line managers accept learning and training as their responsibility?
- Are there going to be personal rewards for learning new jobs and new skills, and for identifying problems?
- Are we going to have more highly skilled and multiskilled people as a result of this change effort?
- How are employees going to capture the learning from this process to use next time?
- Is broad, generalist knowledge rewarded, or do people know that the only way to get ahead is to be an expert in one area?

A Shared Sense of Purpose

In the preceding chapters, we have presented a variety of improvement options we think meet the criteria of drive, flexibility, continuous improvement and learning. It has become clear to us that the fifth criterion, a shared philosophy and purpose, links the four into a powerful force for adjustment and renewal.

There are *two* basically different philosophies about the purpose of organizations and the role of people in the process. The two philosophies, or sets of guiding principles, are contractual and common fate.

The Contractual Philosophy

We see the contractual philosophy lurking behind the twentieth-century managerial model dominating most American firms. We like to think it is dying out, but it is a very slow death.

The contractual philosophy is the belief, dating from the birth of the Industrial Revolution, that a group of shareholders contracts, through its managers, with the employees it hires to deliver a given level of narrowly defined "labor" in exchange for a given level of pay.

A basic assumption of the contractual philosophy is that shareholders are the real stakeholders in the success of the business and that return on investment is the best measure of performance. Management protects the interests of shareholders with elaborate control systems and the job of unions is to protect the interests of employees from management.

Contrast this with a "common fate" organization.

The Common Fate Philosophy

Sometimes called "commitment," "shared destiny," or "mutual growth," *common fate* describes the philosophy of a small but growing number of American firms that believe the interests of employees and customers are as important as the interests of shareholders; some say they even rank higher than shareholders. At a minimum, the internal stakeholders know that their interests will be served if the firm is success-ful. The customers feel the same way: The purpose of the firm is not just to make a profit, but also to serve the customers. Employees of common fate firms

- Understand the business challenges that face the firm
- Are willing to accept broad responsibility for helping meet those challenges
- Respond quickly to opportunities

- Feel a sense of membership and belonging
- Believe their personal interests will be served by the success of the firm and its other stakeholders

It is our experience and belief that when two organizations compete in the market place, one common fate and one contractual, *the common fate organization will have the productivity, quality and competitiveness advantage.*

These are some questions we ask when we begin to work with an organization:

- If you stopped employees at random and asked, "Do you think that this company feels an obligation to you as well as to shareholders?" what answer would you get?
- Are employees willing to make sacrifices when they are told of the need?
- Do employees share in the financial gains when the company is successful?
- Do the employees generally understand and support the company's business and competitiveness strategies?
- Will this change strategy increase the sense of common fate?

USING THE LITMUS TEST

The changes and strategies we have described throughout the private sector Agenda for Adjustment hold the promise of making work more satisfying and organizations more competitive, profitable, and secure. But if a change strategy does not pass the litmus test, management should think long and hard before adopting it.

Of course, passing the litmus test is no guarantee: Being competitive also takes better products and services designed to meet customers' changing needs, and a healthy dose of luck. We agree with Napoleon: "God is on the side with the heaviest cannon." But if adjustment strategies don't pass the litmus test, we don't have a lot of faith in luck and cannons or brilliant product and market strategies.

We deeply believe that the competitiveness race will be won or lost in the private sector. But the private sector does not operate in a vacuum. Government has a role to play. Therefore, we turn to government's agenda for adjustment in the next chapters.

—Part V—
Agenda for Adjustment: Government

—21—

What Government Should Not Do

As the severity of the competitiveness problem increases, the pressure on government to ''do something'' increases.

We counted over the past five years 112 recommendations for government action flowing from twenty-one councils, commissions, Congressional hearings, and study groups on productivity and competitiveness.

''Competitiveness'' has emerged as a new national buzzword and ranks high on the political agenda. The call for a ''more competitive America'' is being sounded by every 1988 presidential candidate, and the Reagan Administration has selected it as a theme for its last years.

Democrats and Republicans alike rise one by one to bash and blame foreigners, issue blackmail ultimatums to trading partners, vie with one another to hold ''competitiveness'' hearings, and flood the legislative agenda with competitiveness and trade bills. The Congressional Leadership Institute identified more than five thousand ''competitiveness'' bills in the last Congress.

247

The underlying assumption behind all this is that there is much that government should—and can—do to improve American competitiveness. We do not agree. Much of what is recommended attacks the wrong cause of the problem, will not work, wastes funds, and makes the situation worse.

Of those things suggested most frequently for government to do, we name in this chapter five things that we think government should *not do* to "help American competitiveness."

1. DO NOT INCREASE PROTECTION

The single worst thing the government can do to harm American productivity and competitiveness is to increase protection.

This is no idle concern.

The United States is already pretty far down the protectionist road, farther than most Americans realize. The United States has erected tariff and nontariff trade barriers against imported steel, autos, textiles, sugar, clothing, color TVs, motorcycles, machine tools, semiconductors, and other products. The United States imposes "Buy American" restrictions, grants subsidies for agricultural exports, and prohibits sales of oil from Alaska and timber cut on national forest lands. United States consumers pay three to four times the world price for sugar because of import restrictions.

Even the Reagan Administration, professing a strong belief in free markets, has succumbed to political pressures for protection in industry after industry. In a perverse twist, many Democrats have wrapped themselves in the posture of free marketeers, having found a neat way to act on their protectionist tendencies under the umbrella of "competitiveness" "market access," and "unfair foreign trade. They are joined by some businessmen who practice "doublethink," publicly defending free markets but privately seeking protection.

Few call protection by that name. It sounds bad. So they call it "reciprocity," "fair trade," "job preservation," "preserving a free America." The most common posture for those advocating protection is to say, "I'm not for free trade, but fair trade." But what is "fair" is always in the eye of the beholders, as witness the centuries-long arguments over what is a "fair price" or a "just wage."

Of course, there *is* protection by other nations, just as there is by the United States. Trade is hardly ever completely "free," and the playing field is hardly ever completely level. Those invoking the litany "free but fair'' often ignore their own protectionism and lack of ''fairness,'' their lack of competitiveness, and suppress data that show that protection hardly ever works, hurts their own consumers, causes loss of export-related jobs, and lowers efficiency. What is really fair is to call it by its real name: protection.

A dangerous scenario has emerged: Businessmen complain, Congress bashes and threatens, the Administration acts to ''get out in front'' or ''forestall worse action.'' It's the game of losers. Each round further weakens the patient—the American consumer and the American economy generally—and increases the danger of a world trade war.

And it isn't only the labor-intensive, low-value-added industries where protection is occurring; *protection is moving up the technological ladder.* First it was agriculture. Then textiles. Then steel. Then autos. Now semiconductors.

The United States is increasingly protectionist and it hurts competitiveness in five ways.

Protection Delays Adjustments

Protection insulates against change. Rather than let competition force change on uncompetitive firms and industries, protectionism does just the opposite—it shelters low productivity, poor management, and poor quality. It locks inefficiency into place.

Washington began protecting in the steel industry in 1968, almost twenty years ago, when Japan and the European trading partners agreed to three-year ''voluntary restraints'' of exports to the United States.

Since then assorted forms of protection have worsened—not helped—the competitive position of steel. Before protection, from 1958 to 1968, growth in compensation, productivity, and investment in steel was about equal to all U.S. manufacturing. *With protection,* from 1968 to 1980, compensation grew more than twice as fast while productivity advanced by only one-fourth as fast, and investment declined.

Contrast that with Xerox.

Xerox almost lost their position in low-end copiers to the Japanese before it decided it had to restructure drastically the way it was organized, the way it manufactured, marketed, related to employees—everything. It successfully fought back. With protection, Xerox would not have undergone such radical changes, a story well documented in the book *Xerox: American Samurai,* by Jacobson and Hillkirk.

Granting protection is like putting an industry on a life-support system. It may prolong life for a while, but it can't restore health.

Protection Spreads Inefficiencies

All industries are interconnected. Protecting one industry raises input costs for another. That makes the second industry less competitive. For example, protection raised the price of domestic steel for auto makers and the price of semiconductors for domestic computer makers, making them less competitive. It also taxes export industries, whose markets are often damaged by retaliation or decreased foreign trade.

Protection by quotas or tariffs is a form of price control, and it works no better in international trade than in domestic markets. The controls penalize consumers, distort markets, and prop up less efficient industries at the expense of the more efficient, *an economy operating in reverse.*

Protection Often Strengthens Foreign Competitors

Protection through voluntary quotas legitimizes foreign government-en-forced cartels, which would be illegal in the United States. Those cartels encourage foreign competitors to raise prices, to "trade up" their product lines, and to pocket more profits so they can strengthen their productivity and quality for the day when protection expires or ways are found around it. The "voluntary quotas" used against Japanese autos is a classic example.

And all that is mostly at the expense of American consumers, who, in the end, pay the bill for protection. Saving one job in textiles and apparel is estimated to cost $42,000 a year to consumers, $105,000 a year in autos, and in dairy products $220,000 a year. Overall, the annual cost to consumers for all protection has doubled from $33 billion in 1980 to $66 billion in 1986.

Protection Is Ineffective

Just as love laughs at locksmiths, most protection ends up being largely ineffective. Competitors invent all kinds of schemes to circumvent the barriers: transshipment, substitution, false certificates of origin, and just plain cheating. The 1986 semiconductor protection agreement was flawed from the beginning with a pricing test any Russian price controller would have been proud of. The scheme was soon riddled with sales to intermediate nations, partially avoided by wiring chips into circuit boards, and neutralized by stepups in production by other nations.

Nations end up haggling over the size of knotholes in plywood, the national origin of Chinese blouses that have buttons added in Hong Kong, or whether fully allocated overhead should be used to determine a "fair" price. Time is spent policing and haggling instead of being productive and competitive. Like all controls, they deteriorate rapidly as markets find their way around them.

Protection Endangers World Trade

Protection invites retaliation, which nullifies the temporary advantage and damages world trade and good relations between nations. Recent examples are the chicken and pasta "wars" with Europe, the Canada-U.S. shootout in lumber and corn, and the Japan-U.S. charges and countercharges in many industries.

The classic example is the Smoot–Hawley tariff of 1930, which raised tariffs an average of 53 percent. It deepened the Depression and provoked a wave of retaliation. Within three years, U.S. industrial exports had dropped 73 percent. Within four years the level of world trade was reduced by two-thirds.

Some protest it can't happen again, because the world has learned its lesson. Apparently not. The United States is now up to 35 percent of its imported goods protected by tariff or nontariff barriers. Bilateral retaliatory actions have already been undertaken by the United States, recently the champion of multilateral trade. Of the top ten products in world trade, four—autos, steel, textiles, and clothing—are largely controlled now by some form of discriminatory agreement. In total, the proportion of world trade that moves under some kind of quantitative restraint is estimated to be between 30 and 50 percent!

And the danger increases of trade wars as Congress and the Administration continue to beat up on foreign competitors and submit legislation any competitive leader should be ashamed of. You even have the embarrassing national spectacle of U.S. Congressmen throwing foreign silverware into a box in the halls of Congress. The political phrase "We're sending a message to Japan" is often a message that "we can't compete on the basis of productivity and quality."

In a world trade shootout, the United States will have a Phyrrhic victory, with dead bodies all around—the Third World being the first casualties—U.S. consumers paying the bill, and American competitiveness declining.

In summary, don't be deceived by the smokescreen of protectionist rhetoric that begins with "fair trade," "competitiveness," "level playing field," "trade policies," and "saving American jobs."

Those labels, usually the preamble to a protectionist recommendation, obscure the fact that (1) many of the accusations about unfair trade are exaggerated or untrue, (2) the United States is about as protectionist as the next nation, and (3) the surest way to destroy jobs, retard productivity, and harm American competitiveness is to increase protectionism, by whatever label.

Protection is like a "poison pill," amounting to economic suicide.

2. Do Not Establish Industrial Policies

"Industrial policies" were hotly debated several years ago, when the economy was in a deep recession. The idea never caught hold, partly because of the economic recovery and partly because of the term's association with "national planning"—anathema to most Americans.

Today, however, the call for industrial policies is being revived. Only this time they are being labeled "competitiveness policies," "trade policies," or "living standards acts."

They are all about the same in purpose: a greater degree of government direction in the economy. *We thought industrial policies were a bad idea when first proposed, and we still do.*

Most of the actions called for giving the government greater power to allocate capital, to intervene in some operating decisions of businesses, to provide subsidies, and to be a guide to national economic adjustment and development. We don't think such actions will work well; we think they will actually worsen productivity and competitiveness:

- Most government personnel are not, by instinct or background, entrepreneurs or managers. Their allocation decisions will be worse than those of the private sector.
- Many of the authors and administrators of policies and laws are lawyers, who are mainly concerned with equity, not efficiency, and economists and other scholars, who know little about actual business operations.
- All government actions are necessarily constrained by considerations of due process, accountability, representation, transparency, and political responsiveness. These will delay adjustments, reduce flexibility, and suboptimize.
- Government cannot plan long range and cannot stay on top of

the *rapid and continuous* adjustments called for in a dynamic market place.

- Despite what some economists may believe, they don't know enough about this complex economy to design a large set of "coordinated policies" that would be any better than Russia's planning policies.

We aren't against *everything* that falls under someone's industrial policy program. In the next chaper, we argue for actions that some would probably include under their version of an "industrial policy." What we are against is an omnibus package as a "coordinated," "holistic" approach—regardless of the label.

3. Avoid Currency Devaluation as a Competitiveness Strategy

Some believe that devaluing the dollar is all that is necessary to restore American competitiveness. We don't agree. It doesn't work well, and it has net negative results.

For one thing, the massive decline in the dollar has not provided much in the way of what was hoped for—a substantial reduction of imports, a large increase in exports, or a rise in capital investment. It has had some impact, helping some industries and hurting others, but nothing like what was hoped for. It is nearing three years since the dollar was at its peak, and it is close to where the exchange rate, in real terms, was in 1981, when the United States had a small current account surplus.

Though the trade deficit is declining slowly, it continues at a high level for several reasons. Foreign competitors sacrifice to hold onto market share, hunker down to greater productivity, live off accumulated profits of earlier years, and build plants abroad. Also, purchases are not made on price alone. A cheaper dollar does not stop Americans from buying foreign products, if they like the design, quality, reliability, and after-sales service of foreign goods.

But besides not working well, driving the dollar down poses risks of renewed inflationary pressures, undermines confidence in the future stability of the United States, reduces what a dollar buys in world markets, and puts American assets on sale at bargain prices, like lowering the price of common stock in America, Inc.

But worst of all, it makes the United States compete on the basis of a lower standard of living. Devaluation keeps knocking the dollar down and down until American wages are cheap enough to compete. That means lowering living standards relative to foreigners and perhaps in absolute terms. The shift in the exchange rates, over the long haul, only recognizes or ratifies the lack of productivity growth—it is the productivity changes that are fundamental for competitiveness, not the exchange rates.

Successive waves of devaluation are likely to follow the first, because fundamental causes are not being worked on. It encourages the perception that things are getting better when the reverse is true. Politicians become "economic hypochondriacs," as Charles Kindelberger describes them, focusing almost obsessively on terms of trade instead of adjustment. Vigorous, growing economies, he points out, can take shifts in competitiveness in stride: price changes and wage rate changes are signals to adjust. To rigid, aged economies, they are signals to protect.

Weak currency strategies didn't help the competitiveness of the British, who tried them at various points in their history, including as late as the 1970s. Dollar devaluation, as a national competitiveness strategy, will cause the United States to become like England, exporting cheap labor and sacrificing living standards as a way to remain competitive.

The futility of trying to restore competitiveness through currency devaluation appears all through economic history. "Economic history," said Paul Volcker, "is littered with examples of countries that acted as if currency depreciation alone could substitute for other actions to restore balance and competitiveness to their economies."

Dollar devaluation make the United States progressively poorer, a losing battle for a nation that wants to continue to be a leader.

4. DO NOT OVEREMPHASIZE CAPITAL INVESTMENT

One of the most popular recommendations by economists, businessmen, and politicians is for governmental policy to help "increase investment." That sounds so unquestionably "good" that many people have come to believe it is the principal route to salvage American competitiveness.

We do not think so.

Quickly, we *stress* that capital investment is not only important for productivity improvement, it is essential. What we argue against is the *overemphasis* and *wrong emphasis* on capital investment.

First, reduced capital investment was not the principal cause of U.S. productivity growth or of its slowdown, and "more" investment does not automatically increase productivity.

U.S. productivity growth *declined* at the same time that capital investment generally remained at a high level. Investment in plant and equipment rose from 9.4 percent of GNP in 1948–65, to 10.5 percent in 1965–78, and was 10.1 percent between 1978 and 1986. As the 1987 Economic Report of the President pointed out, "Business fixed investment set records as a share of real GNP in 1984 and 1985 and remains high by historical standards."

Nor is the direction of causality clear between capital investment and productivity. Though there is a correlation between the two, capital investment may well be the *result* of growth rather than its source. In other words, improved productivity may attract more investment, not the other way around.

Second, when advocates call for "increased investment," they typically mean investment in physical, tangible fixed assets. No question that equipment and structure are important, but this almost total focus on "hard" investment by managers, accountants, and tax codes has led to the relative neglect of investment in the "soft" side of investment—human capital—which is equally or more important for productivity improvement.

Fourth, merely calling for "more" capital investment confuses the volume of capital investment with the productivity of that investment. Expenditures for whatever purpose do not become productive merely by labeling them investment. Often what is needed is not more but *less*.

As we pointed out in Chapter 11 on operating systems, many managers (and economists) are still rooted in concepts inherited from the Industrial Revolution: long production runs, greater volume, bigger factories, more automation. Hence, they believe, if we invest more, we get more.

The Japanese have shown that just the *opposite* can be more productive: investing less results in small batches, small inventories, economies of scope. H. Ross Perot expressed it well: "Our solution is to go out and buy new uniforms. The team looks good, but they still can't play."

Anyone who concludes from reading this that we are saying investment is unimportant has totally missed our point. Investment is critically important. In fact, the Japanese invest more as a percentage of GNP than Americans do. What we are urging is that simply more and more alone is not automatically better, as General Motors sadly found out.

What Hideo Suguera, executive vice president of Honda Motors, said years ago about Detroit could apply equally well to the nation:

> The amount of money they are spending doesn't bother me—capital investment alone will not make the difference. . . . When De-

troit changes its management system, we'll see more powerful competitors.

5. "MORE" R&D IS NOT NECESSARILY BETTER

Much of what was said about capital investment also applies to R&D. Merely increasing the quantity of R&D will not necessarily improve U.S. competitiveness.

The United States is spending more in total dollars on R&D—about $120 billion—than any other nation in the world. However, as a percent of GNP, other nations are equal or very close. In 1986, Japan equaled the United States at 2.8 percent, West Germany at 2.7 percent, and France about 2.4 percent.

The biggest competitive problem, however, is not the *amount* spent on R&D, but on what it is spent, and what is done with the ideas and techniques after discovery.

The United States is still the world leader in originating new ideas. While that is great for the good of the world, what counts in competitiveness is rapid commercialization of new knowledge. And on that score, other nations are copying U.S. ideas, improving them, manufacturing them rapidly at low cost and high quality, and beating the socks off the United States.

The United States shouldn't be indignant about this, for America did the same thing to England in the nineteenth century. England invented during the Industrial Revolution; America copied and manufactured. In the twentieth century, the British continued to lead the world in innovation, even as they were declining in world competitiveness. At the end of World War II, Churchill said in his victory broadcast, "Mark you, our scientists are not surpassed by any nation in the world." British inventiveness continues even today: Cambridge's Cavendish Laboratory alone has produced more than eighty Nobel prize-winners and Britain has won twice as many Nobel Prizes in science per capita as the United States.

With all that, England has remained the least competitive of major developed nations. "When a country falls behind in competitiveness, the last thing they fall behind in is innovation," Harvey Brooks of Harvard University has said. "The first thing is manufacturing and marketing."

That's even more true in the global economy, where widespread technological sophistication and rapid communication cause the comparative advantages between advanced nations to lie less in origination of ideas and more in rapid application. Scientific leadership is no assurance of productivity leadership. The competitiveness edge goes to those who can quickly translate and blend manufacturing with R&D, can develop superior manufacturing methods with involved work teams that make constant adjustments to lower cost and improve quality, and can get to market fast.

One indicator of this focus is that Japan graduates about 70,000 engineers annually, twice the number of the United States on a per capita basis. At the doctorate level, the United States granted as many degrees in psychology as engineering in 1984, leading one of our friends to remark, "We're trying harder to understand what is happening to us, while the Japanese are making it happen."

Some of the problem is that the United States spends about nearly one-third of its R&D on military, space, and basic research—far more than Japan or West Germany. If those are subtracted out, the United States spends only about 1.9 percent of its GNP on civilian R&D, while West Germany spends 2.6 percent and Japan 2.8 percent. Projects with big government funding often have small commercial prospects, whereas commercial application is more likely if it is done and paid for by industry, as it is by our strongest competitors. More U.S. funding of R&D should go to applied R&D.

But that is only part of the problem. U.S. industry has to share a large portion of the blame. U.S. firms are not scouring the world for new ideas in other nations, investing in research with long-term payoffs, or moving from R&D to full production rapidly. The U.S. Defense Science Board, for example, found in its November 1986 report on the Japanese and United States semiconductor industries that "Japanese industry has also, in percentage figures, consistently outspent U.S. industry in Research and Development." It went on to report that Japanese R&D was investing in technology development with a long-term payoff, while American semiconductor firms invested in the design and development of new products with "little direct basis for long-term growth."

No matter how much money is spent on R&D in the United States, it will never improve competitiveness if American firms do not lengthen their investment horizons or adjust their operating systems to convert knowledge into manufacturing with low cost and high quality—and rapidly.

We do suggest more research funds should be spent on a relatively neglected side of technology—"social technology"—the integration of people and organizations with technology. Only 3 percent of federal research funds awarded to institutions by field of science in 1984 were to social sciences, a paltry sum when measured against funding for "hard" sciences.

Simply "more" funding for R&D, then, is not the answer. The Stanford economist Nathan Rosenberg is right when he says, "A first-rate, domestic scientific research capability is neither sufficient, nor even necessary for economic growth." If the private sector cannot convert ideas rapidly to commercialization at low cost and high quality, adding more government dollars directly or indirectly through tax breaks and subsidies will make no difference. If water pours off a duck's back, simply increasing the quantity of water does no good.

SUMMARY

Our list of what the government should *not* do could take up the remainder of this book, for the recommendations are still pouring forth. It is a frightening thought that the 99th Congress had 108 committees and sub-committees in the Senate and 178 in the House, together employing more than 3,000 staff members, all feeling that they must "do something" to help American competitiveness. It keeps us awake at night.

Our view of the limited role for government in increasing American competitiveness is not based on a blind ideological faith in any economic doctrine. If we thought greater government intervention would help, we would recommend a full-blown "action agenda."

We do not.

That does not mean we believe government has *no* role. In the next chapter, we suggest eight things we believe government *should* do.

—22—

What Government Should Do

We recommend eight things that government should do to help improve productivity and competitiveness.

1. EDUCATION

The United States has a glaring and serious competitive weakness: education.

The national focus is on the trade deficit and the budget deficit. But what is much more dangerous is the third deficit: the educational deficit. If Americans do not improve their educational system, there is no way the United States can maintain its economic leadership.

Because we feel education is so important, we devote the entire next chapter to what this nation must do. The prime responsibilities are with the school systems, state and local communities, parents, and business, but there are a few things the federal government can do to assist.

2. INSERT PRODUCTIVITY IN PUBLIC POLICY

The impact of proposed government policy actions on American productivity should be more explicitly considered than it is now. Some officials will protest that they do consider that, but our experience does not bear them out.

In policy discussions about taxes, environmental controls, export controls, protection, inflation, subsidies, and international competitiveness, productivity rarely gets *explicitly* introduced, for three principal reasons.

First, most government officials don't find productivity a very sexy, headline-grabbing topic, nor do they find it an appealing political issue. It is much more fascinating, glamorous, and newsworthy to deal with foreign policy, social issues, and issues of equity and justice, not productivity. Also, politicians worry that if they push productivity, many voters will think they are advocating speed ups, job loss, or greater profits for business.

Second, most government officials aren't comfortable talking at length about productivity except in the most general, "motherhood" sense. They feel it is an economist's province, and they don't understand all their models and arcane language. So they defer to the economists to take care of productivity. And that is where we have the third problem.

Economic public policy-making is too heavily dominated by economists. It sounds odd, we realize, but we believe that is a mistake.

The widely held view is that economists are the only ones who understand how the economy functions. Accordingly, economists dominate economic policy-making (and discussions of productivity) through the CEA (Council of Economic Advisers), the CBO (Congressional Budget Office), and the economists scattered throughout government agencies as decision-makers and staff advisers.

Economists are bright people. But the view most economists, especially in government, hold toward productivity is almost totally a "macroeconomic" view. Their typical remedy for a sluggish economy and slow productivity growth is to alter macroeconomic variables like like demand management, monetary policy, and savings and investment policies. They consider it out of bounds to look inside firms for problems, for in conventional economic theory good firms and managers drive out bad. The economy, therefore, on average always has efficient institutions, managers, and investments.

That is a useful theoretical tool for economic models, and macroeconomic variables do influence the economy. But what influences productivity most over the long run is inside firms. How managers, employees, and union leaders behave and interact is central to productivity improvement, and that involves more than macroeconomics. It involves not only economics, but also other social sciences—psychology, sociology, political science, philosophy—along with business management and engineering. Economics is only one input.

We do not suggest abandoning inputs from economists, for they contribute a lot to our understanding of how the economy works. Their inputs are needed. But that's not all the input we need in economic policy. Economic problems are partly social, partly technical, partly political, yet formal inputs are sought from only one discipline: economics, and macroeconomics at that. Our suggestion, obviously a heretical one to economists, is to expand the membership of the CEA and CBO to *include members from other social sciences as well as practitioners.*

Specifically, we recommend expanding the Council of Economic Advisers to seven (same as Federal Reserve Board) to include an additional three members from other disciplines, say, political science, psychology, and sociology, and one manager. We would also recommend the addition of similar disciplines and practitioners to the Congressional Budget Office staff.

We recognize the unorthodoxy of this suggestion and expect resistance from those who think only economists are "experts" on the economy. But the economy is too important for advice on the economy to be left solely in the hands of economists.

3. PRIVATIZE MORE GOVERNMENT SERVICES

Privatization is a return of government-owned or government-regulated enterprises to competition in the private sector. The reasons are simple: to save money and improve services.

It is a growing trend and should be continued. The federal government has been slow to join it. State and local governments have been at it for years. In fact there is *hardly a city service that not been sold or contracted out somewhere in the United States.*

- Scottsdale, Arizona, contracts for its fire protection at half the cost of government-run fire departments in other cities.

- La Mirada, California, contracts out more than sixty city services and has only fifty-five of its own employees.
- 35 percent of all local governments contract for residential garbage collection; 44 percent for commercial trash collection.

Other communities contract for police protection, jails, waste water treatment, hospitals, and many others. Most report lower costs and better services to the public.

The federal government has already totally or partially privatized or deregulated airlines, railroads, banking, and trucking. It should continue and expand the list to wholesale electric power, moviemaking, postal service, social service centers, hospitals, the naval petroleum reserve, federal crop insurance, among others.

The trend is worldwide. Britain, Japan, Mexico, Italy, France, Brazil, India, and many other countries are following a similar course, albeit very slowly. The International Monetary Fund (IMF) estimated in 1987 that of 1,000 attempts to privatize state-run operations around the world, only 150 have been successful. Politicians hate to give up power and control, especially over jobs. Yet the record is clear that in almost every situation the government can never be as efficient or effective as the private sector.

Privatization will help reduce debt levels, reduce the role of government in economies, and improve national as well as worldwide productivity. Not *every* government service can be privatized, but many more can. The private sector can generally provide the product or service cheaper and better, and can adjust more rapidly to fast-changing technology and market shifts.

4. REFORM ANTITRUST

U.S. antitrust laws and procedures are designed for a world that no longer exists. The whole context of competition has changed in the global economy:

- U.S. firms defined as "large" under U.S. tests of concentration may be tiny compared to global competitors.
- Joint production agreements are legal between GM and Toyota, but not between Ford and GM.
- New entrants from unrelated industries change rigid definitions of competition: U.S. Steel acquired an oil business, Goodyear Tire entered the gas pipeline business, and Sears entered the brokerage business.

U.S. antitrust laws should be changed to recognize that (1) the global economy now exists, and (2) industry definitions and operating systems are radically different, and (3) some cooperative arrangements among firms (e.g., R&D and manufacturing) need not always be uncompetitive.

Relaxing antitrust somewhat does not necessarily lessen competition, nor is it anticonsumer. We firmly believe competition is the greatest force for change. But "competition" is now global. U.S. antitrust laws should reflect that indisputable and inevitable fact.

5. IMPROVE STATISTICS

No nation has a better statistical system than the United States.

However, the data base needs to be expanded and revised to keep up with the rapidly changing shifts in the United States and the global economy.

While everyone acknowledges the importance of data for decision-making, funding statistics get low priority in the federal budget. They are grudgingly allocated, always in small increments and within traditional fields. In addition, budget cuts in recent years have impaired the overall effort. Changes are needed in four areas.

Productivity

The U.S. Bureau of Labor Statistics (BLS) does a good job in publishing productivity statistics, better than any other nation. Still, improvements are needed in:

- Data on services sector productivity
- Measurements of quality of product and quality of services
- Industry productivity data
- International productivity *level* comparisons

Foreign Data: Monitoring and Translation

The United States must increase the monitoring and translation of foreign technical data. The NTIS (National Technical Information Service) does collect some foreign information, but a GAO report found "a virtual dearth of information in the United States on foreign developments.

Foreign publications and research works on manufacturing technology were not routinely scanned, translated, or published in the U.S."

Foreign nations, especially Japan, are producing vast quantities of scientific and engineering knowledge that the United States knows little about. Japan learns from the United States, but the United States doesn't make an effort to learn from Japan. About 10,000 technical journals are published annually in Japan, and only about 20 percent are available in English.

Only about 5 percent of the engineers and scientists in the United States have foreign translation skills, and an even smaller number read Japanese. In addition, because the United States has neglected languages in its educational system, there is a lack of qualified translators in the United States.

Japan has about five thousand scientists and engineers regularly processing thousands of foreign journals and technical reports. All Japanese firms have technical people in the United States to gather information. Japanese tell us, "We subscribe to your journals. Few Americans subscribe to ours."

Japanese firms were asked in a 1985 Japanese survey: "What are your motives for overseas expansion?" The number 1 reason was expansion of markets. But the second item named as most important was *"collection of technological and corporate information."*

Funds for monitoring and translation should be expanded at the governmental level, but the primary responsibility to keep up rests with private firms.

Trade

Statistics about U.S. trade are generally good, except for two areas that need improvement:

- International trade in services is expanding rapidly, but data are lagging in accuracy and scope.
- "Intrafirm trade" statistics are poor—that is, trade between U.S. parents and foreign affiliates.

Standard Industrial Classification (SIC)

The SIC is out of date and needs a major overhaul.

The classification system underlies all establishment-based federal statistics and determine the input–output tables for measuring GNP. Though the economy has drastically changed, the code has lagged. The existing classification system is too heavily skewed toward the goods-producing sector and does not adequately reflect the shift in the economy toward services.

Some revisions were made in 1986, but they were not sufficient. A major reclassification is needed, using new computer technology.

6. IMPROVE PRODUCTIVITY IN GOVERNMENT

Government, like all organizations in the United States, must constantly seek to improve its own productivity and quality.

However, it is unfair to presume, as some do, that government has little or no productivity. Government workers are unfairly stereotyped as lazy, incompetent, and inefficient. To the contrary, the BLS estimated that from 1967 to 1983, federal employees' productivity rose at an annual rate of 1.5 percent, as against 1.4 percent growth in private concerns.

Efforts to improve *are* under way at the federal, state, and city levels. The federal government launched a productivity improvement program in 1986. However, the effort is underfunded, not given high priority, and suffers from the same constraints handicapping all government efforts to improve productivity: political interference, limitations on capital investment, personnel and organizational systems that demotivate, overregulation of efforts, procurement regulations, budget planning, and work environment.

Also, encouraging productivity efforts exist in entire cities, such as Phoenix, and in departments like the New York City Department of Sanitation.

It must be recognized that governments cannot be completely "businesslike," for they must operate under constraints of equity, due process, accountability, and legitimacy. Within those constraints, however, much can be done to improve productivity.

7. USE RHETORIC

Some dismiss rhetoric as "smoke," "hot air," or useless "speechmaking." That's a mistake. Rhetoric can move men's souls—and nations.

We live in a democracy, and in the end public opinion and the ballot box determine the direction of the nation. All of us (including the authors) forget sometimes that when we complain about something "Congress" or the "White House" does that we don't like, the anger should be directed not at the politicians, but at the body politic of the American people. Members of Congress vote what the American people demand, or they wouldn't be elected and reelected.

The so-called failed political will of politicians is not quite accurate; it really is a lack of consensus on the part of the American people as to what should be done. Rhetoric is important in helping to inform people as well as in leading them in directions that truly increase competitiveness—creating a demand for those solutions.

8. CUT THE BUDGET DEFICIT

The United States is in a deadly economic gridlock. The President does not want to increase taxes, Congress does not seem able to reduce spending by much, productivity growth is slow, Americans do not want their consumption to drop, savings are inadequate. The result: continuing high federal budget deficits and overseas borrowing. It can't go on forever. And, as Herbert Stein is often fond of saying, something that can't go on forever won't.

One place to start is to reduce the federal budget by changing any one of the variables mentioned above or combinations of them. It isn't the budget deficit *per se* that is so bad. Japan also runs a large budget deficit. The difference is that Japan's high savings rate is more than sufficient to finance both its deficit and its investment. That's not true in the United States. The United States undersaves and overconsumes relative to what it earns. This nation cannot go on trying to maintain its standard of living growth when it is not earning it.

When Congressmen, Senators, and White House officials ask "What should this nation do?" to restore American productivity and competitiveness, they can start right in their own backyard: the federal budget. Savings rates are not likely to change significantly; the United States has never saved much compared to competitors. Investment could be cut, but not by much if productivity is to increase. Consumption could be cut, but significant amounts might generate a recession. Taxes might be increased some, but too much would depress the economy. Growth through productivity is an attractive route, but high growth for some years to come is not likely.

Our view is that the best way to begin the process is to reduce federal spending. Cuts must be made across the board: in defense, Social Security, Medicare, all entitlements, and the budgets of Washington staffs and expenses. Some of the other factors can be worked on, but the quickest and surest way for now is reduced spending by the federal government.

The fault line ostensibly runs right down Pennsylvania Avenue from Congress to the White House, but the real fault line runs from Bangor to Bakersfield, from Olympia to Orlando. It is the American people who must reduce the federal budget deficit.

Summary

Notice that our list of recommendations for government action is modest alongside the many large-scale government efforts others recommend. The reason is very simple. Most actions have to take place in the private sector.

We think most recommendations that are flying around for government action would be ineffective, would waste funds, and/or would interfere with necessary adjustment. We selected these eight items because we believe they are likely to be of most use.

One of the areas where government can perform a most important task, however, is one the federal government can do the least about— education—the subject of the next chapter.

—23—
Education

Japan's greatest long-term comparative advantage is not its management system, Japan, Inc., or quality.

It is the Japanese commitment to learning.

The Japanese have the most complete, effective, and demanding system of elementary and secondary education in the world. Nor is learning confined to schools. The Japanese emphasize learning from birth to death—at home, in school, at work, and in their daily lives. There is a national consensus on the importance of learning.

In addition, the emphasis on learning is not just for an elite few but for the entire population: As Thomas Rohlen points out:

> The profoundly impressive fact is that [Japan] is shaping a whole population, workers as well as managers, to a standard inconceivable in the United States, where we are still trying to implement high school graduation competency tests that measure only minimal reading and computing skills.

EDUCATIONAL DIMENSIONS

One way to demonstrate the difference in commitment to learning between the two nations is to compare them on five dimensions. The rankings are our own; they are based on years of personal experience and observations of education and training in school systems and businesses:

	Japan Leads	*United States Leads*
Parents and the home	x	
Elementary and secondary education	x	
Higher education		x
Education in business	x	
Education in daily life	x	

Only in higher education does the United States clearly lead.

In fact, the United States is so far ahead in higher education that it attracts a heavy traffic of foreign students. In 1985, 60 percent of all U.S. doctoral engineering degrees were awarded to foreign students. More than 30 percent of full-time engineering and science students at U.S. universities are from abroad, and 23 percent of MIT's student body are foreign nationals.

In all other dimensions, the United States lags in comparison with Japan. It didn't happen overnight.

AMERICAN EDUCATION

Hidden by America's vibrant growth of the Golden 1950s and 1960s was a deteriorating educational system.

First came the beeping of Sputnik, spotlighting the shortage of scientific and engineering skills. Then there was the downward trend in SAT scores.

Startling figures on "functional illiteracy" followed. Exact numbers are debated, but anywhere from 20 to 30 percent of American adults can't function well in a literate society.

The most shocking indictments have come in the past four years in a flurry of reports on deficiencies in the United States educational system, particularly at the elementary and secondary school level: superficial knowledge in many subject areas, especially mathematics, science, and languages; low teacher pay; inadequate teacher skills; high dropout rates; poor reading and writing skills of graduates; and relatively low training investment by American firms. In just about all those indicators the United States is being outdone by foreign competitors. The system is tending, as Barnett said of the English educational system, to become an "education for industrial decline."

Education and Competitiveness

Education is directly linked to competitiveness.

No society can have high-quality outputs without high-quality inputs. Education provides "human capital" to combine with "physical capital" for increased productivity and quality.

That has always been true, but it is even more true in a global technological economy. A competitive nation needs people who have:

- A high degree of average functional literacy
- Some basic competency with mathematics, statistics, and the scientific method
- The ability to observe processes, analyze, interpret, and take action
- A knowledge of the world
- The ability to work together in teams
- The ability to accept responsibility
- The ability to learn continously and adjust to change

Note that the list does not include just "math, science, and engineering," which is the current national push in education. It also includes basic literacy (reading, writing, communication), interpersonal and attitudional skills, and a knowledge of the world (geography, history, economics, language).

In most of those areas, the United States is coming up short: The educational system is not producing a well-educated citizenry or a well-trained workforce.

"We are in a life and death struggle with the Japanese," one electronics industry corporate executive said. "We try to employ high school graduates in our semiconductor plant, but they can't read or write. They don't understand simple graphs, and all too often they can't add, subtract, or multiply numbers." Al Warren of General Motors reported, "It was an awful shock when we assessed the workforce in one of our plants and found that 87 percent of our employees were incapable of doing work beyond the fifth grade and 2 percent were functionally illiterate."

Businessmen are partly to blame, given their belief that managers think and plan whereas "workers" do what they are told. Management accordingly hasn't demanded better-educated employees and hasn't rewarded them or given them responsibility. Business got what it asked for.

The United States is educating very well a bright elite, but not a high *average* level of citizens. The United States wins more Nobels and makes more breakthroughs in science. It has some of the best, most talented, and highest-priced engineers and scientists in the world and a large pool of business school–trained managers. But the best education is available only to a relatively small percentage of United States society.

The result is a narrow pool of U.S. talent, not the deep and wide base, as there is in Japan, of skilled technicians, machine operators, supervisors, and service people who can write computer programs; follow blueprints and technical manuals; build, maintain, and troubleshoot their own equipment; interpret statistics for quality control; work well in teams; and learn as they go. Those skills are needed not by just a small elite but by most of the workforce. The United States relies on using engineers for such technical work (often in isolated offices), whereas even the *average* worker on the factory floor in Japan can understand graphs, charts, and statistics, and can work with some mathematical notation. When Mitsubishi opened a plant in North Carolina, George Gilder pointed out, it had to use graduate students for the statistical quality control done by average line workers in Japan.

In an industry study by Professor Ramchandran Jaikumar of the Harvard Business School comparing U.S. and Japanese factories, more than 40 percent of the Japanese workforce was made up of engineers who had been trained in computer numerically controlled (CNC) machines. In similar U.S. companies only 8 percent of the employees were engineers, and less than 25 percent had been trained on CNC machines. Thurow could be right: A "society where everyone reads and writes will beat a society where most are illiterates and a few are geniuses."

Another problem of the U.S. educational system is that it is not graduating most students with attitudes or skills that make them motivated and disciplined toward work or able to work well with others. Most of the U.S. focus is on developing "cognitive" skills (thinking, reasoning, content) and much less on noncognitive or "affective" skills (attitude, interpersonal skills, diligence, flexibility, determination, self-discipline, responsibility). An effective citizen or employee needs both.

In summary, the U.S. educational system is not preparing the country's students adequately, not only as educated citizens for a richer life, but also, in comparison with competitive nations, for work. The next few pages examines some aspects of the Japanese educational system that prepares citizens well for global competitiveness.

The United States needs to understand what it is up against.

JAPANESE EDUCATION: CRADLE TO GRAVE

Parents

One of the founders of Sony, Ibuka, is a fanatic about education. In his book *Kindergarten Is Too Late,* he emphasizes that learning should begin at birth and continue until death.

Japanese parents try to make sure that happens. Parents consider it a "sacred duty" to provide the best possible education for their children, beginning first in the home environment and then starting them very early in the school system.

About 63 percent of Japanese preschool children attend nursery school (in the United States 32 percent). About 80 percent of all four-year-olds and more than 90 percent of five-year-olds attend kindergarten.

Primary and Secondary Schools

They need this preparation to be ready for the Japanese elementary and secondary system, which is *the most intensive, demanding, and successful system of mass education in the world.*[*]

---

[*] We highly recommend two books in the "Readings" at the end of the book—the books by Rohlen and White—as "must" reading for those wanting to know more about Japanese elementary and secondary education.

	U.S.	Japan
Days/week	5	5½
Days/year	180	240
Weeks/year	36	44
Avg. homework/day	30 minutes	2 hours

Japanese students spend much more time in school and do more homework than do Americans, as the table shows. The Japanese student attends school on Saturday morning (Friday night is a school night), and some stay up to nine hours a day at school. Japanese students go to school 240 days a year; Americans 180.

Japanese students serve themselves their own food, eat in classrooms, and clean the school themselves—there are no janitors in Japanese schools, so there is also a minimum of graffiti.

Teaching is considered a sacred profession, and teachers are more highly paid than in the United States: By law their salaries must be in the upper one-fourth of national incomes. The average teacher's salary in Japan in 1983–84 was 2.4 times the country's per capita income, while the average American teacher's was 1.7 times per capita U.S. income. Japanese first-year teachers are paid more than starting engineers, businessmen, and pharmacists.

In addition to their heavy school schedule, about one-third of all primary school students and one-half of all secondary school students attend *juku* schools for *supplementary* learning. *Juku* schools are not for slow learners, mind you, but mostly for those who are already doing well. Why? To do *better*.

Math, Science, and Language

Japanese schools stress math, science, and languages. Foreign language teaching begins in the seventh grade. Most Japanese students select English, and by the time they finish, most will have studied two languages. The Japanese are generally required to study foreign languages for six years; Americans for two years—if at all.

The Japanese Ministry of Education requires that 25 percent of classroom time in lower secondary schools be devoted to science and mathematics, much more than in U.S. schools.

In Japanese secondary education, most students take three natural science courses and four mathematics courses, including differential calculus. In the United States only one-third of school districts require more than one year each of math and science. International tests of educational achievement show that in both math and science the mean scores of Japanese children are consistently higher than any other nation's.

The demanding curriculum is not for a few honor students (there is no "tracking" for the first nine years in Japanese schools), it is for all. Thomas Rohlen's research shows that what would be considered a superior level of learning of, say, the top 10 percent of the students in the United States or Europe is what is experienced by the majority of academic high school students in Japan:

> The great accomplishment of Japanese primary and secondary education lies not in its creation of a brilliant elite (Western industrial nations do better with their top students), but in its generation of such a high *average* level of capability [emphasis added].

Socialization

One less well understood, but very important, aspect of Japanese education is the socialization process for Japanese life and work, which occurs simultaneously with the cognitive side.

Children are trained at an early age to contribute to and enjoy the benefits of cooperation. They develop habits and positive attitudes toward hard work, discipline, perseverance, orderliness, cleanliness, attention to detail, and importance of effort. They develop interpersonal skills to be able to work in groups, and they are repeatedly told of the importance of education.

Those socialization factors, combined with the cognitive skills, are powerful forces for an educated citizenry and a dedicated, educated workforce.

Japanese Stereotypes

Many Westerners entertain the mistaken and dangerous assumption that Japanese education is only rote memorization and permits no individual thinking. Wrong.

Of course there is rote learning in Japan, just as there is in the United States. But researchers have also found that they also "excel by even greater margins . . . in test subscores tapping understanding, application, and higher processes of science such as hypothesis formulation.''

Another stereotyped view is that Japanese educational success is obtained at the high price of an inhuman regime of forced-march study, with students sitting passively at their desks like automata. Merry White of Harvard's Graduate School of Education, who has studied Japanese schools in depth, explodes that view:

> An American teacher walking into a fourth grade science class in Japan would be horrified: children all talking at once, leaping and calling for the teacher's attention. The typical American's response is to wonder, ''who's in control of this room?'' But if one understands the content of the lively chatter, it is clear that all the noise and movement is focused on the work itself—children are shouting out answers, suggesting other methods, exclaiming in excitement over results.

Americans also hold a common belief that educational pressure causes more youth suicides in Japan than in any other nation. Not so. The 1984 Japanese youth suicide rate for 15–20-year-olds was lower in Japan than in the United States—12.5 per 100,000 in the United States; in Japan 10.8 per 100,000. Also, the suicide rate in Japan dropped 43 percent from 1975 to 1984, while in the United States it rose 17 percent.

The Japanese system *is* definitely a pressure cooker, but children are hardly conformists or unhappy learners. In an international study of twelve nations, Japanese children had both the greatest love of schooling and the highest level of academic achievement.

High School Graduates

In Japan only 10 percent of high school students drop out. In the United States, 26 percent do.

Because of the longer school year, the average graduate of a Japanese high school has the equivalent of four more years of school. In the opinion of some researchers, the Japanese high school graduate has *an education that is roughly equivalent to the average college education in the United States.*

That's the workforce the United States is competing with.

University

Of the Japanese high school graduates, about 35 percent go on to college, as against about 50 percent in the United States.

In the university, the pace is much slower.

The typical four-year Japanese students, except those in professional and scientific-engineering areas of study, spend four years at a more relaxed pace of study with much less rigor.

Continuous Learning

When a youth enters business or government, the learning process continues.

As we discussed in Chapter 17, education occurs not only in classes but in Japanese corporations' rotational system, in quality circles, in team problem-solving, and in trips abroad. As Lawrence and Dyer point out, "Their organizations are learning and social systems as well as production system."

The Japanese send employees to schools all over the world. They send staff members to the Harvard Kennedy School of Government to study political and social trends in the United States. They send engineers to the United States for doctoral or advanced doctoral work. Trading companies become intelligence listening posts.

Learning permeates their daily lives.

In newspapers, the daily circulation in Japan in 1984 was 1.5 times that of the United States on a per capita basis. In new book titles, Japanese publishers turned out about 1.75 times the United States rate on a per capita basis—35,000 in Japan and 40,000 in the United States.

Those are further illustrations that learning in Japan is not just for an elite. Japan is one of the few places in the world, Frank Gibney has said, where you can find a "ditch digger relaxing from work at lunch break reading the local equivalent of the *New York Times*" or, as Scott Runkel personally observed, "an elevator operator reading *Paradise Lost*, a taxi driver interested in Matisse painting, a secretary who reads Stendhal."

Learning never stops.

The thirst for learning is not a recent phenomenon. In the Meiji period of the late nineteenth century, the government declared intellect and learning would be sought across the world. The Iwakura Mission of 1871 traveled for eighteen months across the world, studying educational systems, and the government allocated 30 percent of its education budget to importing faculty ("live machines") from other nations to teach them.

A National Commitment

We devoted this much space to the Japanese national commitment to learning because *we are convinced that many Americans overlook the depth and strength of the Japanese emphasis on learning, and its impact on productivity and quality.*

Most explanations of Japanese success focus on high savings rates, importation of technology, lifetime employment, government–business cooperation, and enterprise unions. All those have had an impact, but the most important single factor is none of them—it is the Japanese people's effective, pervasive, and lasting commitment to learning.

What can the United States do?

If the United States is to match a nation that puts such a premium on learning, it too must become once again a nation that puts high priority on education—in the home, in schools, in firms, and in daily life.

Despite the attention we have given to the Japanese educational system, we do not think it is perfect. The Japanese themselves are questioning some undesirable side effects. Rather, Americans should use the Japanese system as a mirror, and then decide what Americans should do. Our recommendations follow.

RECOMMENDATIONS

Educational change in the United States will not come quickly or easily. But change it must, if the United States is to remain competitive.

1. Parents

Education must begin in the home—a truism American parents often forget and neglect.

We can't emphasize enough the important role that parents play in helping to shape children's education. The parental push and involvement that Japanese parents universally give to education, especially the mother ("education mama"), occurs in only a few exceptional homes in the United States. It's not just setting students down to do homework and occasionally unplugging the TV but, more importantly, setting the climate for learning and personally engaging in their education:

- Reading to them and encouraging them to read on their own
- Asking questions, expressing interest, concern, and excitement about the children's education
- Taking educational trips with children, providing study facilities and supplies
- Pressing school officials and legislators for changes in education
- Attending school events

Too many U.S. parents want the schools to raise their children, to educate them, to discipline them, and to babysit. Yet they are the first to deplore it when "Johnny can't read."

Professor Harold Stevenson of University of Michigan found in a comparison of attitudes about education among United States, Japanese, and Taiwanese mothers that American mothers believed a child's performance in school was determined by *ability,* while Asian mothers ascribed success to *effort.* The Asian system, Stevenson concludes, as more likely to produce hard work than one which holds success to be the product of innate gifts.

2. Schools

At the school level the following changes should be made:

a. Lengthen the school year. At 180 days, there is no way that U.S. schools can match the educational achievements of Asian nations that go 240 days.

The United States should increase the school year to 240 days. Increasing it that much in the United States may seem an impossibility, given the American addiction to the "summer off" and calls for lighter teaching loads. But if Americans want to be competitive in the decades ahead, that is what they are going to have to do. It is not an impossibility, it is a matter of priorities.

The United States used to have a longer school year. In the early nineteenth century, Detroit schools had a 259-day school year, New York 235, and Philadelphia 251. It wasn't until the early twentieth century that schedules started shrinking.

Schools should also move from a six-hour day to a seven-hour day, from a five-day week to a five and a half days, and vacations interspersed throughout the year.

But increasing the school year alone is no guarantee that education will improve. Other changes need to be made.

b. Require the following as minimums for all high school gradu-ates:

- Mathematics   3 years
- Science   3 years
- Reading/writing   4 years of English
- Language   2 years
- History   2 years (1 American, 1 world)
- Geography   1/2 year
- Economics   1/2 year

c. Increase homework from the present average of one-half hour to one and a half hours. A 1986 study of writing in American schools found that 32 percent of the students either had no homework assigned or had it but did not do it. ''Time-at-task'' studies consistently show that homework leads not only to more knowledge but also to more retention.

d. Increase class size from the average twenty-three students to thirty-five. Most people incorrectly believe that the smaller the class, the better the education. After decades of research, *no relation* has been found betwen class size and higher pupil achievement. In Japan, the average class size is thirty-nine. In the United States, it is twenty-three. We recommend that the United States go to an average class size of thirty-five. Back in 1900, average class size in the United States was thirty-seven.

The Economist reported that the average fifteen-year-old Japanese is better educated in mathematics and most testable subjects than the top quarter of British sixteen-year-olds, with double the class size.

Larger classes and more homework would add to teachers' existing loads. But that can be handled. One of the main reasons American teachers are so burdened now is the high percentage of time spent in disciplinary action. In Japan, students spend about one-third more time during a typical class period engaged in learning, and the discipline is achieved without a strong direct exercise of authority by the teacher. Violence is fifty times more likely in American schools, Rohlen calculated, and an increase in discipline would limit the policing role.

Administrative duties are also heavy and time-consuming. Some of them could be dropped altogether, minimized, or altered with computers and different organizational procedures, just as business is having to restructure the way it manages. If absolutely necessary to get the idea of larger class sizes adopted, hire teacher's aides.

e. Reduce social activities and athletics in favor of academics. Reduce extracurricular activities. In an international study of fifth graders, Americans spent 65 percent of their school time on academic studies, Japanese 87 percent, and Chinese 92 percent.

f. Increase project learning, experimental learning, learning how to work in groups, and how to cooperate. Spend more time and methods developing important "noncognitive" attributes: self-discipline, perseverance, cooperativeness, competitiveness, reliability and integrity, habits of work, and priority-setting under pressure. None of those are easy to develop, but they are as important as cognitive areas, perhaps even more important, for responsible citizenship and productive employees.

3. State and Local Governments

Education is the Constitutional obligation not of the federal government but of the states. Of educational spending in 1984, states accounted for 48.7 percent, local communities 44.8 percent, and the federal government 6.5 percent.

Some states have moved vigorously in the past few years to improve education. They are addressing how schools are run, how teachers are trained and certified, curricula requirements, and standards. Many still have not changed or have introduced only minimal changes. We recommend that all states at least do the following:

- Set minimum curricula requirements and statewide standards.
- Strengthen teacher competency and certification tests at the entry level and with periodic testing. The United States will hire one-half of the next generation's teachers in the next six years.
- Fund and support efforts to improve the productivity of education— better-educated students for less funds.
- Raise teachers' salaries to about the average of business middle managers in the state. Pay, hire, and fire on the bases of performance, quality, and merit.

4. Productivity in Education

Education does *not* deserve every penny it can get.

There is no evidence that throwing large sums of money at education will solve the problem. Most of the changes suggested do not necessarily cost more money. Funds for increased salaries and extra teaching hours can be obtained from fewer school administrators, diminished extracurricular activities, fewer and better-used physical facilities, and larger class size. The cry will be that "quality" will suffer, but that does not have to occur here. It does not in Japan.

Japan spends about 5.7 percent of its GNP on education. The United States spends about 6.7 percent. Yet Japanese students consistently outperform Americans at the high school level. Americans have more administrators, smaller classes, and better school and athletic facilities. Japanese have better education.

Educators should be asked to increase productivity as every other economic sector should: more output per input, *including quality*. Improved quality can also mean reduced costs per unit. We are for increased salaries, but they must be matched by greater teacher productivity. We also recommend greater privatization in education for the same reasons we gave in Chapters 21 and 22—better service and product at a lower cost. The "voucher system" would be a way to accomplish that.

5. Federal Government

Education is primarily the states' responsibility, but the federal government can help in several ways:

• *Statistics:* The Department of Education was created by President Andrew Johnson in 1867 for the purpose of collecting educational statistics. Such data are still useful and should be given wider distribution. More longitudinal data are also needed to judge educational effectiveness.

• *Research.* The government should increase its existing research program on educational effectiveness and needs, and disseminate its results more widely. Most educational research of this nature is known only to a few, is in a deadly dull form, and is so awash in academic jargon that it is hard for people to understand or to use.

• *Student aid.* Continue aid to low-income and handicapped students. Continue student loans, but make the loan repayment contingent on income earned over the years.

• *Research.* Continue, perhaps expand, funding of research done by the NAEP (National Assessment of Educational Progress) and the NIE (National Institute of Education).

• *Illiteracy.* The federal government could help by funding a large, long-term program to reduce illiteracy by, say, 50 percent over the next two decades. Much of the money could be channeled to existing private sector organizations to implement literacy programs.

• *Dislocated workers.* Large-scale federal training programs for dislocated workers have not worked and are unlikely to. Two alternative ideas: *one,* allow jobless workers to take unemployment insurance in a lump sum to use for training; *two,* allow employees and employers to contribute tax-free to a training fund (an "individual training account") on which the employee may draw for retraining, job search, or relocation, and which goes to his individual retirement account if not used.

SUMMARY

The main difficulty with getting these changes implemented will be persuading faculty and administrators to initiate some of them, for they resist change as much as any group, perhaps more. And they always invoke "academic freedom" and "quality" to resist external pressure. Parents will be equally hard to change for a different reason: The majority do not want to spend more time with their children's education. Besides, only a few legislators are willing to take on the educational lobby to force radical change.

It seems almost impossible.

Still, we must try. The United States must make changes if it wishes to remain competitive. Education must become, as it is in Japan, a national obsession. The Japanese know their survival has always depended not on natural resources but on human resources. Schools, parents, and students all share the goal of educational excellence. Japanese educational strategy is tuned to an old Chinese proverb: "If you are planning for one year, grow rice; for twenty years, grow trees; for centuries, grow men."

The United States must recall that it once gave higher priority to education and that the "wealth of nations" is truly their human assets. Just as business must adjust its methods and style to fit a new world, so must education.

Of all the challenges facing the United States competitively, improving education ranks at the top. The United States will get the education it wants and gives priority to.

—*Part VI*—
The Competition

—24—
Economic Tectonics

Plate tectonics is the study of the ebb and flow of continents and the forces that affect them—a continuous process of creation and destruction of land masses.

Similarly, forces are at work to produce major changes in world economies, a process we call "economic tectonics."

About 150 million years ago, land on earth was a single solid continent called Pangyrea. It was torn asunder by the flow of physical forces, forming huge land masses that drifted apart like floating rafts on plates, slamming into one another, destroying coastlines, triggering earthquakes. In the process, new continents, volcanos, islands, and mountain ranges were created, a process of destruction and creation still going on today.

We see a like process at work in the rise of the global economy. Enormous advances in transportation and communication, plus widespread education, are collapsing time and geography and redistributing technology at a rapid rate. The results are reshaping international competition, entire industries, notions of comparative advantage, and even the concept of national economies—a destructive–creative process of "economic tectonics."

Instead of breaking apart like the continents, however, economies are flowing together—imploding—becoming more integrated, interrelated, and interdependent. While the world has not yet become Marshall McLuhan's global village, the first outlines of the competitive characteristics of the new global economy are becoming apparent:

1. *Global production:* products made almost anywhere in the world in factories that "float" with shifting economics and technologies
2. *Technology:* technology no longer the monopoly of advanced nations; technology transfer rapid and widespread; copying, improving, and applying equal in value to inventing
3. *Comparative advantage:* dynamic and man-made, not static and fixed by nature; natural-resource-poor nations able to become strong international competitors
4. *Human capital:* the greatest value-added source, not physical capital or natural resources
5. *Financial:* incredible financial power coming from the Orient, especially Japan, the financial powerhouse of the twenty-first century
6. *Flexibility:* a premium on rapid adaptation, not specialized skills
7. *Protection:* increased danger of world trade barriers and retaliatory trade wars
8. *Quality:* ever more important, especially in service- and information-oriented economies
9. *Arbitrage:* jobs and factories moving across nations to obtain lowest costs, highest productivity and quality
10. *Commoditization:* declining importance of traditional commodities; quick commoditization of technological advancements
11. *Pacific Basin:* the economic center of the world in the twenty-first century.
12. *New model:* a new Asian strain of "capitalism" that may prove superior to the U.S. version

As Dorothy in *The Wizard of Oz* said, "Toto, I don't think we're in Kansas any more."

She's right.

GLOBAL COMPETITION

You may as well try to stop the wind from blowing or the sun from setting as stop the global economy. The world is fast becoming a global farm, a global office, and a giant factory, with the sky as the roof and with manufacturing and ownership tangled like a bowl of spaghetti:

- GM's Kadett, manufactured by Opel AG, its West German subsidiary, is assembled by Daewoo of Korea and then exported to the United States. Daewoo imports the majority of the parts from Japan.
- Kodak buys video camera-recorders and videotape from Japan. Honeywell gets the brain for its computer from Japan. Apple makes its PC in Singapore.
- The Nova car is called American even though half of its parts are imported. One out of every four cars driven in the United States is foreign. Honda is now the fourth largest car maker in the United States and is even exporting to Taiwan from Ohio.
- At end of 1986, Japanese had 583 plants in the United States operated by 405 companies.
- Ford's Merkur is assembled in Germany, with an engine from Brazil.

Customers no longer know if brands are foreign, and most wouldn't care if they did know. "Buy America" slogans won't work well in the United States or in Japan. Price, quality, reliability, delivery, design, and after-sales service are what's most important to most consumers, not where it is made.

And it's not just manufacturing that will travel in the global economy. Money and ideas can move to any place on this planet in seconds. Service industries are already moving across national boundaries—advertising, banking, securities, hotels, construction—and more are on the way. Foreign exchange markets are woven together by telecommunications that scarcely acknowledge national boundaries.

The economic center of the world is no longer exclusively in the United States. Powerful challengers to U.S. industries come from all parts of the globe. Traditional competitors in Europe, especially Germany and France, continue to be aggressive. Nations like Brazil and Mexico are competitors in some industries, and there is even sporadic competition from some socialist nations, like Yugoslavia, which sold 35,000 Yugos in the United States in 1986. Automobiles are becoming, as Sir Donald MacDougall predicted in 1954, "the textiles of tomorrow."

But the real dynamic, long-term competitive forces are not coming from Europe or South America. They come from the Pacific Basin.

THE PACIFIC BASIN

The Pacific Basin will be the center of the global economy in the twenty-first century.

By then, six out of ten human beings on the planet will live in the Pacific Basin, and its total economic power will dwarf that of other regions of the world. Already the Pacific Basin is the most important trading region for the United States, and if United States trade grows at its current rate, by 1995 America's trade with the Pacific Basin will be double the size of its European trade. The Pacific Ocean will play the same role as the Mediterranean in ancient times and the Atlantic in modern times.

Fourteen nations are generally considered to be the dominant economic forces in the "Pacific Basin": the United States, Canada, Australia, New Zealand, and the ten nations that are referred to as the "Asian Pacific Rim." That last group are, in our opinion, the strongest new competitors in the global economy and the main challenge to continued U.S. world economic leadership.

The Congressional Research Service issues a lengthy report on the Asian Pacific Rim in August 1986:

- If there is a continuation of current trends, by the year 2000 the Asian Pacific economies will account for 25 percent of the world's production, and North America for a little less than 30 percent.
- It is possible that by the year 2000 Asian Pacific nations will have almost caught up to North America in combined income.
- If current trends continue, equity valuations traded in Far Eastern exchanges could exceed those traded on U.S. exchanges by 1991.

In the past twenty-five years, the unprecedented economic achievements of those nations have transformed the Asian Pacific Rim, leading some to predict that it will eclipse North America and Europe as the center of the global economy in the twenty-first century.

These nations are the focus of this section of the book. They can be roughly classified into four categories in terms of economic strength and competitiveness:

1. *Japan,* the only highly developed nation in the group, with a per capita income of around $17,000.
2. *Asian NICs*—South Korea, Taiwan, Singapore, Hong Kong—rapidly industrializing nations with per capita incomes from $2,000 to $7,400.
3. *ASEAN nations,* Philippines, Thailand, Indonesia, and Malaysia, with per capita incomes from $500 to $1,900 (Not included are New Guinea and Brunei).
4. *China,* more than 1 billion people with a per capita income of about $350.

It is clear that within that arena one nation—Japan—is the dominant competitor, the one with the greatest overall economic strength, the one with the greatest technological skills, the one that has outperformed all developed nations in productivity dramatically over the past three decades and on average for the past 115 years. The main race for world economic leadership is between the leader, the United States, and the challenger, Japan.

The CEO of a large electronics firm recently made a several-hours-long presentation to his board of directors on his five-year strategic plan. When asked by a board member what three things could most likely upset his plans, he answered unhesitatingly, "Japan. Japan. Japan."

JAPAN

Those Americans who have faced Japan in competition or have traveled to Japan are well aware of the Japanese competitiveness and strength. But not enough Americans are fully aware of the depth and magnitude of that challenge:

- Japan is now the second largest economy in the Free World. It produces about 10 percent of the world's GNP, predicted to reach 20 percent by the year 2000.
- Japan's long-term foreign assets at the end of 1986 totaled nearly $397 billion, higher than OPEC's peak holdings of $380 billion in 1983.
- By the turn of the century, Tokyo's financial market is likely to be as large as those of London and New York, and the Japanese yen will be one of the key currencies of the world.
- Nomura Securities is the world's largest securities firm, and it

alone is responsible for financing nearly one-third of the entire 1986 U.S. federal deficit.
- Japan is now the world's largest creditor nation, and if trends continue, Japan will become the largest creditor nation in history with a net creditor position of almost $1 trillion by 2000.
- Seven of the top ten banks in the world in terms of deposits are Japanese. (Only one is American). Japanese banks have 36 percent of the deposits of the world's top five hundred banks; the United States 11 percent.
- Japan is the largest passenger car producer in the world, and by 1988, 17 percent of the cars sold by Detroit under U.S. labels will be made by the Japanese.
- Japan now dominates almost all categories of merchant semiconductor memory chips, and the U.S. Defense Science Board found Japan gaining in American strongholds of microprocessors and other logic chips.
- Japan now has twenty-two billionaires, three of whom are worth more than the richest American, Sam Walton.
- Eight of the ten largest corporations outside the United States are Japanese. Mitsui is now the largest company in the world outside the United States, passing Royal Dutch/Shell in 1986.

In addition to those economic strengths, Japan's record in literacy, social conditions, and quality of life is one of leadership:

- Japan's elementary and secondary school system has already been pointed out as the most demanding in the world.
- Life expectancy in Japan is 75.2 years for men and 80.9 for women, the highest in the world.
- The same number of people die of gunshot wounds in a single day in the United States as in an entire year in Japan. Tokyo averages two robberies a day; New York City 200.

In world markets, the Japanese are experienced and aggressive traders, who have become battle-hardened in fierce domestic competition, described by some as a "Demolition Derby." They are survivors, tough and resilent. They are dedicated with evangelical fervor to continuous improvement, low cost, good services, high productivity, superior quality in the international market place, and all at great speed. Jim Abegglen in *Kaisha* portrayed them as "fierce, investment-driven, market share–obsessed" competitors. They regard global markets as combat zones, and they compete aggressively with all the energy they can. They do it to win.

No wonder Japan was ranked as *the most competitive economy in the world* in the 1986 "World Competitiveness Report," an annual world-wide ranking of twenty-two nations as to competitiveness by the EMF, a nonprofit foundation in Geneva. *Japan was ranked number 1 and has ranked number 1 for six of the seven years that the ranking has been done.*

Japanophiles?

Having said all that, we stress that we are not mesmerized by the Japanese, nor are we apologists for Japan or advocates of its views. We like and respect the Japanese, but we are not blind to their faults or problems.

They are not invincible competitors, flawless magicians, or innocents abroad. They can be infuriating, arrogant, and ruthless. They make mistakes, and they have some very bad, as well as very good, managers.

Nor do we "blame" the Japanese for the economic problems of the United States. Japan did not cause the U.S. productivity slowdown or the U.S. budget deficit, and it is only one contributor to the U.S. trade deficit. The Japanese drive for economic growth does not have to be a win–lose game. The United States did not gain at England's expenses, and Japan does not have to gain at ours. The Japanese will not hesitate to surpass the United States in productivity or wealth, just as the United States did not hesitate to surpass England. The Japanese are formidable and worthy competitors. They work hard, and they are good.

Americans are bombarded with books, article, and TV specials containing many versions of Japan's culture, its strengths, its management system, its weaknesses. Many of the reports conflict, many of the data are obsolete, and American reactions range over the spectrum: "It's all exaggerated." "The Japanese can only copy, they can't create." "They're successful only because of government help and closed markets." "The Japanese are going to win."

The Japanese study the United States carefully and Americans need to do the same of Japan, and sort out from the sound—and sometimes the fury—the myths, strengths, and weaknesses of Japan. They need to ask, "What *is* the truth?

The answer is a modern tale of Rashomon.

A MODERN RASHOMON

It was a chilly evening. A servant of a samurai stood under the Rasho-mon, waiting for a break in the rain.

So begins the tale of Rashomon, a tale of murder and rape in a forest in eighth-century Japan.

> "Yes, sir. Certainly, it was I who found the body. This morning as usual," said the woodcutter in his testimony to the High Police Commissioner, "I went to cut my daily quota of cedars, when I found the body in a grove in a hollow in the mountains . . . a single sword stroke had pierced the breast."

The dead body was that of a samuarai. As the tale by the Japanese author Akutagawa unfolds, the question becomes, What *really* happened in the grove that day? What is the truth? The tale is told three times—first by a bandit, then by the wife of the samurai, and then by the dead samurai himself, told through a medium.

Each time the reader begins to "believe" one version, another tale is told—slightly different—that seems equally true. The lesson of Rashomon, made famous in a classic film by Akiro Kurosawa, is that there are many "truths," many explanations of the same event—each believable, all similar in many ways, but each also different. It becomes difficult to distinguish between subjective and objective, truth and fiction, illusion and reality.

In the end, the viewed is left with a gnawing question: What is the real truth? Or is there even a "truth?"

So it is with the "truth" about Japanese competitiveness. It is a modern tale of Rashomon, a mixture of truths, half-truths, exaggerations, and myths. And, as Robert Coles reminds us, we shouldn't make the mistake of confusing "what is most distinctive" with what is most important. It is important to try to understand as much as possible about such a strong challenger, to discover what we can about (1) the myths, (2) the strengths, and (3) the weaknesses of Japanese competitiveness, the subjects of the next three chapters.

—25—

Myths About Japan

In this chapter we discuss the five myths that we feel are the most dangerous for Americans to believe about Japanese competitiveness.

As with Rashomon, in every myth there is some truth; in every truth, there is some myth.

Myth 1. The Japanese are brilliant imitators, but they are incapable of originality and innovation.

This is simply not true. There are four errors associated with this myth.

First, we have shown that nations throughout history—including the United States—have copied and adapted from one another, especially in their early developmental years. But the fact that nations copy does not mean they cannot also be creative. Were that so, the United States would not be a creative nation today.

Second, the Japanese have always been creative. The world's first novel, *The Tale of Genji,* was written in Japan in the eleventh century. Calculus was invented by a Japanese—Seiki Takakazu—before Newton and Leibnitz. Edwin O. Reischauer has pointed out the tremendous vitality and creativity of Japanese culture in symphony orchestras, theater, dance, architecture, painting, and pottery.

It also isn't true that Japanese science and engineering always lag behind the United States. Justin Bloom, who spent six years as Counselor for Scientific and Technological Affairs in the American Embassy in Japan, testified before Congress:

> I have discussed the quality of Japanese science with literally hundreds of American scientists and engineers who work directly with their Japanese counterparts in a wide variety of technical fields, and almost invariably I have been told that the Japanese are working at or close to the leading edge of these fields.

The Japanese are also expanding basic research, exploring areas like electron beams physics, biotechnology, molecular electronics, and software science. Since 1980, Japan has been planning and constructing twenty-six large-scale, ultramodern, high technology "technopolises," scattered across the nation. Each technopolis (*"tech*nology," plus *polis* for city-state) will have R&D centers, manufacturing plants, a venture capital base, industrial parks, schools, art and culture centers, highway and airport systems, all linked throughout the archipelego by NTT's Information Network System (INS). These technopolises have been jointly planned by the prefectures and MITI for almost eight years, some are under construction now, most are scheduled for completion by the year 2000, and all are aimed at producing creative technologies to surpass the West—Japan's economic engines for growth in the twenty-first century. Tatsuno in *The Technopolis Strategy* points out that the United States faces a "patent deluge" of immense proportions in the decades ahead.

Third, it is an error to associate creativity and innovation only with invention. Technological innovation depends on invention, but also on development *and* application. The English invented, Americans improved and applied. Americans invented transistors, semiconductors, color TV receivers, commercial videotape machines, and numerically controlled machines. But the Japanese copied, adapted, improved, and thought of commercial applications the Americans overlooked. Scientific success is not necessarily equated with economic success or competitiveness.

Implementation also requires creativity. The Japanese have shown themselves to be innovative in manufacturing processes—kanban, just-in-time, flexible manufacturing systems—that require integration of "hard" and "soft" technologies. They are also innovative in marketing, management systems, and training. Neglect of these areas of innovation is one of the main reasons that automation of American plants is often unsuccessful.

Many important inventions were discovered not in "basic research" labs or in isolated think tanks but in the bustle of application. Japanese engineers spend time on the factory floor and become members of teams alongside marketing, design, and manufacturing personnel, inventing and applying.

The fourth error is to assume that only individuals can be creative, as opposed to groups.

It is probably true that the supergeniuses Americans idealize—the Albert Einsteins—are not as likely to emerge from the Japanese system, which prizes group-oriented work. But groups can assemble minds in an interactive, supportive way that provides not only novel solutions but solutions that can be implemented because of group participation in the process.

In fact, the image of Thomas Edison as a lone wolf inventor isn't true. Edison was one of the pioneers of team research. As the stock of knowledge becomes so vast that only groups can effectively master knowledge, international comparative advantage swings more and more to team research. "Innovation," Michael Polanyi has said, "occurs on a crowded stage."

The drawbacks from continued belief in this myth are that the United States (a) continues to underestimate the Japanese, (2) focuses only on basic and hardware research, neglecting application and organizational innovation, and (3) assumes that the Japanese have "copied all they can" and are therefore condemned to stay behind.

"I get very uneasy when people talk about the Japanese not having the ability to be creative," says Ralph Gomory, IBM's chief scientist, "I suspect it's just wishful thinking."

Myth 2. Japan's success has been engineered by Japan, Inc.

A common notion is that Japan's competitiveness is largely due to the workings of "Japan, Inc.," a cabal of government, business, and labor working together almost as a national corporation.

It is true that in the 1950s and 1960s government played an active and strong role in Japan's development. There were stringent government export and exchange controls, a multitude of government-directed financial support devices, and government administrative guidance from the Ministry of Finance, the Bank of Japan, the Economic Planning Agency, and the Ministry of Industry and Trade (MITI).

But most observers, including ourselves, believe (1) the government–business–labor network never masterminded Japanese competitiveness, and (2) the extent and effectiveness of such collaboration have been far overstated and overrated. Furthermore, what influence the collaboration did have has diminished as companies have become stronger and as MITI has been stripped of many of its legal powers. Many Japanese businessmen openly complain about government meddling, controlling, and interfering with the market, and sometimes refuse to cooperate.

It is not a myth, however, that the Japanese government *does* work more cooperatively with business than does the American government. It would be a mistake, when noting that MITI has made errors and has lost some of its powers, to conclude that it is ineffective and powerless. MITI is very active and respected, and it still serves as a useful catalyst to bring government and business together around selected issues—cajoling, persuading, discussing, disagreeing, and providing information, assistance, and seed funding for some projects.

MITI gives far less direct financial aid than most Americans think. It does give some, but its main role is to goad business, to collect and disseminate information, to push hard for consensus, to push and help declining industries reduce capacity and restructure, and occasionally to operate government-enforced cartels forced on the Japanese by the United States (e.g., autos and semiconductors).

For the most part, however, it is the market, not Japan, Inc., that is the force driving Japan's competitiveness. If MITI went out of existence tomorrow, Japanese competitiveness would be only marginally impaired.

Myth 3. The main reason for the U.S. trade deficit with Japan is Japanese protectionism.

Japan protects and restricts access to some of its markets by tariff and nontariff measures. That is not a myth. It is true.

But around that truth are some dangerous myths: (1) Japanese protection causes the U.S. trade deficit, (2) Japanese protection is very large, and (3) Japan is far more protectionist now than the United States.

First, the large U.S. trade deficit is not mainly due to Japanese protectionism. *Complete elimination* of all Japanese trade barriers—tariff and nontariff—would reduce the trade deficit with Japan by an estimated $6 billion, roughly 10 percent, C. Fred Bergsten, Director of Washington's

International Institute of Economics, says. If all Japanese meat and citrus import quotas were removed, U.S. Secretary of Agriculture Richard Lyng estimates, the United States would sell only an additional $1 billion annually in exports to Japan in the next few years.

Even the most ardent protectionist in Congress, Representative Gephardt from Missouri, estimates trade barriers at only 15 percent of the U.S. trade deficit with Japan. That would still leave at least a $50 billion trade deficit with Japan, and a $162 billion deficit in the worldwide trade balance.

That the U.S. trade deficit with Japan is largely caused by Japanese protection is a myth. It is caused by a host of other factors, such as exchange rates, U.S. budget deficits, capital flows, competitiveness, and differences in growth rates.

Second, much of the impression of Japan as a protectionist nation lingers from the years when it did have high protection. From the 1950s to the early 1970s, Japan used tariffs, quotas, subsidies, exchange controls, customs hassles, and other techniques—the whole ball of wax—to protect its markets.

But beginning in the 1970s, Japan began to lower its tariffs, drastically cutting by almost 2,000 items the number of commodities on which it had import restrictions. By 1985, Japanese average tariffs at 3 percent were actually lower than the 4.2 percent rate in the United States, and 4.9 percent in the EEC.

But neither is Japan as completely an open market as some Japanese profess. The Japanese do use nontariff barriers, which are a form of *de facto* protectionism. Even so, Professor Hugh Patrick of Columbia, who has been a longtime observor and researcher on Japan, has concluded: "My judgment is that, overall, Japanese government restrictions on imports of manufactures from the United States are, on balance, no more severe, and possibly less severe, than United States protection on imports from Japan."

Americans forget that the United States is also protectionist, as we pointed out in an earlier chapter. Almost one-third of everything that Americans import are subject to some form of American tariff or nontariff barrier. Daniel Goleman cites a *New Yorker* cartoon where a king sits in a medieval castle surrounded by knights and says, "Then we're in agreement. There's nothing rotten here in Denmark. Something is rotten everywhere else."

Both nations protect. Both sides have their share of horror stories and finger-pointing: metal baseball bats, ski equipment, peanut mush, automobile and steel "voluntary" quotas, textiles, color TVs, and cars with steering wheels on the righthand side. On balance, the two are probably about the same in protectionism today. The danger in believing that Japanese protectionism is the cause of the U.S. trade deficit and declining U.S. competitiveness is that we thereby divert attention from solving the underlying problems.

Myth 4. The Japanese business system is closed to foreigners.

The belief that American firms are frozen out of Japanese markets is also exaggerated. U.S. exports to supposedly closed Japanese markets in 1986 were larger than American exports to England, West Germany, and Italy combined. And Japanese consumers spend three times as much per capita on foreign brand goods as American consumers do on goods from Japanese firms.

Yet in every myth there is some partial truth.

It is true that there are some subtle forms of barriers to Americans doing business in Japan by bureaucratic maneuvers, certification standards, and restricted bidding. The Japanese business network is also capable from time to time of hindering entrance of American products, especially through the relations between large companies and their networks of contractors and suppliers. But the total amount of such "closed markets" is small, and the United States engages in informal barriers of the same kind itself.

For many of the examples cited of closed markets, there are also many examples of firms that for decades have operated very successfully in Japan. Estimates from various sources are that U.S. companies in Japan produced more than $50 billion in goods and services in 1985—more than the U.S. trade deficit with Japan in that year. The following are 1982–83 market shares of some American firms doing business in Japan:

	Market Share
Nestlé instant coffee	63%
Kellogg cereals	34
Johnson floor wax	30
Coca Cola	60
IBM computers	40
Schick razor blades	70

McDonald's started doing business in Japan in 1971. Many said it couldn't succeed, that after two thousand years of eating rice and fish, the Japanese would not eat hamburgers.

McDonald's reached 100 billion yen in annual sales in 1984 and is the number 1 "eat out" company in Japan. The world's largest McDonald's is in Kyoto. Another successful fast food company is Kentucky Fried Chicken, so Japanized that the company conducts a Shinto religious ceremony every July in honor of the souls of the chickens that earn KFC's living.

It is true that it is not easy to do business in Japan, but a large part of that is due to the language difficulty and the high standards of Japanese consumers for quality, design, and service. Not all American firms are willing to make the effort. While it is estimated that 50,000 marketing executives from Japan are in the United States, only 1,200 from the United States work in Japan. In 1985, while Detroit sold only 1,300 cars in Japan, BMW sold nearly four times as many. (Among other things, the German firm puts the steering wheel on the righthand side; the Japanese drive on the left, as do the British.)

Clyde Prestowitz was, until May 1986, a key person in the U.S. Department of Commerce negotiating trade issues with Japan. He said at the time of his resignation, "The biggest obstacle to selling more goods in Japan is not trade barriers, but the USA's growing lack of competitiveness."

Jim Abegglen, a longtime American consultant in Japan and author of several books on Japan, concludes: "Japan's markets are at least as open as the average among the other developed nations and far more open, for example, than the French or Italian economies." While the Japanese are not completely "clean" on this issue, the belief that American firms can't do business in Japan is mostly a myth.

Myth 5. High Japanese productivity results from unique cultural factors; therefore Japanese methods are not transferable.

The "cultural uniqueness" argument for Japanese management practices is exaggerated.

It is true the every culture is somewhat unique, including the culture of the United States. There are also many similarities, however, and many practices, philosophies, and concepts that are transferable. The myth is that Japanese productivity methods are so ancient and bound to culture that the United States cannot learn from them.

First, many current Japanese management practices have not always existed as a part of Japanese culture. They are partly derived from historical customs, partly the product of the American Occupation after World War II, and partly created by necessity driven by the poverty, turmoil, and destruction of postwar Japan.

Many of the so-called Japanese unique business practices—harmonious labor–management relations, lifetime employment, quality circles—did not spring fullblown from Japanese culture. They were forged out of necessity:

- From 1945 to 1960, Japanese labor relations were among the worst and most violent in the world.
- Some managers fought every step of the way before they adopted (limited) "lifetime employment."
- Kanban and just-in-time were postwar productivity inventions born of the necessity for simplicity and reduction in waste in inventory.
- Labor–management cooperation was born of mutual frustration, destructive strikes, and the need to get to work.
- Quality improvement sprang from Japan's desire to sell in higher-value-added world markets.
- "Quality circles" were no cultural artifact; they originated with employees meeting together to try to learn statistical quality control techniques.

It is true that some practices fit well with some Japanese cultural characteristics, but they were not inherited from a mystic cultural past. They were created to fit the times.

Japan has a culture. So does the United States. Rather than concentrate on what is different or distinctive about the two cultures, Americans should concentrate on what is most important, similar, and adaptable. In our opinion, a high percentage, perhaps 80 percent, of the basic ideas the Japanese use for productivity and quality gains are transferable with adaptation to the American business system.

Now, what are the Japanese strengths?

—26—
Strengths of Japan

We pointed out in Chapter 6 that the ''real'' causes of the U.S. productivity slowdown were not the butler or the usual macro-economic ''suspects'' but were much deeper, more fundamental, more long-term causes.

We feel the same about the real sources of Japanese competitive strengths.

Japan's competitive strengths flow not from protection, MITI, or Japanese imitation but from more deep-seated strengths: education, drive, ability to adjust, a less adversarial society, and emphasis on productivity and quality.

Strength 1. The single most important source of Japanese productivity growth is the emphasis on learning.

We have already discussed the Japanese emphasis on learning in Chapter 23. We won't repeat it here, except to stress again that we believe it is the single most important long-term competitive strength of Japan.

The emphasis on learning exists not only in the schools but continues throughout life in extensive training inside firms and government ministries, in the home, and in daily lives. It is a sad and bitter fact that the average Japanese is better educated and better equipped to learn than the average American.

Strength 2. The Japanese adjust rapidly to changing conditions.

"We are crisis eaters," one Japanese said.

Everything that happens to the Japanese is described as a "shock"— the Nixon Shock, the Soybean Shock, the Oil Shock, the Dollar Shock. But they go on. Adversity heightens their sense of unity. Japan has survived invasion, civil wars, earthquakes, fires, typhoons, isolation, bombings, the American Occupation, energy "shocks," food embargos, and a 50 percent rise in the yen. Each is a setback, but the Japanese have adjusted to them all remarkably well, while maintaining a distinctive sense of identity and continuity.

They even regard defeat as an impetus. Setbacks are opportunities. Defects are treasures. The Japanese are not a people to dwell long on disasters, defeat, or lost causes—"no use biting your own navel."

They are a nation of survivors.

One source of this strong ability to adapt to rapidly changing conditions is the people's pragmatic approach to life, their lack of a fixed ideology or fixed principles. "Isms" don't exist. Morality is not viewed as black-and-white.

Another source may be their fear of being so isolated in a small archipelago in the Pacific Ring of Fire, without many raw materials, with their survival dependent on their ability to adjust.

Finally, their artistic and philosophical sense about time assists their attitude toward change. The Japanese prize both timelessness and impermanence in their art, their gardens, their homes, their products. Change, improvement, and adjustment are natural rhythms. Buddhist thinking emphasizes that nothing is permanent, that life is changing. "All things change," one calligrapher said, "and they are beautiful precisely because they change."

The ability to adjust continuously to changing conditions in world markets, to changing technology, and to setbacks is a great competitive strength of the Japanese, a strength second only to education.

Strength 3. Japan's "drive" is a competitive strength.

As we said in the "litmus test" in Part IV, "drive" is universally acknowledged as a critical ingredient for achievement in almost anything, including international competitiveness.

Defining drive is similar to the problem of defining pornography. It's hard to put into words, but you "know it when you see it."

And we see it in Japan.

Most American businessmen who visit Japan come back marveling at the way workers swarm problems, their attention to little details, their pursuit of the "last grain of rice." "When workers finish their break, they run back to work," Ford's president Polling says. David Kearns, the chairman of Xerox, has said: "Every time I go [to Japan], I come back invigorated and scared to death."

Ask those who have faced the Japanese in competition. "When the Japanese enter your markets, nothing is the same any more," said one manager. Ask those who have worked with them in a joint venture. They see markets as battlefields. They "attack" markets, regarding competitors as honorable enemies, but someone they must defeat in unrelenting, single-minded pursuit. They obtain reams of information from everywhere, ask endless questions, have countless members of their team visit and talk, produce huge quantities of figures, analyze hundreds of possible outcomes, work long hours, drink until late, then go back to work the next day to work hard again.

That drive flows in part from the Japanese home life and the educational system, which teaches from birth that success is primarily due *not to ability, but to effort.* Merry White points out that in kindergarten the Japanese children learn to bear hardship, in the middle grades to persist to the end and with patience, and in the upper grades to be steadfast and accomplish goals undaunted by obstacles or failures. Graduates from all that are the human capital that America is competing against.

No wonder that a 1985 *New York Times* survey reported that many Americans now believe the Japanese are more determined, work harder, and pay more attention to detail. James Fallows, an *Atlantic Monthly* editor, reported from Tokyo in August 1986: "The fundamental problem we've had in competing against the Japanese is obvious after only a few days here: the Japanese all work much harder than we do."

Strength 4. Japan is a less adversarial society than the United States.

Japan's fourth strength is that it has less adversarial relationships between individuals, within business firms, and between the private and public sectors.

We quickly point out that (1) Japanese relationships are not free of conflict, and (2) not all American relationships are adversarial. The differences are relative.

Conflicts do exist in Japan. One can find vicious infighting among groups and factionalism in government, in political systems, and within organizations. What is different is how the conflicts are handled.

Americans prefer to resolve conflicts through a system built on rights protected by law and due process, along with a business contractual system that relies much more on written agreements, legal proceedings, and confrontational tactics. Relationships and rights are defined in formal contracts, where every word is scrutinized for implications and detailed rules are spelled out in an attempt to anticipate every future event. If things don't work out, parties resort to lengthy and costly adversarial, win–lose judicial proceedings to resolve differences.

As a result, the United States is a much more adversarial and litigious society, with a huge supply of lawyers. More than 25 million lawsuits are filed each year in the United States, and one estimate is that about one-fourth of U.S. population at any given moment is suing or being sued.

Almost two-thirds of all the lawyers in the world are in the United States. The country has about 2.5 times as many lawyers as Britain, and five times as many as Germany. There are about 680,000 lawyers in the United States now. An additional 53,000 paralegals bring the U.S. total of legal personnel close to three-quarters of a million. By the mid 1990s or sooner, there will be more than a million. Right now, New York City alone has 47,000 lawyers; California 84,000; Washington, D.C., about 44,000.

Japan has fewer lawyers. Figures are often cited showing only about 12,000 lawyers in the whole of Japan, which means there is one lawyer to serve roughly the number of people served by twenty-five lawyers in the United States. That doesn't accurately portray the situation, however. While Japan does have only about 12,000 attorneys specializing in criminal defense and civil law ("bengoshi"), it also has quasi-legal persons (scriveners, legal advisers) and special tax attorneys, bringing the total of legal personnel closer to 80,000—still far fewer than in the United States.

The difference is that the Japanese rely far less on the legal system to settle disputes and protect rights. Law is not an absolute but a framework for discussion. They rely much more on personal relationships and mutual obligations. Many Japanese live and die without ever using a lawyer. Whereas Americans think of rights, the Japanese think in terms of duty; they strive constantly for harmony, consensus, and compromise. One study of Tokyo taxicab companies showed that from a total of 2,567 accidents causing injury or damage, only two suits were filed. Barely 2 percent of the divorce cases ever find their way to court.

Japanese companies think of a contract not so much as a legal instrument but as a statement of the beginning of a relationship. An oral commitment is more important than a written contract. A businessman is uneasy with long, detailed written contracts that are *de facto* statements of distrust, which remove flexibility, prevent the ability to adjust to changing conditions, and pull people apart in adversarial proceedings. Many big Japanese corporations have no legal counsel on their staff and use outside lawyers only when they have to.

The same thinking affects how individuals and groups work together inside firms to improve productivity and quality:

- Employees and managers begin with an attitude of trust and common fate, and then seek more ways to work together than to oppose one another.
- Individuals' feelings are sought and respected, giving them a sense of common purpose toward group effectiveness.
- Functions such as marketing, sales, and engineering still have conflicts, but they search for consensus rather than defend turf and waste time in compartmentalized conflicts.
- Unions and management can still have conflicts resolved through collective bargaining, but they cooperate around competitiveness.

Among firms, there is more joint R&D, joint production, and cooperation in the face of global competition. Yet rival firms also compete ferociously, reverse engineer one another's products, gather intelligence about competitors, battle it out in the market with "destructive pricing," and do everything possible to destroy opponents. The fierce competition has been likened to a barroom brawl with no mercy shown, a Demolition Derby, and all-out war.

Thus, while cooperation and competition exist side by side in Japan, they are not seen as necessarily contradictory behaviors. The Japanese believe that you can have *both competition and cooperation* ("both/ and"), in contrast to the American belief that competition and cooperation are pretty much opposites ("either/or"). Cooperation in the United States is viewed with some suspicion as being possibly collusive against the public interest, violating someone's rights, or "selling out."

In reality, each society has elements of each. Americans cooperate and have some communitarian values, too. However, Americans clearly

are more on the individualistic scale and Japanese more on the communitarian scale. The Japanese seem better able to blend the two, partly
perhaps because of a Confucian philosophy that places a high value on
agreement and harmony, and also defines the concept of self through
relationship to groups. The school system reinforces this.

That outlook also affects relationships between government and the
private sector. In the United States, the relationship between the two
sectors is formal, controlled by numerous laws, fraught with mutual
suspicion, and viewed as best handled by arms-length relations, checks
and balances, administrative law, and adversarial proceedings. In Japan,
contact between business and government is frequent, less formal, less
defined by regulations and laws, and less adversarial.

Few nations have been as successful as Japan at obtaining the values
of both cooperation and competition, reducing the amount of time and
resources spent on litigation, increasing flexibility and responsiveness
to change, and permitting more cooperative relations among individuals,
groups, and the government—all important strengths of Japan for competitiveness.

*Strength 5. Japan stresses productivity and quality to a greater degree
than other nations.*

No other nation in the world gives the degree of emphasis to both
productivity and quality that Japan does. Neither emphasis is a ''program''
or an overlay on top of other responsibilities, but more a way of life, a
philosophy. As the Japanese say, ''Quality is a state of mind.'' ''Productivity is a way of practicing virtue.''

We've already given concrete examples of how those philosophical
statements get translated into operating procedures inside Japanese firms,
but we can also illustrate how much they are part of the national ethos
by briefly describing the establishment of two Japanese institutions dedicated to productivity and quality: (1) the Japan Productivity Center,
and (2) the Deming Prize for Quality.

Japan Productivity Center (JPC). In 1954, leaders in Japanese business and government recognized the necessity of a nationwide movement
to raise the productivity of Japanese industries. The government approved
the idea of establishing a national productivity center but directed by a
vote of the Diet that it be located and funded not in government, but
in the private sector.

The Japan Productivity Center was established in March 1955 as a
nonprofit, nongovernmental, tripartite center. The U.S. government as-

sisted with technical aid that totaled $6.4 million. Labor was suspicious at first about participating in the JPC but agreed to become involved after the JPC adopted three crucial guiding principles that still hold today:

1. "We believe that improvement in productivity eventually leads to expanded employment opportunities. Temporary redundancy should be dealt with to the extent possible by reallocation, thus minimizing the risk of unemployment."
2. "We believe that specific steps for improving productivity should be studied by joint consultation between labor and management."
3. "We believe that the fruits of improved productivity should be fairly distributed among management, labor, and consumers."

Those three principles contributed to the emphasis on (1) lifetime employment, (2) joint consultation in labor relations, and (3) a broad sharing of economic gains, which has given the Japanese one of the most egalitarian distributions of income in the industrialized world.

JPC began by sending teams of Japanese abroad to study operations in other nations. Since then, more than 25,000 Japanese participants from all strata of society have traveled abroad, and hundreds of foreign specialists have lectured in Japan. Ironically, the very first team from Japan came from the steel industry, which in a few years began to overtake the American steel industry.

JPC is *the largest productivity center in the world*. Its 1986 budget was over 7 billion yen (approximately $45 millin at a 150 yen/dollar rate, and it has a full time staff of 325 people. Its main offices are in Tokyo, but it also has nine regional centers in Japan, as well as offices in Washington, D.C., London, Paris, Rome, and West Germany. JPC has also taken a leading role in helping to establish the "Asian Productivity Organization" to help other Asian nations improve productivity.

JPC is a symbol of the commitment of Japanese businesses to the improvement of productivity. Though Japan's explosive productivity growth since 1950 was the best in its history, it has had a long record of productivity improvement. If productivity growth is averaged over a very long time, Japan comes out higher than any nation in the world. The following table, graphed in Figure 26–1, shows the average annual productivity growth rates of the various nations from 1870 to 1985:

	Growth in GDP/Hour
Japan	3.0%
France	2.6
Germany	2.6
United States	2.2
Netherlands	2.1
England	1.9

Japan had the highest average rate of productivity growth of all nations in the world over the entire 115-year period.

The Deming Prize. In the early 1950s, Japanese leaders recognized that "Made in Japan" meant low quality to world markets. People associated Japanese products with little toy umbrellas in their drinks and with the failure of the Toyopet, the first Toyota car imported into the United

Figure 26–1. GDP PER HOUR, 1870–1985

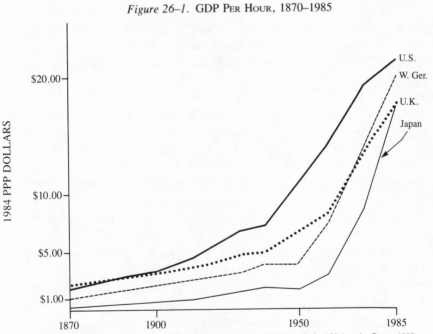

SOURCE: Angus Maddison, *Phases of Capitalist Development* (Oxford: Oxford University Press, 1982), Appendices A, B, and C. Also, Bureau of Labor Statistics, U.S. Department of Labor, December 29, 1986. Based on 1984 purchasing power parity exchange rates and adjusted for frontier changes.

States, which could hardly negotiate the hills of San Francisco. Like the Germans in the late nineteenth century, the Japanese knew that they had to improve the quality of goods if they were to ever become a force in the world export markets.

The Union of Japanese Scientists and Engineers (JUSE) began a national program of quality improvement. As one of its steps, it invited an American, Dr. W. Edwards Deming, to come to Japan to deliver a series of lectures on quality improvement. Dr. Deming had for years urged American firms to become more interested in quality but had been largely ignored.

Dr. Deming, in July 1950, gave an eight-day course to a group of 340 Japanese research workers, engineers, and plant managers. In addition, senior executives of fifty leading manufacturing firms were invited to a special session and listened well when Dr. Deming told them it would take at least two years to revise Japanese ideas of quality, precision, and uniformity; five years more to establish a reputation for quality, precision, and uniformity; and an even longer time to overcome the reputation for inferior quality that Japanese products had built up before the war.

The Japanese accomplished in a relatively short period one of the most remarkable turnarounds in history of a nation's quality image. Today, they rank number 1 in quality in most international polls.

Americans should not regard the rise in Japanese quality as a stolen "American idea." The Germans over the years have paid attention to quality more than Americans. The Japanese had started to work on quality before Dr. Deming's arrival. What the Japanese did was to acknowledge their shortcomings, listen and learn from others, and then merge other ideas with some of their own, ending with a quality approach distinctively Japanese.

However, the Japanese never forgot the contribution of Dr. Deming. JUSE in 1950 established the Deming Prize in commemoration of Deming's contributions to quality improvement in Japan. Each year since then, the Deming Prize has been awarded to a very small number of corporations and plants (sometimes an individual) that have exhibited unusual quality achievements. In the thirty-four years that the Deming Prize has been given, only 119 have been awarded, an average of only *four a year*.

The Deming Prize is now the most coveted and prestigious award for quality in Japan, sort of a Japanese Superbowl of quality. Even the Emperor comes now and then to the nationally televised awards ceremony.

None of the strengths we've presented is intended to paper over the faults, problems, and weaknesses of Japan. It has them, as all nations and peoples do.

In the next section, we present seven areas where we think the Japanese have problems and weaknesses that could hurt their world competitiveness.

—27—
Japan's Problems

If you ask Japanese if they face economic and world competitive problems, be prepared to spend the evening. They would have you believe that the economy is almost doomed and that the island will probably sink into the ocean next week.

Some of their response is based on the perpetual sense of impending disaster that permeates Japanese consciousness, but some of the problems are real and serious.

In this chapter, we list seven problems we think Japan faces.

Problem 1. Japan's greatest problem is rising world protectionism.

It is unparalleled in history for one nation to have such large trading surpluses—$101 billion in FY 1987—and world protectionism against Japan's is its single biggest immediate problem.

The United States has already taken protectionist steps against Japan in autos, machine tools, motorcycles, color TVs, steel, and semiconductors. After every monthly announcement of the trade figures, the U.S. Congress, the Reagan Administration, or Europe threatens some additional form of protection or retaliation.

If such protectionism increases, it will hurt Japan, but it will not be its economic Waterloo. Japan could survive economically with lowered exports. Only about 16 percent of Japan's GNP depends on exports of goods and services, contrasted with 25 to 30 percent in Germany, France, England, and Italy, and around two-thirds in The Netherlands and Belgium. However, its export industries are some of its strongest and most productive, so it would hurt its productivity, GNP growth, and bid for world economic leadership.

Japanese firms have been well aware of the danger for some time now and are doing as much as they can to offset it. Many firms have already moved, or are moving, production facilities to other nations, forming joint ventures with firms in other nations, and working even harder at home to improve productivity and quality in existing facilities—"wringing the dry towel once more," as one Japanese described it.

The single most effective thing the Japanese government could do would be to follow the advice of Japan's own leading business organization, Keidanren, and remove *all* trade barriers, tariff and nontariff. That would not be easy, for Japan, like the United States, has strong political factions and its own internal bureaucracy. But if Japan wanted to do one single thing to minimize its greatest danger, that would be it.

Even that, however, would not stop all the protectionist steps by other nations, for trade barriers in Japan are not the primary causes of the trade deficits of other nations. Other nations would continue to blame Japan to some degree, because they need a scapegoat, and they would use some other justification—defense, saving jobs, equity, "fairness," or reciprocity. Still, complete elimination of all barriers would go a long way toward defusing the issue.

Problem 2. The NICs (newly industrializing nations) are challenging Japan in productivity and quality.

"We do worry about foreign competition," a Japanese business leader has said, "but not from the United States. The countries we worry about are South Korea and Taiwan."

And they should.

The Asian NICs (South Korea, Taiwan, Hong Kong, and Singapore) have become world-class competitors, exporting such high-quality manufactured products as computers and autos, along with traditional exports of textiles and footwear.

None of this is lost on the Japanese. "Japanese industry is no longer competitive in the lower levels of industrial activity where proprietary technology is not a factor," Sukeo Kohno, chairman of Hitachi Metals, says.

Some Japanese industries, such as steel and synthetic fibers, are phasing down capacity and moving into higher-priced, custom-designed, higher-value-added markets, such as pharmaceuticals, software, biotechnology, microprocessors, and rocketry, regarded by many as the last bastion of U.S. competitive strength.

Also, Japan cannot afford to overlook Australia, which has a long history of high productivity, or the ASEAN nations of Malaysia, Thailand, and Indonesia, which have the potential to catch fire, and NICs elsewhere in the world, such as Brazil. Even economically backward nations like China and India, while not a competitive force today, certainly have the capability to become so in future years.

We list competition by other nations, especially the NICs, as a "problem" for Japan, in truth, it really might be classified as hidden strength, for the competitiveness of those nations will keep Japan on its toes.

Problem 3. Japan still has some inefficient sectors in its economy that are a drag on overall productivity.

Like the United States, Japan's greatest gains in productivity come from its manufacturing sector. If manufacturing is considered alone, Japan's productivity is estimated to be about equal to or even better than that of the United States in output/employee and close to the United States in output/hour.

But when distribution, agriculture, and transportation are added in, Japan's overall relative productivity drops to about 70 percent in terms of output/employee and about 60 percent in output/hour.

If Japan is to maintain a high growth rate, it must find ways to increase the productivity of those relatively inefficient sectors, particularly the services sector, now almost 60 percent of Japanese GNP (U.S. = 68 percent). The U.S. record in productivity of the services sector is very poor. Unless Japan can improve productivity in agriculture, distribution, and transportation, its overall growth will continue to be pulled down by its inefficient sectors.

Problem 4. The "graying" of Japan poses a threat to its future productivity growth.

Japan is aging at a faster rate than any other nation in the world—two to four times faster than France, Sweden, Germany, or England. By the year 2025, its population will become one of the oldest in the world, exceeded only by Germany's.

The problem isn't only the number of elderly (sixty-five and older), it is the incredibly rapid rate at which that number increases. The United States also faces a rising aged population, but nothing like the rate in Japan. Whereas Japan will double its aged population percentage in twenty-six years (from 7 percent in 1970 to 14 percent in 1996), a doubling of this figure is expected to take seventy years in the United States (1945–2015), and 130 years in France (1965–2095).

The proportion of elderly will continue to climb to an estimated 21 percent by 2025, with some estimates going as high as 24 percent. The rise is mainly due to a greatly increased life expectancy (the highest in the world at 75.2 years for men and about 80.9 for women) and a very low fertility rate of 1.8 percent.

The extremely rapid "graying" that Japan is beginning to experience has no parallel in human history. It will have powerful effects on businesses, savings rates, tax rates, and governmental social expenditures.

The International Monetary Fund (IMF) estimates that Japanese government pension and medical care costs will rise from 9 percent of GDP in 1980 to 21.5 percent in 2025. At that point, there will be only about three working age persons for every retiree, instead of the 7-to-1 ratio now. To meet the costs, Japan's Ministry of Finance predicts that Japan's overall tax burden of 36 percent in 1986 may rise to as high as 50 percent of GDP in the next forty years, and the personal savings rate could decline from its current level of 16 percent to only 10–13 percent. That is one of the reasons the Japanese do not want to give up their high savings rates now, abandon fiscal restraints, and consume more as the United States is urging.

At the firm level, the aging work force will strain Japan's management system:

- "Lifetime employment," already limited to 25 percent to 33 percent of the workforce, may become even more limited as firms fear being stuck with older workers.
- Promotion opportunities could dwindle as the managerial ranks become crowded with older workers at the top.
- Attitudes of workers and managers may become more conservative with more aged employees.
- Firms will have higher pension costs as larger numbers of workers hired during the high expansion years of the 1950s and 1960s retire. The retirement age has already crept up from fifty-five to near sixty.

Japanese firms are well aware of these trends and of the consequences if they do nothing. They have slowed the hiring of new graduates. Nissan and others are spending more of their capital investment budget to make older workers more productive. Some firms are also already creating subsidiaries to absorb older workers.

If Japan does not find a way to "renew" itself, it faces a very serious drag on future productivity growth as an "aging nation."

Problem 5. Japan could succumb to the "advanced nation's disease": changed values and stagnation from affluence.

One of the greatest fears of the Japanese is that the same spirit of sacrifice, hard work, and high savings that brought them such success may now be fading—a loss of drive. Or, as Jim O'Toole put it, "Alas, nothing fails like success."

As we pointed out in the earlier chapters, the eroding influences of affluence appear over and over in history. Will Japan now come down with the advanced nation's disease, wanting to enjoy "the good life," slowing savings, increasing consumption, investing and working less? Japan has been an extremely goal-oriented society. What will challenge it when it has achieved most of those goals?

Many of the features of the Japanese management system were forged out of the devastation and hardships of postwar Japan—out of necessity. The necessity is disappearing. The Japanese are now almost right on the historical affluence track now: questioning high savings and low consumption, asking whether hard work, group cohesion, pay and promotion systems, and a demanding educational system are really desirable. The United States is adding to the pressure, urging the Japanese to become more like grasshoppers, less like ants.

The Japanese are moving, as Ray Dalio of Bridgewater Associates puts it, from a nation that "becomes rich, but still thinks of themselves as poor" to a nation that is "now rich and thinks of themselves as rich."

The United States is just leaving that stage. It is entering the stage of becoming poorer and still thinking of itself as rich. England has been there for years.

As yet, Japan is not showing many symptoms of the negative side of affluence. It is a long way from Marx's goal of "hunting in the morning, fishing in the afternoon, rearing cattle in the evening, and criticizing after dinner."

One of the factors that will help to keep Japan's eye on the ball is the strong competition from the NICs, which by working even longer hours at lower wages and producing almost equal quality are providing stiff competition. They may save Japan from the gout of affluence.

Being Japanese, they worry. If history is any guide, they should.

Problem 6. Success can bring overconfidence and arrogance.

The successful are also often afflicted with rising overconfidence in their abilities and increasing arrogance. Japan has shown such tendencies in the past, and it is easy to see how it might happen again.

Japan has reason to be proud. From a nation with a per capita GNP of only $188 at the end of World War II it has risen to the second largest economy in the Free World.

But from pride and self-confidence it is but a short step to overconfidence and arrogance. On recent trips to Japan and in the press we have seen early signs of the "Victory Disease"—growing arrogance, the same disease that turned some Americans into "ugly Americans."

That arrogance is beginning to show as part of the increasingly bitter exchanges over charges about "unfairness" in trade. Europe and the United States accuse the Japanese of trading unfairly or failing to open their markets to foreign firms. The Japanese say foreign imports don't sell in Japan because they are of poor quality, that other nations are just making excuses for their lack of competitiveness ("sour grapes"), that the world "needs" Japan as a model for hard work and quality, and that their methods are clearly superior. Behind it all is a thinly veiled attitude of cultural, moral, and intellectual superiority.

In private, a few Japanese say "Americans are stupid," "European products are junk," or "Europe is a boutique; America is a farm." The feeling grows that Europeans and Americans want to blame their consumption policies and lack of competitiveness on a scapegoat, Japan. The United States feeds such attitudes when it bashes, for it appears to be blaming Japan for its own failings, breeding disdain. The Japanese know full well they are not to blame for the bulk of the U.S. trade deficit, and it puts the United States in an inferior position, similar in their mind to a loser blaming an opponent for his own shortcomings and accusing him of cheating to win.

This feeling of being bashed and dumped on unfairly by other nations can grow into paranoia, a siege mentality, which runs all through Japanese history anyway. Every child is taught in school that "constant vigilance" is required for self-preservation. They vacillate between an inferiority and a superiority complex. History also shows that the Japanese can change their views like quicksilver, and it is but a short journey from the Yin of confidence to the Yang of arrogance.

"The strong," an old Japanese proverb says, "should walk on tiptoes." The Japanese would do well to remember their own proverb.

Problem 7. Japan's sense of "separateness" from the world could block it from world leadership.

The Japanese believe they are a unique people, separate from the rest of the world.

That attitude had its deepest expression in their incredible isolation from the world that began in the seventeenth century with the Tokugawa period, when Japan slammed the door on the world and withdrew into itself. The government "forbade overseas travel by Japanese on pain of death and even refused readmittance to Japan of shipwrecked Japanese fishermen rescued by foreign ships. Commerce was outlawed with all nations except China and Holland, and citizens of no other nations were allowed in Japan. The Dutch were confined to a small island . . . Under no circumstances were the 'red-haired people' . . . allowed into the rest of Japan; they were even forbidden even to bury their dead on Japan's sacred soil."

Japan stayed locked up like that for more than two centuries, until the seclusion was shattered in 1853, when Commodore Matthew Perry sailed into Japan with seven black ships and demanded at gunpoint that the Japanese open up their country and trade with the world. Arthur Koestler described what happened next as the breaking of the window in a pressurized cabin.

In the Meiji Restoration that followed, Japan went out and learned from the world, but always maintained its homogeneity—culturally, racially, and in spirit. Even today, Japan remains one of the purest gene pools in the world, with the United States referred to as a "genetic brawl."

The Japanese are still uncomfortable around foreigners, calling them all "gaijin"—outside people–and even requiring the fingerprinting of aliens. About 85 percent of Japan's "foreign" residents are Koreans, three-quarters of them born in Japan. But "most Japanese still look down on Korean–Japanese as colonials or think of them as gangsters," the *Economist* reports. Some corporations will not hire or promote Koreans.

The Japanese took in very few Vietnamese boat people, and foreign businessmen report difficulties in ever being accepted into the Japanese social community. A leading Japanese editor reported that Japanese will often speak of their affinity for their "fellow Asians," but in all but a few Japanese, no such affinity exists.

Toynbee pointed out that it is an error for any nation to try to create a "national culture" free and separate from foreign influence in a global world. The Japanese, if anyone, are prime candidates to commit that error. That raises the question of whether Japan is capable of becoming a world leader.

It may be that there is no clear number 1 in the world ahead. Instead of Pax Britannica or Pax Americana, it will be a Pax Consortia—a number of nations of nearly equal strength. But if there is a number 1 (and history says there generally is), the most likely candidate to replace the United States would be Japan. And many people, including the Japanese, wonder whether Japan can take or wants the job?

Being number 1 includes:

- A commitment to sustaining world free trade
- Being a leader, lender, and mentor to the developing nations of the world
- Exercising an openness and integration in world social, political, and economic institutions
- Building and maintaining military power, and a willingness to use it.

Many people wonder whether Japan could ever overcome its current feelings of "separateness" from the world and its underlying suspicion that the world is "out to get it." Japan is a world trader but not yet a nation of international dimensions in its thinking or institutions.

A wide perception exists that the Japanese have no lasting ideology that can be a standard bearer for the world, no political acumen. And there is a world suspicion of Japan left over from its military adventures of the 1930s and 1940s, a question whether Japan only adopted democracy because of defeat and occupation, like the "rice Christians" of China.

Japanese leaders are asking themselves many of those same questions. "Japan is like a runner," one Japanese official said, "who after making a headlong dash, finds himself unexpectedly in the lead." Both business and government officials are calling on Japan to assume more of a role as a world leader—increased defense, internationalization of the yen, further market opening, and aid and relief programs for developing nations.

For years Japan did not have to face those questions. But now Japan may have no choice. As Kahn and Pepper put it, Japan will be forced to consider its role not just as a "superstate" but as a "superpower."

Our belief is that it probably can. But of all nations that have assumed the role in the past, Japan may find it more difficult than any other. Being number 2 is one thing. Being number 1 is another.

SUMMARY: WILL THE BICYCLE FALL OVER?

With all these problems–now and in the future—is Japan destined to slow down and fall behind? Japan's economy has been compared by some to a "bicycle economy": It works only at high speed.

Japan has already slowed from the blistering 6 to 8 percent annual productivity gains of earlier years. It is now in the 3–4 percent range. Given the continuing problems outlined in this chapter, some are forecasting (and hoping) that Japan's bicycle will slow and perhaps fall over.

We don't believe that, for four reasons.

One, the Japanese have met strong setbacks before, such as the oil embargo and energy price shocks of the 1970s. Hard times, fear, disaster, destruction, and adversity seem to increase their competitive response and ingenuity.

Two, some of the changing factors favor them, such as lower prices for energy and cheaper components from countries like South Korea and Taiwan, whose currencies are linked to the dollar. The Japanese are taking steps to live with a high-value yen: forming alliances, building plants overseas, moving offshore, and reducing costs at home. Honda, for example, has initiated a three-year plan to be competitive at even 120 yen to the dollar.

Three, they have incredible financial power with a strong yen and extremely high savings rates. They face these problems with a rock-hard financial base. They are investing at home and around the world in higher-value-added industries to move up the productivity ladder, thus strengthening their competitiveness. They still have in their workforce a high average technical sophistication, a blend of discipline and flexibility, and a work ethic that calls for hard work and long hours. Abbeglen and Stalk calculate that the leading Japanese firms in major industries spend more than 5 percent of sales on R&D, as against 3.7 percent of sales for their U.S. counterparts. Continuous quality improvement is almost a religion. They have a national passion for education and learning. They cherish harmony and cooperation as well as competition.

Four, Japan does not have to slow just because it has almost "caught up" to the United States. The catchup process is not automatically self-terminating. David Landes has pointed out that throughout history the effort of catching up "calls forth entrepreneurial and institutional response that, once established, constitute powerful stimuli to continued growth." The English didn't stop when they neared the Netherlands in productivity. The United States didn't stop as it neared the English productivity level. Both sailed right on by the leader.

In sum, we believe that Japan's bicycle will *not* fall over, that it will average 1.5 to 2.0 percentage points in productivity growth above the United States for the next decade or so, sufficient to pull past the United States shortly after the turn of the century—*provided the United States doesn't accelerate.*

The United States must remember that while Americans are working hard to improve productivity and quality, so are the Japanese. They are not sitting there paralyzed. With all their problems, they are pedaling furiously. Japan is likely to emerge from its current problems leaner, fitter, richer, and even more of a formidable competitor than before. The United States underestimated the Japanese in the past, and it would be a grievous error to underestimate them again.

One reason they are running so hard is not just to pass the United States but to survive the hard charge by other Asian nations that are challenging both the United States and Japan.

The global economy is heating up.

—28—

Asian NICs

Hard on the heels of Japan and the United States are the Asian NICs, the "newly industrializing countries" of South Korea, Taiwan, Hong Kong, and Singapore.

"NICs" might equally well stand for "next in competitiveness," for while developed nations have been battling it out among themselves, these hard driving "four dragons" have recorded incredibly high growth rates (see Figure 28–1) and have moved rapidly in head-to-head competition with the developed nations.

Their trade with the world has soared, their exports growing from $2.7 billion in 1965 to $113.4 billion in 1985, not just in labor-intensive goods but also in capital-intensive, high-tech, and knowledge-intensive goods. Their share of world exports more than doubled from 1960 to 1985, from 2.5 to 6.4 percent. They are fully capable of competition on a global scale.

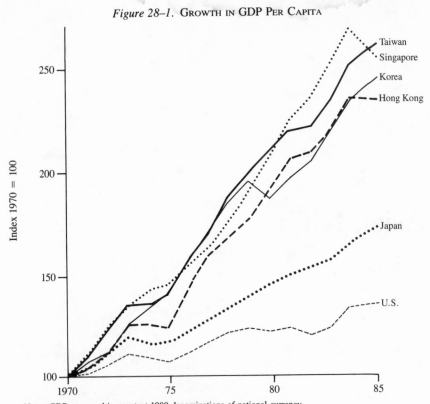

Figure 28–1. GROWTH IN GDP PER CAPITA

NOTE: GDP measured in constant 1980 denominations of national currency.

SOURCE: International Monetary Fund, *International Financial Statistics Yearbook 1986*, pp. 152–55, 420–21, 432–33, 598–99, 690–91; and Wharton Econometric Forecasting Associates, *World Economic Service Historical Data*, pp. 203–4, 215–16.

The U.S. merchandise trade deficit with the Asian NICs is larger than that with the entire European community, and per dollar of their GNP, the NICs export to the United States three times more than the European community. Their economies account for more than half of the U.S. trade deficit. They are already powerful competitors, and American business is now realizing it. They are a force to be reckoned with.

A *Business Week*/Harris poll of 1,000 American executives in December, 1986 showed that the overwhelming majority (69 percent) felt that the "emerging nations" such as South Korea, Taiwan, and Brazil were the "greatest threat" to U.S. manufacturers in the next five years; 76

percent agreed it would be the same in the year 2000. Though the NICs do not like the label, they are the "little Japans."

The following statistics show the NICs' income per capita, growth rates, productivity, compensation, and capital formation as a percent of GNP, together with U.S. figures:

	GDP/ Capita 1984	Real GNP Growth 1980–84	Labor Productivity 1975–83	Mfg. Pay 1986	Capital Formation as % GDP 1984
United States	$15,660	2.3%	0.9%	$12.97	17.9%
Taiwan	3,005	6.7	5.1	1.45	N/A
South Korea	2,052	5.3	4.9	1.41	30.1
Hong Kong	6,300	7.8	9.4	1.78	22.3
Singapore	7,260	8.7	4.0	2.41	47.0

Time periods are not all exactly the same because of gaps in the available data, but the figures are reasonably accurate. Together, they show quite a remarkable track record of growth and a powerful combination of low pay and high productivity for continued competitiveness. The NICs' technology is advanced and sophisticated, their cost structure is a fraction of that for the United States, and their workforce is young, hungry, and not burdened with high living standards, rigid work rules, or conventional management wisdom.

All four have in common a commitment to growth, a willingness to work long hours, entrepreneurship, a disciplined and reasonably skilled labor force, and a high level of education. But each is also different in some ways.

SINGAPORE

Singapore, an island only about 25 miles long and 14 miles wide, has had for almost two decades one of the most explosive growth curves in the world, averaging almost 9 percent a year. It has the highest national savings rate in the world—42 percent of GDP—and the highest per capita income in Asia (Brunei and Japan excepted). Per capita income in Singapore is higher than in Spain, Ireland, or Italy. Proportional to GNP, it has the highest import and export trade levels in the world. In 1984 it passed Rotterdam in tonnage to become the world's biggest port.

The Singapore economy is based on trade, the refining and shipping of oil, and relatively light manufacturing. However, there is a trend toward increasing concentrations of manufactured goods, making it a recent entry into capital-intensive world markets.

The Prime Minister discusses ''productivity'' almost constantly, saying in his speeches, "Productivity is the only way we can survive." Singaporeans believe that their future lies with better-educated workers, more and better machines, and positive attitudes—people who are willing to work hard.

HONG KONG

Also a tiny island, Hong Kong (HK) has exhibited a similar strong 8–9 percent growth. HK is the world's third largest financial center after New York and London, and thrives on trade (180 percent of GDP), banking, communications, and shipping.

HK also has a manufacturing component, primarily textiles and clothing. Other manufacturing includes electronics, toys, and electrical equipment, but very little heavy industry.

HK's strengths lie in its open markets, a bustling free market spirit, low taxes, no trade restrictions, and a ''welcome'' sign for foreign investment. Its future in world competitiveness is now heavily linked to the role it will play for and with China when the takeover occurs in 1997.

Hong Kong and Singapore are more ''entrepot'' (trading) nations; Taiwan and South Korea are more manufacturing-oriented.

TAIWAN

The standing joke in Taiwan is that one of every eight Taiwanese is a member of the board of directors of a corporation.

That dramatizes the fact that most Taiwanese businesses are small entrepreneurial enterprises (Taiwan has 50,000 manufacturing enterprises, ten times as many as South Korea), mixed with increasingly heavy foreign investment. Taiwan is one of the fastest-industrializing and most export-oriented nations in the world. Nearly 50 percent of its GNP depends on exports, about 48 percent of which went to the United States in 1985. Imports from Taiwan into the United States equalled U.S. imports from Germany in 1985. And it has, for its size, an embarrassment of riches: a staggering $62 billion in foreign exchange reserves, larger than Japan's.

Taiwan is moving rapidly out of textiles, toys, and footwear into industries requiring higher levels of technology, such as automobile manufacturing. It is already attracting investments from Ford, Nissan, and Mitsubishi Motors. It also aims to be a factor in high technology, having established in 1980 a science research park that houses fifty-nine companies at work on new high-tech businesses. It has also sent nearly 100,000 of the country's brightest graduates to the United States for advanced study, and of those nearly 10,000 have earned Ph.D.s, mainly in the sciences.

The Taiwanese are already a force in U.S. markets and will steadily move up the higher-value-added manufacturing curve. However, of the four Asian NICs, the next nation—South Korea—is the one that will, in our opinion, be the strongest challenger, not only to the United States but also to Japan.

SOUTH KOREA

Many Americans have an image of Korea (in this section, "Korea" refers to South Korea) as a poor nation, still suffering from several wars, with people living in crowded slums and huts, mostly uneducated, poorly paid but eager workers.

That outdated image arises largely from memories of a Korea that was devastated after World War II. Some Americans remember, for example, when Koreans had to eat tree bark to stay alive in 1945–46. Seoul was just a pile of bricks. As late as 1961, Korea's GNP/capita was $93. A nation that once claimed rice as its main product now challenges both the United States and Japan in automobiles, steel, TV sets, VCRs, computers, and semiconductors.

"The Koreans are driving right through the wall and into the living room—and not even using the door," Paul Rossel, Director of International Planning at DuPont, says. "We see Korea as the Japan of fifteen years ago," says Denis Root, director of Chrysler-Korea. "Who would have said that Japan fifteen years ago would have challenged the U.S. market?"

When Koreans first entered world trade, they exported wigs (first made of human hair, then of synthetics), textiles, clothing, and small electrical appliances. Not content to follow the usual slow labor-intensive development cycle, they decided to break out by concentrating on manufacturing and technology. They formed the Korea Productivity Center in 1957 and began work, as Japan was doing, to improve productivity and to correct the impression that all Korean goods were of inferior quality.

They copied, borrowed, licensed technology, and created joint ventures. They set up "listening post" firms in Silicon Valley and formed joint ventures with some of the most sophisticated firms in Japan and the United States. Korea became a competitive powerhouse.

- Korea is now the thirteenth largest exporter in the world; it ranks seventh among U.S. trading partners—bigger than France or Italy.
- Korea's estimated 1987 GNP of $120 billion was larger than the GNP of half the OECD's members.
- Two Korea companies—Hyundai and Samsung—are on *Fortune's* 1985 list of the 100 largest industrial companies in the world.
- In shipbuilding, Korea had 4 percent of the market in 1980; in 1985, it had 14.4 percent and was climbing.
- Pohang Steel is the largest and most efficient steel mill in the world; the world's largest shipyard is in Pusan, Korea.
- Manufactures as a percentage of total exports increased from 61 percent in 1965 to 92 percent in 1984.
- Korea's rate of fixed capital investment has been about 30 percent of GDP, and R&D about 1.3 percent.
- Only eighteen months after entering the Canadian market with its Pony subcompact, Hyundai pushed aside Toyota and Honda to become Canada's leading car import.

Koreans are teaming up with some of the largest corporations in Japan and the United States. Ricoh and Seiko Epson have begun assembly of integrated circuits in Korea. Japanese firms are licensing VCR production. General Motors put $400 million into joint ventures with Daewoo. Kia Motors is building the Ford Festiva. AT&T owns 44 percent of Goldstar Semiconductor. Not only do Koreans make products under their own names that are slowly becoming known to Americans—Lucky Goldstar, Hyundai, Samsung, and Daewoo—they manufacture U.S. brand names for RCA and GTE. Even vehicles bearing the famous Caterpillar yellow and logo may be Korean.

And they have moved production into the United States.

Goldstar has two plants in Huntsville, Alabama, turning out color TVs and microwave ovens, operating the plant under a Korean management style. Samsung Electronics has a similar plant in Roxbury, New Jersey. According to the U.S. Bureau of Economic Analysis, the average American worker at a Korean-run plant in the U.S. produced $94,000 in goods in 1984. Comparable plants owned by U.S. companies produced $87,000. At Japanese-run U.S. plants, however, American workers produced $155,000.

The U.S. BLS normally includes no Asian NICs in its international comparisons, but because of Korea's growing competitiveness, in 1986 the BLS added Korea. In GDP/capita Korea was at 27 percent of the U.S. level. In productivity (GDP/employee) it was at 33 percent of the U.S. level. Though still far back, Korea is roughly where Japan was relative to the United States in 1960, and Korea's annual growth rate of 5.2 percent in GDP/employee from 1973 to 1986 was ten times the U.S. rate, almost double Japan's, and by far the highest of the thirteen nations compared.

The average Korean manufacturing work week is fifty-four hours (United States, forty; Japan, forty-one). Many of the manufacturing operations are on a six-day schedule, with two shifts of twelve hours each, and three vacation days a year. It is not uncommon for Koreans to work on Sundays. The Koreans "work harder, longer, and have more of a can-do attitude than anywhere else in the world I've seen," George Cobbe, president of Samsung Hewlett-Packard, says.

Even the Japanese complain: "They work too hard." Korean managers work seventy to eighty hours a week; Japanese sixty to seventy, and American about fifty. "We play on Sundays," Hiroshi Takeuchi, the head of Japan's Long Term Credit Bank says, "while the Koreans work . . . and they work far more fiercely."

Average hourly compensation costs (market exchange rates) for production workers in Korea is $1.75 per hour, as against $12.82 in the United States and $10.26 in Japan. Korean engineers earn about one-fifth of a U.S. engineer's pay. It's a little bit of irony to hear the Japanese say, "The Koreans ought to get their wages up."

However, Korea's workforce is not just cheap and hardworking. It is smart and well educated. Korea, like all Confucian societies, has always stressed education. Almost all Koreans are literate, and teenagers in Korea are more likely to finish high school than teenagers in Italy or Britain. The labor force, as in Japan, has been taught both at home and in school to be obedient and to work long and hard. As one Korean mother said, "If my sons work hard and study, they will get rich. That is my dream."

Korean managers often have degrees in electrical engineering and computer sciences; many are U.S.-trained. If the Korean Development Institute is correct, Korea has the highest number of Ph.D.s per capita in the world. The third nation to develop a 256K RAM chip was not Germany, France, or England, but Korea.

None of these attitudes, cultural strengths, or capabilities suddenly burst on the scene after World War II. The Koreans are an ancient and distinguished race. Most American know almost nothing of the history of Korea, being unaware that three Korean kingdoms existed at about the time of Christ's birth; that the Yi Dynasty was founded 100 years before Columbus landed in America; that the Japanese copied ideas, technologies, and painting from Korea; and that the Koreans produced the first metal type known to history in 1403.

Americans, we hope, will not repeat their mistake of underestimating a challenger, as they did with the Japanese, and neglect the growing strength of Korea.

Korea is the most dragonlike of the four dragons. And behind it, as shadows on the wall, are China and India.

ASIAN COMPETITION

"A race without a finishing line" is what David Landes called international competition for wealth. The "pursuit goes on. . . . No one wants to stand still; most are convinced that they dare not."

The United States dares not. The Asian competition is not just *more* competition. It is *different* competition. It is not just the challenge of a nation, it is the challenge of a region. Nations have effectively absorbed and improved U.S. technology, worked with government, increased the average level of education, created a national spirit of growth, learned to think for the long term, and combined all this with an incredible work ethic, drive, and a low standard of living. A powerful combination for competitiveness.

Some see this increased development as a desirable and vital engine for world growth. Some see it as a threat to America's economic supremacy. Whatever one's attitude, no one can any longer ignore the Orient.

"OUR ORIENTAL HERITAGE"

For almost two thousand years, the center of the world has been, for Americans and Europeans, Western civilization. The Mediterranean was originally the reigning arena. About 1600, the balance of power shifted north to Europe, and then the Atlantic nations rose to power and spread over half the world.

Because of that Westward orientation, few Americans can tell you anything of the histories of Oriental nations much beyond that of military excursions (Genghis Khan), quaint customs (tea ceremonies and bowing), and a few interesting tales of Marco Polo. Many do not realize that when the Pilgrims were landing at Plymouth Rock, most Oriental nations had been in existence for thousands of years, were economically and militarily powerful, and, for their period, were technologically sophisticated.

That lack of understanding of Eastern civilizations weakens American competitiveness. Most Americans simply are unfamiliar with the cultural, philosophical, and motivational backgrounds of their strongest challengers—a world so unfamiliar, so ancient, and with such a different philosophical and religious orientation to everything, including business.

Yet these nations, as Hofheinz and Calder pointed out in *The Eastasia Edge,* have longer recorded histories and more collective experience in business and trade than the rest of the world combined. They are driven by a sense of historical destiny and have a synergy of political, economic, and social dimensions and institutions that is hard for most Americans to understand.

In fact, if it were admitted, most Americans simply cannot conceive of a non-Western nation leading the world! They have a smug, thinly conceived belief that the Far East (it's really the Far West, but the United States takes its orientation from Europe) is really "backward" and incapable of achieving a Western standard of living or thinking. Yet the very first book of Durant's eleven-volume history of the world is *Our Oriental Heritage.*

The nations that now have zoomed up in competitiveness cannot be ignored or passed off as a temporary surge. Ancient mapmakers drew dragons on their charts to warn explorers of dangers ahead, and now the "dragons" of the Orient have come alive again economically. Lurking in the background is the gnawing question; increasingly asked: "Have the Asians come up with a more competitive system?"

AN ASIAN STRAIN?

Is it possible that Japan and other Asian nations have come up with a variation on capitalism—an Asian strain—that is better than the American version? Or is there no difference—Americans just went to sleep for a while, and once awake, they can take up where they left off?

At first we dismissed the idea that perhaps there might be a new "Asian strain" of capitalism: *Capitalism is capitalism.* But the more we think about it, the more we believe the thought must be entertained lest the United States dismiss an important development, like the mutation of a new species on the planet.

Peter Berger, in *The Capitalist Revolution,* raises the same question, also believing that it is possible that the Asians have come up with something different—a "second case," he calls it—not just an extension of Western capitalism, but something *different,* perhaps even better. "It is analogous to . . . a zoologist . . . who suddenly comes on a second environment in which the same species is flourishing."

The United States has always assumed that a nation will always win if it has the basic tenets of capitalism—freedom of entry, private property, market pricing, consumer information—and a culture that stresses individualism, has checks and balances, and minimum government interference with the economy.

The Asian version, although like the Western one in many ways, is also different and challenges some of those assumptions. The idea of variants of capitalism and governance shouldn't be surprising or shocking. The United States adapted many features of its economic and political system from the British, and the British from the Graeco-Roman system.

The Japanese copied from the United States and Europe in the nineteenth century, but it was capitalism without all of the Western ideologies. They built on their particular strengths—high savings, elite goverment bureaucracy, zaibatsu-keritsu business relationships, and a homogeneous society. They also build on their belief in the priority of personal relationships and mutual obligations over rights.

Accordingly, the notion that the state and the individual are adversaries is not a strong part of their ethic, nor are adversarial proceedings between individuals the main way of resolving differences. Government is more active, not controlling or planning the economy, but working with the private sector and nudging it. Peter Berger concludes, after examination: "The East Asian evidence falsifies the thesis that a high degree of state intervention in the economy is incompatible with successful capitalistic development."

Some refer to it half-jokingly as Confucian Capitalism or Communal Capitalism. Call it what you will, the label on the outside may say "capitalism," but on the inside, it's not the same. Phrased in managerial terms by Takeo Fujisawa, cofounder of the Honda Motor Company, "Japanese and American management is 95 percent the same and differs in all important respects."

The differences are subtle, perhaps even metaphysical: The whole counts for more than the parts; unity prevails over dualism; both/and is better than either/or; interconnections are more powerful than distinctions. To use the language of Gestalt, Westerners seek the meaning of the picture in the figure, when the secret lies in the background.

It is perfectly fine for Americans to say that they don't want any part of those things and don't want to copy them. They don't have to.

Why should we raise this question in this book?

Because of competitiveness. *If* the Asian strain has different and better features, then, as Bruce Scott, George Cabot Lodge, and Ezra Vogel of Harvard University (among others) have suggested, the United States is employing a less effective set of tools, concepts, and institutional frameworks. The Asian strain would have a "comparative advantage," and the dynamics of capitalism would transfer the leadership of the world economy there. After all, capitalism is not faithful to any particular georgraphy. "It pits," David Halberstam says, "our highly creative, highly individualistic capitalism against something genuinely unique in our experience, the state-guided capitalism of Japan."

That is why we have stressed throughout the book that Americans should study the Asian nations not as a model, but as a reference point, and see what ideas they can adopt or adapt to the American framework of American individualism, entrepreneurship, creativity, and adversarial proceedings.

We are definitely not saying (1) that the so-called Asian strain is better, or (2) that the Americans would want to—or could—adopt it if they wished. But it is a legitimate question well worth asking, and there are undoubtedly things Americans can learn from them. The United States must, like all nations in history, constantly learn from others and adjust.

As Will Rogers said, "Even if you are on the right track, you will get run over if you just sit there."

—29—

It's Up to Us

This book isn't about the Japanese or Asian challenge. It is about the productivity challenge.

Even if there were no Japan, no South Korea, no competition, our American standard of living would still not have grown much, simply because our productivity is stagnant. Further, it is primarily because our productivity is stagnant that challengers pose a threat to U.S. economic leadership.

The importance of productivity to the health and competitiveness of the United States is hard to exaggerate. Productivity is the key to a rising standard of living and to maintaining world economic leadership. That is why we have adopted it as *the* benchmark of U.S. competitiveness.

This last chapter is an opportunity for us to offer a few parting words of encouragement and optimism.

GLOBAL ECONOMIC TECTONICS

"For the first time in our history, we can neither dominate the world, nor escape from it," Henry Kissinger has said.

Economic tectonics have reshaped the world, drawing once distant nations face to face in the market place as buyers, sellers, and competitors.

Raising productivity and standard of living is not a zero-sum game, an international Super Bowl where the United States, Japan, Germany, or Korea wins at the others' expense. *Each nation earns its own standard of living through its own productivity growth.*

A win-lose game happens only if nations are unable to grow through productivity and they resort to "beggar thy neighbor" tactics like protectionism and artificial manipulation of exchange rates. Equally dangerous, bashing and threats do real harm to relationships, especially between the two greatest economic powers in the free world, Japan and the United States. We should remember that Carthage and Rome were friends until they became equals.

The United States and Japan together now account for about 38 percent of the world's GNP and about 35 percent of total world foreign investment. The relationship is too important and too mutually beneficial to allow it to end in acrimony.

David Halberstam put it well: "The Soviets challenged the theory of the American dream unsuccessfully; the Japanese are challenging how we live up to that dream."

OPTIMISTS OR PESSIMISTS?

Throughout this book we have tried to convey our sense of urgency and alarm about America's eroding competitiveness. On the other hand, we are basically optimists, not pessimists.

We are optimists because we see people all over America taking action, challenging accepted practices, willing to learn and create better, more productive organizations. We have given many examples of them throughout this book. The goal we set of 2.5 percent average gain in productivity for the next decade is ambitious. It will be difficult to obtain, but not impossible.

New operating systems are emerging. The power of involvement is expanding to real business issues. Sophisticated automation is spreading. Rigid job classifications and work rules are being replaced with broader, more satisfying roles for employees. Restructuring has reduced staff work and slimmed bureaucracy. Quality is improving.

It is not yet enough. The mind-set of too many managers stops at traditional measures. Many still cannot conceive of fundamental, sweeping revisions: entirely revamping the operating systems; making pay systems flexible; combining engineers, R&D, and manufacturing people into design-to-build teams; learning languages and selling abroad; doing away with remote and closed offices and alienating status symbols. Many are still short-term-oriented, still focused on quarter-to-quarter earnings.

Many managers, employees, unions, politicians, and parents are simply not ready—yet—to make the kinds of sacrifices that are required to restore productivity growth and competitiveness. It is for them that we are sounding the two-minute warning.

THE CREW HAS CHOICES

Our two-minute warning should be taken in the same way that Joseph Schumpeter, the economist, characterized a report that a ship is leaking and is in danger of sinking.

The warning is not a "Doomsday" bulletin. It is a report. The crew has choices.

One, the crew members can fail to respond. They can dismiss the report as unreal and ignore the warnings. Or, they can believe it, but do nothing: (1) blame one another, (2) tidy up their cabins until the outcome is decided by the passage of time or by somebody else, or (3) go to the bar and curse the sea and their bad luck.

Their other choice is to "rush to the pumps," repair the leaks, and sail on. The United States has choices. There is no inevitability about its decline, it has no "appointment in Samarra." It's up to us.

The English faced a similar choice and did little. That does not have to happen to Americans.

The seeds of renewal are there; America is strong, there are remarkable changes under way, and we have competition to spur us on.

AMERICA'S STRENGTHS

If the United States tries to solve its competitiveness problem with inflation, protectionism, devaluation, and government programs or tax incentives, we will decline. None of those approaches does anything to increase long-term productivity growth, and that is the key.

In Chapter 6, we listed the deep-seated underlying causes of the American productivity decline: affluence, aging, adversarialism, the conflict between politics and economics, and lack of competition. Our competitors have eliminated the last one; the first four we shall have to take care of ourselves.

Those weaknesses tell only half the story. America has deep-seated underlying strengths upon which it can draw.

Diversity

American is a great melting pot of ideas, talents, and cultures. Like a rich gene pool, within that diversity lie the attributes that can "fit" the new global economy. Among our managers, employees, entrepreneurs, and new immigrants are those with the "eye of the tiger," the drive and the will to win.

Pluralism

Americans not only have diverse points of view, they are remarkably tolerant of that diversity. Our system of government and our philosophy of individual freedom support the clash of ideas in the political arena and in the market place. From that clash can come creative synthesis: new products and services, new institutions, and new solutions.

Size and Wealth

American firms sit in the middle of the wealthiest economy and the largest market in the world.

- Total U.S. GDP is three times that of our nearest Free World competitor, Japan, and more than eight times that of Britain.
- GDP per capita is the highest in the world on a purchasing power parity basis.
- Americans per capita own more color TVs, automobiles, and telephones than any other nation in the world.

Response to Crisis

When faced with a serious threat, Americans have shown themselves able to rally together toward a common purpose. Managers, union leaders, and employees have turned around almost hopeless situations by sheer drive and willingness to cooperate.

It may sound corny, but the last four letters in American are ''I can.''

AMERICAN ACHIEVEMENTS

Those strengths have produced remarkable results.

Just as there are warning signals indicating danger, there are encouraging signs promising hope.

- The quality of Detroit's automobiles has tripled in the last five years, bringing them closer to world standards for mass-produced vehicles.
- Productivity growth in segments of the economy have been strong; nonelectrical machinery, rubber, food, textiles, chemicals, and electrical machinery have all exceeded an annual rate of 3 percent growth for six years.
- Americans are slimming inventory and work-in-process. The national ratio of inventory to sales has declined in the last two years, when the business cycle would historically have said it should be higher.
- Inflation is down, and employment, as a percentage of the working-age population, is the highest among all leading industrialized Free World nations.
- The number of days of work lost in labor disputes has fallen by a factor of five in the last fifteen years. In 1985, it was the lowest since the Department of Labor started compiling the statistics in 1947.
- Automation and new operating systems are making it profitable to manufacture in the United States. Firms such as GE, who had sent production offshore, are bringing it back to the United States.
- Black & Decker, Harley-Davidson, Xerox, and others are winning back market share from foreign competitors by getting productivity and quality up and introducing better products faster. Xerox and Black & Decker did it without trade protection. Harley-Davidson will soon.
- World-class quality knows no borders. Texas Instruments won the Japanese Deming Prize for quality in 1985.

- Many American firms compete successfully in tough international markets: McDonald's, IBM, Kellogg, Hewlett-Packard, Warner Lambert, Boeing, and others.

But resting on past laurels, even the recent past, is precarious. As encouraging as all these indicators of change and progress may be, they are not yet sufficient in breadth and depth throughout the economy. America does not "own" any industry; look what happened to steel and autos. Leadership in any industry belongs to those who can compete, and the heat from continued foreign competition may be the best way to re-ignite America's productivity growth.

VALUE OF COMPETITION

Andrew Grove of Intel said a couple of years back that "the principle thing this company has going for it is that it's never had a moment without competition."

The rate of productivity is highest where there is competition and lowest where there is none. Competition is the spur to growth and improvement. The drive of competitors can be contagious, and their practices are instructive. America will not be more productive through protection, retaliation, or bashing foreign competitors. We can learn from them, correct our weaknesses, and build on our strengths.

Our advice is to first go visit plants and offices in the United States that are restructuring. Then get on a plane and go to Europe, Japan, South Korea. Visit the plants, talk to the workers, go to offices and schools. Understand at first hand the competitiveness you are facing, learn, and then come back and adapt to your own situation.

Without competition, an affluent nation can easily decline without recognizing the symptoms before it is too late. To pick up the analogy of the "boiled frog" from Chapter 2, without competition, the water would heat so slowly our American frog will never jump.

IT'S UP TO US

Will Durant said, "When we ask what determines whether a challenge will or will not be met, the answer is that this depends upon the presence or absence of initiative and of creative *individuals* with clarity of mind and energy of will . . . capable of effective response to a new situation."

Make no mistake—it is not the same challenge as in the past. It is an entirely new challenge, in a new arena, with different rules, different players, and a different tempo in the game. The United States must not only respond, it must respond sufficiently.

It is also important to remember that "America" doesn't do anything. Americans do. Organizations don't do anything. Individual employees and managers do. Government doesn't do anything. Voters, politicians, and government employees do.

When individuals understand that they have the responsibility and the outcome depends on them, they rise to the challenge.

It is up to us as individuals—as managers, as union leaders, as elected representatives, as government employees, as parents, as teachers, and as voters—to make the private and public sector Agenda for Adjustment a reality.

Now, while we still have two minutes, we must change the American game plan.

Many Americans have the will and the willingness to change. There is a new breed of managers and employees who find challenge exciting and continuous improvement satisfying, who are inspired by the idea of providing high-quality goods and services.

The capabilities and opportunities for reviving American productivity to a 2.5 percent growth exist right now in almost every organization in the United States. Firms do not have to wait for a government program to assist them or a crisis to force them to change. All around them are undeveloped and underutilized resources of people and talent to muster for renewal.

The late Francis Bello, an associate editor of *Scientific American,* reminded us that the only reason a four-minute mile was not run earlier was that men didn't think it possible. Lindberg could have flown to Paris sooner, and there was no reason man could not have launched a satellite early in the twentieth century. Arthur Clarke also pointed out that cavemen froze to death on beds of coal for essentially the same reason. People didn't know, didn't think it possible, didn't try.

But it won't happen overnight.

Like turning a 50,000-ton tanker plowing through the open sea, it will take a long time to change the direction of the U.S. economy. It took almost twenty years to get into our current shape, and it will take another five to ten years to start pulling out. But it surely won't happen at all if we don't get started. Atlas must do more than shrug.

The time to start is now, before it's too late.

No Timeouts Left

"The pitiless crowbar of events," to borrow Solzhenitsyn's phrase, is forcing American minds open to what they must do. And the key factor that will determine the final outcome will be productivity.

We firmly believe that if the United States does *not* respond to the two-minute warning within five years—well, as Don Meredith used to sing near the end of a football game whose outcome was almost certain, "Turn out the lights, the party's over."

The party is far from over. As Yogi Berra said, "It ain't over till it's over."

Stay tuned.

Epilogue

We close as we began, with the words of Thomas Wolfe:

I believe that we are lost here in America, but I believe we shall be found. . . . I think the true discovery of America is before us.

I think the true fulfillment of our spirit, of our people, of our mighty and immortal land, is yet to come . . . and that this glorious assurance is not only our living hope, but our dream to be accomplished.

Dear Fox, old friend, thus we have come to the end of the road that we were to go together. My tale is finished—and so farewell.

. . . A wind is rising, and the rivers flow.

You Can't Go Home Again, pp. 741, 743.

References

...

Preface and Acknowledgments

page

xi   "Can the U.S. Compete?" *Newsweek,* April 21, 1972.

xi   "Can America Compete?" *Business Week,* April 20, 1987.

xii   Tom Peters, "There are No Excellent Companies," *Fortune,* April 27, 1987, p. 341.

xii   "Will the U.S. Stay Number One?" *U.S. News & World Report,* February 2, 1987.

xiv   Fred A. McKenzie, *The American Invaders* (London: Howard Wilford Bell, 1901), pp. 6–7.

Chapter 1 THE TWO-MINUTE WARNING

page

3   E. E. Williams, *Made In Germany* (London: William Heinemann, 1896), p. 1.

4   McKenzie, *American Invaders,* p. 6.

11   Williams, *Made In Germany,* p. 19.

14   *Business Week,* April 20, 1987, p. 68.

16   Ross Perot speech before the Economic Club of Detroit, December 2, 1986.

16   Petach quote: *New York Times,* September 6, 1984.

16   George Butts quote: speech, May 1984.

16   Williams, *Made In Germany,* p. 69.

Chapter 2 CONSEQUENCES

page

17   Sheridan Tatsuno, *The Technopolis Strategy* (Englewood Cliffs, N.J.: Prentice-Hall, 1986), p. xviii.

19   Frank S. Levy and Richard C. Michel, "The Economic Future of the Baby Boom," *The Urban Institute,* December 5, 1985, p. 14.

20   *Ibid.,* p. 10.

22   Lester Thurow, *Zero Sum Solution* (New York: Simon & Schuster, 1985), p. 34.

22   Joseph L. Bower, *The Two Faces of Management* (Boston: Houghton Mifflin Company, 1983), p. 161.

23   Richard Rosecrance, *The Rise of the Trading State* (New York: Basic Books, 1986).

23   J. J. Servan-Schreiber, *The American Challenge* (New York: Atheneum, 1968), p. 29.

24   C. Fred Bergsten, "Economic Imbalances and World Politics," *Foreign Affairs,* Spring 1987, p. 772.

Chapter 3 PRODUCTIVITY

page

43   Isaac Asimov, *Would You Believe?* (New York: Grosset & Dunlap, 1981).

48   James Brian Quinn and Christopher E. Gagnon, "Will Services Follow Manufacturing into Decline?" *Harvard Business Review,* November–December 1986.

Chapter 4 THE DECLINE AND FALL OF PRACTICALLY EVERYBODY

page

49   The title of the chapter is taken from a book of the same name by Will Cuppy, *The Decline and Fall of Practically Everybody* (New York: Holt, 1950).

50   Herman Kahn, *The Coming Boom* (New York: Simon & Schuster, 1982), p. 47.

52   Angus Maddison, *Phases of Capitalist Development* (Oxford: Oxford University Press, 1982).

53 Norman Gall, "The Rise and Decline of Industrial Japan," *Commentary*, October 1983, p. 29.

53 Carlo Cipolla quote: *ibid.*, p. 29.

54 David Landes, *The Unbound Prometheus* (Cambridge: Cambridge University Press, 1969), p. 124.

55 *Times* editorial: Ross J. S. Hoffman, *Great Britain and the German Trade Rivalry* (Philadelphia: University of Pennsylvania Press, 1933), p. 80. We are grateful to Ezra Vogel for bringing this book to our attention.

55 Quote from British workman: *ibid.*, p. 75.

55 Quote from Colonial Office: *ibid.*, p. 93.

55 *Times* editorial; *ibid.*, p. 82.

56 Williams, *Made In Germany*, p. xiv, 135.

Chapter 5 THE RISE AND STALL OF THE UNITED STATES

page
57 Steven Schlossstein, *Trade War* (New York: Congdon & Weed, 1984), p. 3.

59 Lester C. Thurow, *Management Challenge* (Cambridge: MIT Press, 1985), p. 1.

59 McKenzie, *American Invaders*, pp. 11–13.

59 *Ibid.*, pp. 59–61.

60 Maddison, *Phases of Capitalist Development*, p. 212.

60 Landes, *Unbound Prometheus*, pp. 244, 269.

61 Frank Gibney, *Miracle by Design* (New York: Times Books, 1982, p. 47).

62 Schlossstein, *Trade War*, p. 4.

62 Interview with Tom Peters, *Quality*, May 1986, p. 15.

63 *Time*, July 14, 1975, p. 42.

Chapter 6 WAS IT THE BUTLER?

page
69 Thurow, *Zero Sum Solution*, p. 67.

70 Ross Perot quote: *Fortune*, February 16, 1987.

70 Landes, *Unbound Prometheus*, p. 336.

70 Arnold Toynbee, *A Study of History* (New York: Weathervane Books, 1979), p. 141. A one-volume edition, revised and abridged by the author and Jane Caplan.

71 Arthur M. Okun, *Equality and Efficiency* (Washington, D.C.: Brookings Institution, 1975).

72 Alfred L. Malabre, Jr., *Beyond Our Means* (New York: Random House, 1987), p. 8.

72 Will Durant and Ariel Durant, *The Lessons of History* (New York: Simon & Schuster, 1968), p. 19.

REFERENCES FOR PAGES 73-91

72   Joseph L. Bower, *The Two Faces of Management* (Boston: Houghton Mifflin, 1983), p. 203.

73   Charles Kindelberger, "An American Economic Climacteric?" *Challenge,* January–February 1974, p. 41; and "The Economic Aging of America," *Challenge,* January–February 1980, p. 48.

75   Charles Kindelberger, "Historical Perspective on the Decline in U.S. Productivity," *Dimensions of Productivity Research,* Volume I, Proceedings of the Conference on Productivity Research at the American Productivity Center, Houston, April 21–24, 1980, p. 724.

75   John Gardner, *Self-Renewal* (New York: Harper Colophon Books, 1965), p. 1.

Chapter 7 LESSONS FROM HISTORY: THE LEADER'S PERCEPTIONS

page

80   Durant and Durant, *Lessons of History,* p. 52.

80   Soren Kierkegaard, in *Bartlett's Familiar Quotations,* 14th Edition (Boston: Little, Brown, 1937), p. 676.

82   Carroll Quigley, *The Evolution of Civilizations* (New York: Macmillan, 1961), p. 88.

82   Toynbee, *Study of History,* p. 277.

82   E. J. Hobsbawm, *Industry and Empire* (Middlesex: Penguin Books, 1969), pp. 187, 191.

83   Toynbee, *Study of History,* pp. 169, 275.

83   Landes, *Unbound Prometheus,* p. 336.

83   *Ibid.,* p. 327.

84   Joseph A. Boyd, "The Competitive Challenge Facing the U.S. Semiconductor Industry," speech in Orlando, Florida, June 3, 1985.

84   Williams, *Made in Germany,* p. 19.

87   Durant and Durant, *Lessons of History,* p. 41.

88   Ustariz quote: Fernand Braudel, *The Perspective of the World* (London: Fontana Press, 1985), p. 177.

88   *Ibid.,* p. 324.

88   Ross Perot speech, Economic Club of Detroit, December 2, 1986.

Chapter 8 LESSONS FROM HISTORY: THE WAYS OF THE CHALLENGER

page

91   Samuel Johnson quote: Don Gevirtz, *Business Plan for America* (New York: G. P. Putnam's Sons, 1984), p. 146.

91   Williams, *Made in Germany,* p. 156.

91   Landes, *Unbound Prometheus,* p. 334.

91   McKenzie, *American Invaders,* p. 24.

92   Williams, *Made in Germany,* pp. 135, 152, 154.

93   Landes, *Unbound Prometheus,* p. 344.

93   Ralph L. Pounds and James R. Bryner, *The School in American Society* (New York: Macmillan, 1967), p. 51.

95   Braudel, *Perspectives,* p. 55.

95   Angus Maddison, *Phases of Capitalist Development* (Oxford: Oxford University Press, 1982), p. 34.

95   Williams, *Made in Germany,* p. 67.

Chapter 9   LESSONS FROM HISTORY: THE CHALLENGER CLOSES IN

page
98   Landes, *Unbound Prometheus,* p. 267.

98   Charles Kindelberger, "The Aging Economy," a lecture by the author at the Institut fur Weltwirtschaft, Kiel, Germany, July 5, 1978, p. 482.

99   *Ibid.*

99   "Changing content": Landes, *Unbound Prometheus,* p. 344; "British visitors": also Landes, pp. 267–68.

99   Williams, *Made in Germany,* p. 128.

99   Landes, *Unbound Prometheus,* p. 267.

100   Williams, *Made in Germany,* p. 158, 159

100   McKenzie, *American Invaders,* p. 53.

100   Ken-ichi Imai, Ikujiro Nonaka, and Hirotaka Takeuchi, "Managing the New Product Development Process: How Japanese Companies Learn and Unlearn," in Kim B. Clark, Robert H. Hayes, and Christopher Lorenz, eds., *The Uneasy Alliance* (Boston: Harvard Business School Press, 1985), p. 385.

101   Alvin Rabushka, *From Adam Smith to the Wealth of America* (New Brunswick, N.J.: Transaction Books, 1985), p. 4.

102   Landes, *Unbound Prometheus,* p. 328.

102   Chamberlain quote: Jagdish N. Bhagwati and Douglas Irwin, " 'Fair Trade' Could Trap the Democrats," *New York Times,* June 22, 1986.

102   Landes, *Unbound Prometheus,* p. 269.

105   Robert B. Reich, *The Next American Frontier* (New York: Times Books, 1983), p. 281.

106   McKenzie, *American Invaders,* p. 130.

106   Kindelberger, "An American Economic Climacteric?" *Challenge,* January–February, 1974, p. 35.

Chapter 10   THE AGENDA FOR ADJUSTMENT

page
112   We have taken liberties with Elisabeth Kübler-Ross's description of "working through" the stages of the grief experience. Daniel Yankelovich, in his book

New Rules, also borrowed the term when describing the process of how Americans in the 1970s reacted to the simultaneous shocks of slowing growth and cultural upheaval.

113   CEO survey, *Business Week,* August 26, 1986.

115   "Reagan to Celebrate Harley's Success," *Washington Post,* April 23, 1987.

116   J. Richard Hackman, "Designing Research that Works," technical paper, Yale University, 1984.

117   Lionel and Rawlings examples: *Wall Street Journal,* October 14, 1986.

117   GE announcement: *Wall Street Journal,* February 13, 1987.

Chapter 11 INTEGRATED OPERATING SYSTEMS

page
122   "High Tech to the Rescue," *Business Week,* June 16, 1986.

122   "For IBM, Automation Means 'Made in the USA,' " *Business Week,* June 16, 1986.

122   Gary Jacobson and John Hillkirk, *Xerox: American Samurai* (New York: Macmillan, 1986).

122   Sherwin-Williams: E. J. Poza and M. L. Markus, "Success Story: The Team Approach to Work Restructuring," *Organizational Dynamics, 8,* no. 3 (1980): 3–25.

123   There are many excellent sources for information on sociotechnical system theory and design, including Eric Trist, *The Evolution of Socio-technical Systems,* Ontario Ministry of Labour, Paper No. 2, June 1981; Richard E. Walton, "From Hawthorne to Topeka and Kalmar," in E. L. Cass and F. Zimmer, eds., *Man and Work in Society* (New York: Van Nostrand Reinhold, 1975); and James C. Taylor, "Employee Participation in Socio-technical Work System Design: A White Collar Example," UCLA Technical Report, 1976.

125   "How Ford Hit the Bull's Eye with Taurus," *Business Week,* June 30, 1986, pp. 69–70.

126   See Jacobson and Hillkirk, *Xerox.*

126   Goodyear example: Donald B. Thompson, "Everybody's a Boss," *Industry Week,* February 23, 1987, p. 16.

126   *Rolm & Haas Reporter,* Winter 1985.

127   "Cooperative Entrepreneurs at American Transtech," *World of Work Report,* April 1985.

127   First National Bank of Chicago: F. K. Plous, "Redesigning Work," based on *World of Work Report,* November 1986.

129   J. B. Myers, "Making Organizations Adaptive to Change: Eliminating Bureaucracy at Shenandoah Life," *National Productivity Review, 4,* no. 2 (1985): 131–38.

129   Hamtramck case reported in *Wall Street Journal,* May 13, 1986.

130   Speech by John Clancy, McDonnell Douglas Information Systems Group, 1976.

130   Ramchandran Jaikumar, "Postindustrial Manufacturing," *Harvard Business Review,* November–December 1986, pp. 69–76.

131   Thomas M. Rohan, "Bosses—Who Needs 'Em?" *Industry Week,* February 23, 1987, p. 15.

132   Poza and Marcus, "Success Story," p. 22.

Chapter 12 REDESIGNING THE ORGANIZATION

page
135   Kodak example: "Managing," *Fortune,* April 27, 1987, p. 26.

136   Goodyear example: Thompson, "Everybody's a Boss," p. 16.

138   Bruce Lee quote: *Fortune,* July 9, 1984.

138   Thomas J. Peters and Robert H. Waterman, Jr., *In Search of Excellence* (New York: Harper & Row, 1982), p. 275.

139   "Loss of Middle Management Jobs," *Wall Street Journal,* December 23, 1986.

140   Tom Peters, "There Are No Excellent Companies," *Fortune,* April 27, 1987, p. 341.

140   Theodore Leja quote, *Fortune,* April 28, 1986, p. 52.

140   Richard E Kopelman, *Managing Productivity in Organizations* (New York: McGraw-Hill, 1986), p. 152.

141   Bro Uttal, "Speeding New Ideas to Market," *Fortune,* March 2, 1987.

142   Susan Fraker, "High Speed Management for the High-Tech Age," *Fortune,* March 5, 1984, pp. 62–68.

Chapter 13 THE QUEST FOR QUALITY

page
145   Xerox example is drawn from a variety of sources, including presentations by and personal correspondence with Frank J. Pipp, vice president, Diversified Business Group. See also Jacobson and Hillkirk, Xerox.

147   Robert Hayes and Kim Clark, "Why Some Factories Are More Productive than Others," *Harvard Business Review,* September–October 1986, pp. 66–73.

148   Portions of Harley-Davidson and Xerox examples based on *Fortune,* June 9, 1986.

152   Quality training: Japanese Union of Scientists and Engineers, personal communication, 1985.

152   Motorola: Michael Brody, "Helping Workers to Work Smarter," *Fortune,* June 8, 1987, p. 87.

153   L. L. Bean: "Where the Customer Is Still King," *Time,* February 2, 1987, pp. 56–57.

153   *Survey on Service Quality,* American Society for Quality Control, 1985.

153   *Quality: Observations and Six Case Studies* (Houston: American Productivity Center, 1986).

154   Corning experiences: Thomas Howitt, Jr., *World of Work Report,* Work in America, 1985.

155   Data on quality ratings of automobiles: *Fortune,* February 2, 1987.

Chapter 14   COMPETITIVE COMPENSATION

page
156   Carla O'Dell, *Gainsharing: Involvement, Incentives and Productivity* (New York: AMACOM, 1981).

159   Poll results: Carla O'Dell, *Sharing the Productivity Payoff* (Houston: American Productivity Center, 1984).

159   Japanese bonuses: computed from *Japan 1986: An International Comparison* (Tokyo: Keizai Koho Center, 1986).

163   O'Dell, *Gainsharing,* pp. 1–20.

163   Survey results: Carla O'Dell and Jerry McAdams, *People, Performance, and Pay: A National Survey on Non-Traditional Reward and Human Resource Practices* (Houston: American Productivity Center, 1987). Research was supported by the American Compensation Association, the Xerox Foundation, and Towers, Perrin, Forster & Crosby.

Chapter 15   EMPLOYMENT STABILITY AND FLEXIBILITY

page
171   Hallmark example from Bill Saporito, "Cutting Costs Without Cutting People," *Fortune,* May 25, 1987.

172   Bureau of Labor Statistics, *Monthly Labor Review,* November 1986.

172   Ronald E. Berenbeim, *Company Programs to Ease the Impact of Shutdowns* (New York: the Conference Board, 1986).

174   Data on the costs of turnover and advantages of greater stability can be found in Roxanne Dean and Daniel Prior, "Your Company Could Benefit from a No-Layoff Policy," *Training and Development Journal,* August 1986, pp. 38–41.

174   O'Dell and McAdams, *People, Performance, and Pay,* p. 28.

176   Hallmark example: Saporito, "Cutting Costs."

178   For more information on how a wide variety of companies use peak period and downturn strategies, see Jerome Rosow and Robert Zager, *Employment Security in a Free Economy* (New York: Work in America Institute, Pergamon Press, 1985); Diane Riggan, "Employment Security Revisited in the '80s," *Personnel Administrator,* December 1985, pp. 67–74; and James F. Bolt "Job Security: It's Time Has Come," *Harvard Business Review,* November–December 1984, pp. 115–22.

179   For discussion of the possible negative effects of employment security on a fluid labor market, see Audrey Freedman, "The Case for a Free Labor Market," *Across the Board,* January 1985, pp. 42–48.

Chapter 16   EXPANDING EMPLOYEE INVOLVEMENT

page

185   Directory of Labor–Management Committees, Department of Labor, 1983.

185   Information and training in expanded EI, American Productivity Center, 123 N. Post Oak Lane, Houston, TX 77024. (713) 681–4020.

185   O'Dell and McAdams, *People, Performance, and Pay,* p. 25.

186   Xerox example: Peter Lazes, "Employee Involvement Activities: Saving Jobs and Money Too," *New Management,* vol. 3, no. 3, Winter 1986.

187   Rockwell: "The Reading Redesign Story," presented at the Ecology of Work Conference, Pittsburgh, June 10, 1986.

188   "Meeting Customer Needs at FMC Through Workplace Redesign Within a Traditional Union Environment," presented at the Ecology of Work Conference, Pittsburg, June 9, 1986.

188   White Collar Productivity Improvement: Sponsored Action Research 1983–1985 (Houston: American Productivity Center, 1985).

190   *McDonnell Douglas Electronics Company,* Case Study No. 56 (Houston: American Productivity Center, 1987).

192   For issues in expanded EI, see Donald Ashkenas and Todd Jick, "Productivity and QWL Success Without Ideal Conditions," *National Productivity Review,* August 1982, pp. 381–88; and Edward Cohen-Rosenthal, "Orienting Labor-Management Cooperation Toward Revenue and Growth," *National Productivity Review,* Autumn 1985, pp. 385–96.

193   Robert H. Hayes, "Strategic Planning: Forward in Reverse?" *Harvard Business Review,* November–December 1985, pp. 111–19.

Chapter 17   TRAINING AND CONTINUOUS LEARNING

page

195   Merry White, *The Japanese Educational Challenge* (New York: Free Press, 1987).

195   Literacy data: Jonathan Kozol, *Illiterate America* (New York: New American Library, 1985).

196   Company examples: Kumar Naj, "The Human Factor," *New York Times,* November 10, 1986.

196   Ken-ici Imai, Ikujiro Nonaka, and Hirotaka Takeuchi, "Managing the New Product Development Process: How Japanese Companies Learn and Unlearn," in Kim Clark, Robert Hayes, and Christoper Lorenz, eds., *The Uneasy Alliance: Managing the Productivity–Technology Dilemma* (Boston: Harvard Business School Press, 1985), p. 374.

198   Mazda example: "The New Cutting Edge in Factories: Education," *The Washington Post,* April 14, 1987.

199   "Training Magazine's 1986 Industry Report on Training," *Training Magazine,* October 1986, pp. 26–60.

200   *Ibid.,* p. 45.

200   IBM and Motorola: Michael Brody, "Helping Workers to Work Smarter," *Fortune,* June 8, 1987, pp. 86–88.

201   Nancy Foy, "Action Learning Comes to Industry," *Harvard Business Review,* September–October 1977, pp. 158–68.

203   Andrew Grove, "Why Training Is the Boss's Job," *Fortune,* January 23, 1984.

203   Ford remedial program: Irwin Ross, "Corporations Take Aim at Illiteracy," *Fortune,* September 29, 1986, pp. 47–54.

204   Herbert E. Striner, "Retraining as a National Capital Investment," *Productivity Brief* (Houston: American Productivity Center, 1982).

204   Retraining/adjustment data: *New York Times,* August 10, 1986.

204   GAO: reported in "Job Aid Program Rates High," *Houston Post,* March 15, 1987.

Chapter 18 ACCOUNTING SYSTEMS

page
207   Robert S. Kaplan, "Must CIM Be Justified by Faith Alone?" *Harvard Business Review,* March–April 1986, pp. 87–91.

207   Allen-Bradley example: *Fortune,* May 26, 1986.

208   C. Jackson Grayson, "The Use of Statistical Techniques in Capital Budgeting," in Alexander A. Robicheck, ed., *Financial Research and Management Decisions* (New York: Wiley, 1967).

210   James Abegglen and George Stalk, *Kaisha: The Japanese Corporation* (New York: Basic Books, 1985).

214   Michael Sheppeck and Stephen Cohen, "Put a Dollar Value on Your Training Programs," *Training and Development Journal,* November 1985.

214   Xerox example: *Industry Week,* March 4, 1985.

215   Weyerhaeuser example: "Accounting in the Real World," *Harvard Business School Bulletin,* December 1986.

Chapter 19 SYMBOLS, STATUS, AND MEMBERSHIP

page
217   Ross Perot quote: *Wall Street Journal,* July 22, 1986.

218   Andrew Grove, *High Output Management* (New York: Random House, 1983), p. 93.

219   Syntex: *Wall Street Journal*, February 27, 1985.

220   Chrysler Jefferson Avenue plant: *Fortune*, November 24, 1986.

220   Ken Iverson interview: *Inc. Magazine*, April 1986.

221   Frank Gibney, *Japan: The Fragile Superpower* (New York: Meridian, 1985).

222   Thomas Allen, "Communications in the Research and Development Laboratory," *Technology Review*, October–November 1967. Cited in Peters and Waterman, *In Search of Excellence*, p. 220.

223   Livonia example: *Business Week*, May 16, 1983.

224   Servan-Schreiber, *American Challenge*, p. 233.

Chapter 20   A LABOR–MANAGEMENT PARTNERSHIP

page
226   Union membership data: *The Economist*, February 14, 1987; NLRB votes: *Wall Street Journal*, August 26, 1986.

228   John Wolf, speech on November 6, 1986, in Houston.

229   "Now Unions Are Helping to Run the Business," *Business Week*, December 24, 1984, p. 69.

229   "Developments in Industrial Relations," *Monthly Labor Review*, June 1986.

231   "LTV Knocks the Rust off Its Labor Relations," *Business Week*, December 23, 1985, p. 57.

232   *The UAW-GM Report*, Special Saturn Issue, Summer 1985.

234   "AT&T's Hard Bargain: A Watershed for the Industry?" *Business Week*, June 30, 1986, p. 37.

235   Robert R. Rehder and Marta Smith, "Kaisen and the Art of Labor Relations," *Personnel Journal*, December 1986, pp. 84–94.

235   "How Power Will Be Balanced on Saturn's Shop Floor," *Business Week*, August 5, 1985.

SUMMARY: THE LITMUS TEST

page
239   Internal document, 1986, used with permission of John McDonnell.

243   Richard E. Walton created the most influential descriptions of the two philosophies in his article "From Control to Commitment in the Workplace," *Harvard Business Review*, March–April 1985, pp. 77–84.

Chapter 21   WHAT GOVERNMENT SHOULD NOT DO

page
250   Estimates of total cost to consumers are by Gary Hufbauer, Professor of Finance, Georgetown University. Estimates of job loss per industry by Hufbauer and Howard Rosen, a research associate at the Institute for International Economics, Washington, D.C., *Fortune*, May 11, 1987.

254   Kindelberger, "Aging Economy" (see Chapter 9), p. 411.

254   Paul A. Volcker quote: *New York Times,* February 4, 1987.

255   *Economic Report of the President* (Washington, D.C.: U.S. Government Print-
        ing Office, January 1987), p. 3.

255   Ross Perot quote: *New York Times,* July 22, 1986.

256   Hideo Suguira quote: Peters and Waterman, *In Search of Excellence,* p. 34.

256   Winston Churchill quote: Correli Barnett, *The Pride and the Fall* (New York:
        Free Press, 1986), p.3.

256   Harvey Brooks quote: *Washington Post,* April 13, 1987.

257   Final report, untitled, Defense Science Board Task Force on Semiconductor
        Dependency, to the Secretary of Defense, November 30, 1986.

258   Nathan Rosenberg quote: *Washington Post,* April 13, 1987.

Chapter 22   WHAT GOVERNMENT SHOULD DO

page
264   "Manufacturing Technology: A Changing Challenge to Improve Productivity,"
        General Accounting Office, June 3, 1976, p. 83.

Chapter 23   EDUCATION

page
268   Thomas P. Rohlen, *Japan's High Schools* (Berkeley: University of California
        Press, 1983), p. 322.

270   Corelli Barnett, *The Pride and the Fall* (New York: Free Press, 1986), 201.

271   Al Warren quote: Harvard Symposium on Productivity, *Harvard Business
        School Bulletin,* December 1984, p. 65.

271   George Gilder, "Chip Sense and Nonsense," *Wall Street Journal,* April 2,
        1987.

271   Jaikumar, "Postindustrial Manufacturing" (see Chapter 11), p. 75.

272   Thurow, *Zero Sum Solution* (see Chapter 2), p. 124.

275   Herbert J. Walberg, "Scientific Literacy and Economic Productivity in Interna-
        tional Perspective," *Daedalus,* Spring 1983.

275   Merry I. White, "Japanese Education: How Do They Do It?" *The Public
        Interest,* Summer 1984, p. 96.

276   Paul R. Lawrence and Davis Dyer, *Renewing American Industry* (New York:
        Free Press, 1983), p. 262.

276   Gibney, *Japan: Fragile Superpower,* p. 221.

276   Scott F. Runkle, *An Introduction to Japanese History* (Japan: International
        Society for Educational Information Press, 1976), p. 52.

278   Harold W. Stevenson, "Making the Grade: School Achievement in Japan,
        Taiwan, and the United States," a talk given on April 29, 1983, published

in the 1983 Annual Report of the Center for Advanced Study in the Behavioral Sciences, Stanford University.

279   Rohlen, *Japan's High Schools,* p. 298.

Chapter 24   ECONOMIC TECTONICS

page

288   Sir Donald MacDougall quote: Kindelberger, "Aging Economy," p. 416.

288   Congressional Research Service, "Economic Changes in the Asian Pacific Rim: Policy Prospectus," Washington, D.C., August 1986.

292   Robert Cole, *Work, Mobility, and Participation* (Berkeley: University of California Press, 1979), p. 31.

Chapter 25   MYTHS ABOUT JAPAN

page

294   Justin Bloom quote: *Manufacturing Productivity Frontiers,* September 1984.

294   Tatsuno, *The Technopolis Strategy,* p. 224.

295   Michael Polanyi quote: Gevirtz, *Business Plan* (see Chapter 8), p. 158.

295   Ralph E. Gomory quote: *Fortune,* March 30, 1987.

297   C. Fred Bergsten quote: *Fortune,* April 27, 1987.

297   Secretary Lyng's estimate: talk by Gerald Marks, former Director, Chicago office of the U.S. & Foreign Commercial Service, April 14, 1987.

297   Statement attributed to Gephardt in *Wall Street Journal,* April 28, 1987.

297   Hugh T. Patrick, "U.S.–Japan Political Economy: Partnership in Jeopardy?", in Kermit O. Hanson and Thomas W. Roehl, eds., *The United States and the Pacific Economy in the 1980s* (Indianapolis: Bobbs-Merrill, 1980), p. 94.

297   Daniel Goleman, *Vital Lies, Simple Truths* (New York: Simon & Schuster, 1985), p. 181.

299   Clyde Prestowitz quote: *USA Today,* April 28, 1986.

Chapter 26   STRENGTHS OF JAPAN

page

303   Polling quote: *Business Week,* November 4, 1985; Kearns quote: *USA Today,* April 30, 1986.

303   White, *Japanese Educational Challenge,* p. 17.

303   Survey results in "U.S. Workers Say Japanese Are Superior," *New York Times,* September 1, 1985.

303   James Fallows, "Letter from Tokyo," *Atlantic Monthly,* August 1986.

Chapter 27 JAPAN'S PROBLEMS

page
313   Sukeo Kohno quote, *Fortune,* August 4, 1986, p. S-78.

315   James O'Toole, *Vanguard Management* (Garden City, N.Y.: Doubleday, 1985), p. 56.

315   Ray Dalio, January 23, 1987, Newsletter from Bridgewater Associates, Wilton, Connecticut.

317   Jared Taylor, *Shadows of the Rising Sun* (New York: William Morrow, 1983), p. 35.

317   *The Economist,* August 23, 1986.

318   Herman Kahn and Thomas Pepper, *The Japanese Challenge* (New York: Thomas Y. Crowell, 1979), p. 121.

319   Abegglen and Stalk, *Kaisha* (see Chapter 18), pp. 119, 121.

319   Landes, *Unbound Prometheus,* p. 336.

Chapter 28 ASIAN NICs

page
323   *Business Week,* January 12, 1987.

325   Paul Roessel quote: *Industry Week,* July 7, 1986.

325   Denis Root quote: *Houston Chronicle,* January 6, 1986.

327   George Cobbe quote: *New York Times,* April 7, 1986.

327   Hiroshi Takeuchi quote: *Business Week,* December 23, 1985.

328   Landes, *Unbound Prometheus,* 538.

329   Roy Hofheinz, Jr., and Kent E. Calder, *The East Asia Edge* (New York: Basic Books, 1982).

330   Peter L. Berger, *The Capitalist Revolution* (New York: Basic Books, 1986), p. 141.

331   David Halberstam, "Can We Rise to the Japanese Challenge?" *Parade,* October 9, 1983, p. 7.

Chapter 29 IT'S UP TO US

page
333   Henry Kissinger quote: David Rockefeller, "America's Future: A Question of Strength and Will," *Atlantic Community Quarterly,* Spring 1979, pp. 14–19.

333   Halberstam, "Can We Rise to Japanese Challenge?"

334   Joseph A. Schumpeter, *Capitalism, Socialism and Democracy,* Second Edition (New York: Harper & Brothers, 1947), p. xi.

337   Durant and Durant, *Lessons of History* (see Chapter 6), p. 91.

338   Francis Bello, "The Technology Behind Productivity" (book source unknown).

Additional Readings

The "References" section includes books and articles we cited directly in the chapters. Over the years, there have been many other authors whose works directly and indirectly influenced our thinking and, in turn, this book.

We cannot cite all magazine articles and newspaper stories that have informed us—the list would run into the thousands. But we would like to cite and recommend *additional* books we have found particularly valuable.

The following list has been categorized to correspond to various parts of the book, but many of the works have subject matter making them appropriate for several parts.

Finally, this list is not to be considered exhaustive. Readers will find here only the beginning and pointers for where to go further.

Parts I and II

Abernathy, William J.; Kim B. Clark; and Alan M. Kantrow. *Industrial Renaissance*. New York: Basic Books, 1983.

Ayers, Robert U. *The Next Industrial Revolution*. Cambridge: Ballinger, 1984.

Committee for Economic Development. *Productivity Policy: Key to the Nation's Economic Future*. Washington, D.C.: CED, 1983.

_____. *Strategy for U.S. Industrial Competitiveness*. Washington, D.C.: CED, 1984.

Denison, Edward F. *Accounting for Slower Economic Growth*. Washington, D.C.: Brookings Institution, 1979.

Kanter, Rosabeth Moss. *The Change Masters*. New York: Simon & Schuster, 1983.

Kendrick, John W. *Improving Company Productivity*. Baltimore: Johns Hopkins University Press, 1984.

_____, ed. *International Comparisons of Productivity and Causes of the Slowdown*. Cambridge: Ballinger, 1984.

Lawrence, Robert Z. *Can America Compete?* Washington, D.C.: Brookings Institution, 1984.

Lodge, George C., and Ezra F. Vogel, eds. *Ideology and National Competitiveness*. Boston: Harvard Business School Press, 1987.

McGraw, Thomas K., ed. *America Versus Japan*. Boston: Harvard Business School Press, 1986.

Porter, Michael E. *Competitive Strategy*. New York: Free Press, 1980.

President's Commission on Industrial Competitiveness. *Global Competition: The New Reality*, Washington, D.C.: Government Printing Office, 1985.

Scott, Bruce R., and George C. Lodge. *U.S. Competitiveness in the World Economy*. Boston: Harvard Business School Press, 1985.

Thurow, Lester C. *Dangerous Currents*. New York: Random House, 1983.

Yoffie, David B. *Power and Protectionism*. New York: Columbia University Press, 1983.

Part III

Durant, Will. *Our Oriental Heritage*. New York: Simon & Schuster, 1954.

Gibbon, Edward. *The Decline and Fall of the Roman Empire*. New York: Modern Library, n.d.

Glubb, Sir John. *The Fate of Empires and Search for Survival*. Edinburgh: William Blackwood & Sons, 1976.

Hoffman, Ross J. S. *Great Britain and the German Trade Rivalry*. Philadelphia: University of Pennsylvania Press, 1933.

Melko, Matthew. *The Nature of Civilizations*. Boston: Porter Sargent, 1969.

McNeill, William H. *Mythistory and Other Essays*. Chicago: University of Chicago Press, 1986.

_____. *The Rise of the West*. Chicago: University of Chicago Press, 1963.

Robbins, Keith. *The Eclipse of a Great Power*. New York: Longman, 1973.

Rosenberg, Nathan, and L. E. Birdzell, Jr. *How the West Grew Rich*. New York: Basic Books, 1986.

Starr, Chester G. *A History of the Ancient World*. New York: Oxford University Press, 1983.

Vanished Civilisations. Sydney: Reader's Digest Services, 1983.

Wells, H. G. *The Outline of History*. New York: Garden City Books, 1956.

Part IV

Crosby, Philip B. *Quality Without Tears: The Art of Hassle-Free Management*. New York: McGraw-Hill, 1984.

Doyle, Robert J. *Gainsharing and Productivity*. New York: AMACOM, 1983.

Grove, Andrew S. *High Output Management*. New York: Random House, 1983.

Walton, Richard E., and Paul R. Lawrence, eds. *HRM Trends & Challenges*. Boston: Harvard Business School, 1985.

Juran, J. M. *Managerial Breakthrough*. New York: McGraw-Hill, 1964.

Lawler, Edward E. *High-Involvement Management*. San Francisco: Jossey-Bass, 1986.

Miller, Lawrence M. *American Spirit: Visions of a New Corporate Culture*. New York: Morrow, 1984.

Mills, D. Quinn. *The New Competitors*. New York: John Wiley & Sons, 1985.

O'Toole, James. *Vanguard Managment: Redesigning the Corporate Future*. Garden City: Doubleday, 1985.

Reich, Robert B. *The Next American Frontier*. New York: Times Books, 1983.

Schuster, Michael H. *Union-Management Cooperation: Structure-Process-Impact*. Kalamazoo, Mich.: W. E. Upjohn, 1984.

Simmons, John, and William Mares. *Working Together*. New York: Alfred A. Knopf, 1983.

Townsend, Patrick L., with Joan E. Gebhardt. *Commit to Quality*. New York: John Wiley & Sons, 1986.

Weitzman, Martin L. *The Share Economy: Conquering StagFlation*. Cambridge: Harvard University Press, 1984.

Part V

Brown, B. Frank. *Crisis in Secondary Education*. Englewood Cliffs: Prentice Hall, 1984.

Houle, Cyril O. *Patterns of Learning*. San Francisco: Jossey-Bass, 1984.

Kozol, Jonathan, *Illiterate America*. New York: Anchor Press, 1985.

National Commission on Excellence in Education. *A Nation at Risk*. Washington, D.C.: Government Printing Office 1983.

Olson, Mancur. *The Rise and Decline of Nations*. New Haven: Yale University Press, 1982.

Rohlen, Thomas P. *For Harmony and Strength*. Berkeley: University of California Press, 1979.

Part VI

Abegglen, James C. *The Strategy of Japanese Business*. Cambridge: Ballinger, 1984.

Allen, G. C. *The Japanese Economy*. New York: St. Martin's Press, 1981.

Benedict, Ruth. *The Chrysanthemum and the Sword*. New York: New American Library, 1946.

Braddon, Russell. *Japan Against the World 1941–2041*. New York: Stein & Day, 1983.

Christopher, Robert C. *The Japanese Mind*. New York: Linden Press, 1983.

Christopher, Robert C. *Second to None: American Companies in Japan*. New York: Crown Publishers, 1986.

Clark, Rodney. *The Japanese Company*. New Haven: Yale University Press, 1979.

Ishikawa, Kaoru. *What Is Total Quality Control? The Japanese Way*. Englewood Cliffs, N.J.: Prentice-Hall, 1985.

Johnson, Chalmers, ed. *The Industrial Policy Debate*. San Francisco: ICS Press, 1984.

Johnson, Chalmers. *MITI and the Japanese Miracle*. Stanford, Calif.: Stanford University Press, 1982.

Moritani, Masanori. *Japanese Technology: Getting the Best for the Least*. Tokyo: Simul Press, 1982.

Ohmae, Kenichi. *The Mind of the Strategist*. New York: McGraw-Hill, 1982.

Pascale, Richard Tanner, and Anthony G. Athos. *The Art of Japanese Management*. New York: Simon & Schuster, 1981.

Pepper, Thomas; Merit E. Janow; and Jimmy W. Wheeler. *The Competition: Dealing with Japan*. New York: Praeger, 1985.

Reischauer, Edwin O. *The United States and Japan*. Cambridge: Harvard University Press, 1970.

Vogel, Ezra F. *Japan as Number One: Lessons for America*. Cambridge: Harvard University Press, 1979.

————. *National Strategies: Japanese Style, American Style*. New York: Simon & Schuster, 1985.

Wheeler, Jimmy W.; Merit E. Janow; and Thomas Pepper. *Japanese Industrial Development Policies in the 1980s: Implications for U.S. Trade and Investment*. New York: Hudson Institute, 1982.

Zimmerman, Mark. *How to Do Business with the Japanese*. New York: Random House, 1985.

Index